This book is co-authored by 34 inspiring women

Sallie Warman-Watts, Jenni Hallam, Lesley Readman, Mikel Ann Hall, Jennifer Levers, Angela Pepperell, Lynette Marie Allen, Andrea Jackson, Mairi Taylor, Julia Anastasiou, Ali Hutchinson, Stevie Jane Foster, Angie Gifford, Ann Ball, Emily Madghachian, Mykela McAlpine, Katie (KaT) Thomas, Louise Edwards, Francesca Yogini, Kirsten 'Kimama' Lapping, Alexandra Fraser Duran, Mahala Gehna, Lou Moore, Beverley Ross, Louise Harris, Jagdeep Kaur (Jags), Eleshia Harris, Maila Salmaso, Virginia Gonzalez Pinto Medrano, Ashleigh Guthrie, Casey Mauro, Wakanda Rose, Pascale Huart, E Birch

Curated and edited by Lynette Allen, Medicine Woman, Author and founder of 'Gather the Women'

DEDICATION

This book is dedicated to sisters around the world.

While the women who wrote this book, all sat with Gather the Women, there are many, many other sister circles of all names and kinds around the world. Sometimes, they're official sacred gatherings, other times, they are just women supporting women through crisis and that's where the benefactors of this book, the charity Bali Street Mums (based in Bali) comes in.

Several years ago, a Balinese woman called Ibu Ketut left her husband. This is most unusual in Balinese culture. Their marriage was a violent one and so, gathering her five children, pregnant with her sixth, she decided to take what she could carry and leave. When a Balinese woman marries, she leaves her family of origin and lives with her husbands' family. She leaves her family temple (each family and home have their own temple) and she adopts the temple of her husband. She lives there with her in-laws, her husband and their children. This is Balinese culture and for many women, their integration into their new family is welcomed, blessed and a beautiful blend of ritual and ceremony for the new generation of their family. For a Balinese woman, this is now her home.

For a woman to leave her husband in Balinese culture means she leaves that home, she leaves that temple and she has no place of safety. Rarely is she allowed back into her family of origins home.

Ibu Ketut bravely left her husband's family and temple. She made herself homeless, regarding it as a better and safer existence on her own. She had no money, no food and no plan. A woman on the street in a country where exploitation is rife, where the weather

3

is either scorching hot and dry or caught in tropical rainstorms, she was in dire straits.

Some of the Javanese women who lived on the city's rubbish dump, found Ibu Ketut and her children. They took her in. Culturally, the Javanese and the Balinese stay separate and help their own but these women took Ibu Ketut into their small private community, a group of shacks surrounding one of the city's largest and busiest rubbish dumps. They take their living from there, climbing over the rubbish looking for recycling to sell, food to eat or things to use. And they showed Ibu Ketut the ropes.

Kim, the founder of Bali Street Mums, an Australian woman who came to Bali many years ago, supports and knows the women at the rubbish dump very well. When she saw Ibu Ketut for the first time, she was barefoot and in late pregnancy clambering over the rubbish dump to earn her keep. They met and, in their smiles, they instantly found a connection. Kim had seen a YouTube video on how to make glasses from recycled bottles and she told Ibu Ketut about it. Together they tried it.

They sat on the dirty mud floor of her hut, with a candle and some bottles watching YouTube trying to figure out how to make these glasses! They laughed, they tried over and over, they got it wrong, they broke bottles, they tried again, the next day and the next and the next. It became a 'thing'!

Enjoying each other's company, every day Kim would visit and together they would try again. Until one day, Ibu Ketut did it. She had made her first glass, that could be drunk from! She made more and Kim took them to the local western market for tourists to buy. They bought them all. So Ibu Ketut made more. And she made more and more. With the help of Bali Street Mums, her glasses are now being sold all over the world, regular orders coming from

4

restaurants and families from American to Australia! Ibu Ketut's monthly wage is now approximately eight times the normal monthly wage of someone in Bali! With some of that money, she bought a car, which she keeps a ten-minute scooter ride from the rubbish dump, at the Bali Street Mums safehouse in case they need it urgently for one of the children. And if she wants to use it, she rides her scooter to the car and then takes it for a while.

On top of that Ibu Ketut gives back to her community of sisters at the rubbish dump, she's taught them all how to make glasses, which ones to collect and she pays them well. All the women here have blossomed because of their care and attention in taking Ibu Ketut in.

Kim recently spoke to her about upgrading her accommodation. She can now afford something with more privacy, something cleaner that isn't next to the rubbish dump, she can afford a place with her own bathroom and shower now but Ibu Ketut has made it clear, she's not going anywhere. She won't leave her sisters or her community. They share food, they cook together, they share childcare, they laugh and they look after each other.

Sisterhood is sisterhood, the world over

For information on buying Ibu Ketut's glasses, you can contact Bali Street Mums or donate to them at any time. They are a very small charity, run by Kim and her tiny team, they are completely transparent in how they spend the money donated to them. At the writing of this book, they currently looked after 75 children at their safehouse and feed many more families, delivering food, water and supplies all over Bali.

Any support you feel called to give is deeply appreciated.
www.balistreetmums.org/donate
@balistreetmums_project

All profits from this book go to Bali Street Mums

There are 34 women here from all walks of life,
spanning five decades,
consider them your teachers and guides,
helping you to access what may be hidden from view.
They each have a gift for you.
Hold this book close to your heart and ask what you need to hear,
then open the book and where it lands
will be words of wisdom for your heart.

FOREWORD
By Lynette Allen

At the beginning of my journey into the world of sister circle, plant medicine and ritual, I sat with ayahuasca. For those first ten journeys at least, she took me deep into slumber. 'Rest', she said 'You do too much...sleep'. She was right, I did do too much.

A wife, a mother, a daughter, a sister and back then, I classed myself as a business woman too. Of course I was busy! I LOVED being busy. I got things done and I had a lot to do. I had a team of women I led into corporates to teach women in male dominated environments how to find their voice. It was a company I loved, everything about it, I loved. I loved our programmes, I loved our trainings, I loved the travel – Europe and all over the UK, TV, radio, magazine articles covered our work, I regularly met with bosses of some of London's top corporates in glass fronted offices! I loved every single thing. Above all, I loved the women I worked alongside, my team, I loved them deeply. I felt like I had sisters, who got me and understood me.

And they did. Until they didn't.

My journey into plant medicine was considered... distasteful, worrying, frowned upon for sure. I'd gone from the woman who'd never even smoked a cigarette, to immersing myself in one of the world's strongest psychedelic plant medicines! Even I was surprised...but I was being called to this...I had to be there. Fascinated by shamanism and intrigued by the blessings, the healing stories I was hearing, the revelations, the learnings, the deep uncoverings, the chants, the smells of incense, the candlelight and the opportunity to be by myself, to stop everything…was, I considered, a necessity.

Being busy, was not giving me time to consider anything outside of my then 'what's next' mentality. Meditation was a mystery to me. Plant medicine…terrifying yet intriguing. My inner workings stopped at what I considered was my intuition and I'd dove no further than that.

This was my initiation. I drank many dozens of times in the end, spending hours deep in the medicine, with shamans, brothers and sisters. By candlelight, in deepest reverence to this beautiful spirit of ayahuasca, we would do our work, the internal work of understanding one's self on a far deeper level than our left brains would otherwise allow us to go. This was the brave work of having the blindfolds of society, our pasts, our culture and our images of ourselves carefully taken off. This was the brave work of stripping the ego bare and leaning into the fine line of the veil between worlds. The world of spirit, of messages, of insights, of visions. An underworld of knowing and of letting go of the fractals of material that make us feel whole in our human form. It's the cracking of the mirror.

It was also the brave work of travelling that path alone, of releasing those around me and I lost so much. I lost my sisters (most of them), I lost connection, I relinquished my company, I burned every scrap of professional paper and notes that I'd kept with me for twenty years and I watched the flames flicker everything I knew away.

At times, I felt entirely and completely on my own.

It was in one of those nights that I became aware that there were three aspects to me. The girl I used to be, the woman I was at that moment in time and the woman I was yet to become. Always three aspects.

For the girl I used to be, she could be that forty something year old woman I was yesterday or that little girl of five years old from the 1970's in her school uniform. I was always with the woman I am now...for when I grow...she grows too, every second that passes, I am the woman I am now. And for the woman I am yet to become, she is always one step ahead of me, she has walked this path, she knows me so intimately, what I want, what I crave, what I need, my secrets and my dreams.

I began to try to sense into her whereabouts in those medicine filled nights, to sense where she was in relation to me...physically as well as energetically. I could feel her close, like a big sister, a mentor, the older wiser version of me, always beckoning me forwards, running slightly ahead, just out of sight, laughing and encouraging me...she knows the way, she knows exactly where I am and what's ahead. And she delights in showing me. I'd asked the universe for a mentor at that time, I hadn't been aware that I was calling in plant medicine to show me my own internal mentor – the me of the future but it's clear now, I was.

And I remembered that little girl I used to be, the essence of her, how she felt, the games she played in her mind, the thoughts she thought, the worries she had. And I would sit with her and love her, from the future.

As for the woman I was then, at that time, she was less graspable. I saw her obviously, in the mirror, in real life and I liked her. I knew her. I loved her. She had a good life, she did good in the world, I saw her, a gentle mother, a devoted wife, a focused messenger for those in her business world. A writer. A teacher. Articulate. She loved those around her with all of her heart and more. But she didn't know what she could do, what she was capable of. She didn't know her power and her life was changing so fast, she was being scooped up by the universe, her birth chart, mother ayahuasca and she was being put under immense pressure. And she didn't know why. And it was confusing. And so...with a foot in both camps still...the corporate busy world of 'doing' and 'thinking' and this new medicine path that was opening up, one of stillness, consciousness and connectivity, I asked the women I knew back then, about the girls they used to be, the women they were at that time and the women they were yet to become.

I didn't know how to assimilate the words I heard. They were in tears, they barely knew how to answer but they felt those questions, they landed and they almost stopped their breath. They told me about their childhood hurts, their regrets, their fears, what they'd say to the little girls they used to be.

They told me they weren't sure who they were, that they felt lost.

As for the women they were yet to become, they didn't know. It seemed they had never considered an actual future projection of themselves before, that woman was an anomaly. I spoke to them, I read their words and I closed the book.

I had no answers. It seemed I had my own work to do.

My own work took me to the brink of all that I had considered to be safe and true. And it took me to the other side of the world to Bali, the land of the Gods, a precious, intensely beautiful and powerful island of volcanic energy, daily prayer, offerings, ritual and ceremony.

Swapping ayahuasca for ceremonial cacao, the most beautiful of heart-opening plant energies, I was taken to a deeper level again, this time a deeper level of support, of integration, of assimilation

11

and of placing all of the parts of me down, back in a different order, the order of the medicine woman within.

I became the medicine, I wrote. I wrote and wrote and wrote, all of my integrations and portals described, channelled in the midst of cacao, I wrote. And I published them. Three books, a trilogy...A Woman's Blessing, HELD and Sacred.

And right in the middle of those channellings, early one morning, as the final in the trilogy, Sacred, was in the metaphorical womb, I sat in meditation with cacao. Barely breathing, free of thought, I flew out of that state with a sharp inhale of breath as my eyes whipped open.

I understood. I understood the girl I used to be, the woman I am now and the woman I am yet to become. I understood them and it was as clear as day how to access them. I understood the rituals needed to find them, I understood the power of lighting a candle, of women in ceremony and of serving plant medicine.

I understood the process of drinking cacao every day, I understood the beauty of breaking and of being rebuilt and of why the ability to access those three aspects is so vital to the heart beat of the wild and wise feminine.

And most of all, I understood the power of sisterhood in medicine, the ancient, ingrained echo, the yearning and need for women to gather.

So, Gather the Women was born. A 22-day rite of passage. 22 days of sitting with cacao, in ritual, in ceremony, with sisters from around the world. Women who had never met, women who had never thought much about the girls they used to be, women who weren't sure how to look at themselves, how to stare into their eyes and see themselves fully and completely in the mirror. Women who hadn't considered the prospect of calling in their future, wiser self, of sitting with all of their three aspects together, as one union, gathering all of the women within them at once.

But one by one, each woman said yes. And we gathered. We talked. We cried. We heard each other. Each woman held, each woman's reputation remaining intact as she broke sometimes in front of us, sometimes behind the scenes, sometimes while hearing another woman's beautiful and much needed wisdom.

Working with Sacred Eldership, where our elders speak first, where we honour the passing of time and the depth that comes with grey hair, post-menopausal bliss, bodies changing shape and the growing into the crone years. Sacred Eldership where we listen to those who have walked a different, yet equally untethered path, we give status to the elders in our sister circle. Recognition is given to them in this rite of passage.

Gather the Women has been and still is, a rite of passage to finding the medicine within, of sitting in sister circle and reconnecting in the same way our ancestors did, so many moons ago. Sister circle is not new, it's ancient, its tribal, its steeped in natural medicine and in ritual.

There are many, many beautifully held sister circles throughout the world, Gather the Women is just one of them and there are courageous medicine women spanning the globe who hold space for the feminine in circle. Each one of them has been guided to this position of space holder, because they know, as I do, that it is imperative to the future of women, for our daughters that we speak openly, without competition and in the sincerest of love for each other.

Our great grandmothers and *their* grandmothers, the medicine women and space holders of the past, knew how to conjure with their words, they knew the power of their sacred stick, they journeyed together, they sat in circles, marked and declared them as sacred and they drank their herbs, mixtures and brews in presence of one another. They cast their spells with the written word, in candle wax and their menstruation blood. These journeys are a remembering.

The stories of these women have been life-changing, for me and for all of us in these sacred spaces.

And those women decided to write their stories, for you. They wanted to inspire you, they wanted you to know that you are not alone, they wanted you to know that you are an incredible being, that you need no other to bless you, to announce you, to find you. They wanted you to know, through their own brave and daring stories that they found versions of themselves they did not expect to find and that means, that you can too.

They have no special powers, luck or status bestowed upon them. We were not interested in and neither did we discuss, our career status, how much money we earned or what car we drove. I still have no idea where these women live or who they are, other than, in that circle, I heard their words, I listened to their stories, their awakenings and bore witness to their blossoming.

Each one of them have discovered their own sacred portals, their words, their voices, their breath. Each one of them have stared at themselves deeply, through cacao, ritual and our ceremonies and they have recognised themselves. They have been reunited with their most magnificent feminine power, power they never imagined they had.

The women who wrote these stories are you. They are in their twenties, thirties, forties, fifties, sixties and almost approaching their seventh decade. Some had never tried ceremonial cacao before, some had never known ritual, some were so nervous they almost didn't come!

This is not their rags to riches story, these stories are real, messy, still in progress, not fully wrapped up and neither will they be. They were bleeding and going through life as they wrote, some women wrote in English even though it's not their mother tongue. All were writing with tears falling on the page or keyboard as they typed. And in giving me (as the respectful curator and editor of this body of work), their release to print their words…hitting that permission button was done with closed eyes, in slow motion and virtually no breath. Trust me when I say, these women have put themselves on the edge of their comfort zones to try to explain and do justice to the power of this work.

This is the power of gathering with women, this is the power of sister circle, a power you may not have met yet.

These are my sisters, they are among the bravest women I know and they have written their stories just for you.

82

She learned to expect her transformation to be messy,
turbulent, seemingly lawless.
There were times when she sobbed,
fighting for breath and praying for gravity
to connect her to the earth.
Yet even in those moments,
she felt everything coming together for her highest good.
Even in those moments,
she felt held by a thousand women behind her.
Ancestors, spirits, witches, crones, children,
all whispering goodness.
Filling her with spirit,
for she was forging the way ahead for her grandchildren.

from A Woman's Blessing

In order of Sacred Eldership...our elder speaks first

Sallie Warman-Watts

53

In her silence she explored so much,
entertaining every single sacred thought,
dancing in delicious, yoni-melting glorious delirious, wild and
wonderous love
and licking it up – very, very slowly.

from 'Sacred'

Trust

At some point in my life, I had decided that trust between females did not exist...on any level, at any age. Instead, I had only witnessed and felt betrayal, assassination and the removal of anything resembling loyalty and friendship. I understood this to be a default trait of the female form, from which there appeared to be no escape.

And so, as I sat in the opening ceremony in a circle of women, placing myself right at the heart of my own fear-based trigger, I became aware that I was leaning into the need to release that sense of fear and rejection, that sense of dismissal, of humiliation and of worthlessness. I tentatively held out a hand to this new circle of women, reaching for something I couldn't quite grasp, only knowing that my heart was eager to find a home in sisterhood, to stay a while at the fire hearth of affection and build my strength for what was to come.

I held on, hoping to tangibly disassemble those heightened emotions that swung between trust and distrust, to maybe move into a harbinger of pure friendship and belief of change.

There were Sister Promises at our opening ceremony. We made promises to hear each other, to listen to each other, to not presume to know each other's story or to see one another as broken. Sacred vows to be spoken by each woman in turn, not forced but honestly spoken in love and authenticity. As elder, I uttered mine first. I was sincere in my promises but between the thinking and the speaking of these sacred words, a thought flashed across my mind. 'How would I know that *their* promises would be sincere?'. I shifted my body nervously. I was uncomfortable but I had to know for certain.

I interrupted the process.

I opened my mouth and tears fell down my face as the words fell out.

I stopped the ceremony.

My breath caught in my throat; I needed to know with absolute clarity.

'Is this real? Is this true? Are you really saying to me, that this is possible, that trust can really exist between women? That women can come together to celebrate each other genuinely, sincerely, with heartfelt intention for each other, with no ulterior motive?'

Each woman listened. Each woman had fallen silent. Each woman heard me. I saw them bring their hands to their hearts with tears in their eyes too.

And then they answered clearly and one by one.

'Yes!'

'We promise'

'We will hold you'

My eyes widened then slowly closed shut, tears fell like burning candle wax moving their way to the end of my chin where I wiped them with the back of my hand, up into my hair taking a sharp breath in and straightening myself.

And so, that sacred space was opened.

Our journey had begun.

I learned to step into the unknown, to feel those fears of insecurity and work WITH them in order to overcome what was, by this point, my own prejudice. As the unfolding began with 'the girl I used to be', it soon became clear that this sister circle was honest and sincere. We foraged together in our gardens for our rituals and altars, to make 'the girls we used to be' happy. We painted hearts and fingers in bright colours on paper and laughed at our silliness. Then one morning I woke up and felt lost,

21

distracted, sad even. I was struggling. There were some painful memories moving through me from when I was a child, memories I thought I'd dealt with or at the very least forgotten.

My normal coping strategy would be to swallow the pain but this day I decided to share it with my sisters, I felt intuitively drawn. It took me a great deal of courage to step out and step up to be heard but heard I was and held as I explained my thoughts and feelings. My beautiful sisters thanked me for my honesty, for trusting them with my true and authentic painful self, that they loved me and held me in their healing light.

After the years of mistrust began to melt away, it was so relaxing for that space to be replaced with unquestionable authentic love. It was alien and yet the most beautiful of sensations. It was true, it was sincere, they really did and do, keep their sister promises, even to this day.

Inner deepening

So here I am, in my seventh decade unashamedly asking my sisters to accept me for who I am. As the elder of my sister circle and as the elder of this book offering, I can finally see my value, my place in sister circle and what I offer to my younger sisters.

I have been where they have been, I have walked where they have walked and my thoughts will have been so very similar to theirs. I've loved, I've laughed, I've cried, I've died a little at times and I've married, I've divorced and I've birthed children. I have lost children too, I've had careers, I've had jobs, I've loved desperately until it hurts. I've been peri, post and through menopause, I've had a life of extremes but through it all, there was always the 'knowing': I am that longing, I am that aching heart, I'm

22

the pull towards the searching, I'm that part of every woman who is just out of reach, I am the connection missed, I'm that part that needs acceptance, I am that part of who seeks the truth and I'm the part who is desperate to know love.

I feel now this is all of us, this is the collective WOMAN, I feel this is women preparing themselves for this time of awakening.

When I breathed into the mighty medicine of cacao, when I was held in sister circle when we gathered, I took solace in meditation. I found my heart with ritual. I healed with reiki and I began to rise. Such is the power of when the women gather. I had so many expectations but how to meet those when I began my journey, felt most important. I asked myself questions such as 'What might I find buried deep inside, what could happen if my perceived path changed and would I like who I became if I changed?'.

In my life, there have been certain words that have helped to bring a certain loving clarity into my world;

Hope, Optimism, Love, Dedication, Loyalty, Grace, Peace and finally, Listen.

From sitting in sister circle, I've realised these words are like spells, weaving their way through my mind, conjuring up my thoughts, beliefs and intentions. Mantras to set my course by.

Hope, for me, at its best, is a beautiful feeling of expectation. A visualization of a dream yet to come. A sense of trust in a given situation that it will come to pass.

At its worst, hope has been a longing for proof of a gift...an imminent desire and the thought of its arrival was almost too much to bear.

Optimism, I believe is the best of everything wrapped up in a smile or the confidence of the young when undertaking a difficult task, it's when I'm held in trust when I think I can't.

23

Dedication I feel is my commitment to myself. When I am my own sovereignty and my sister circle became part of my rituals and dedication.

Loyalty, in my world is the wanting to support those who would commit to me; your faithfulness to the sacred cacao plant and those who would be part of my healing journey.

Grace, is 'gentleness' for me, a serenity in all things, my acceptance of the inevitable but without surrender.

Peace, I would wish this state of being for all both inside and out. My tranquillity of mind, body and soul, my place to be still and calm. It's my platform to not only aspire to but to grow from within.

Listen, is my most favourite of words. This has been difficult for me, to be quiet, to be still and to listen. But slowly I've taught myself and the less I've talked, the more I've listened. I have become better at understanding and learning.

And love is the foundation of my expectations of myself, I have used that analogy often, in all ways, to sustain, ground and nurture me.

When my thoughts catch me unawares, it's how I know my expectations are being met. When I light a candle just before I begin my rituals and the thoughts that push forward are of ancient times, when my ancestors also lit candles, I feel they become a bridge between both worlds. They are incantations over the flame, symbols of light shone for my searching for a way home.

I had a knowing that the fallen branch that became my sacred stick called to me, she appeared in front of me, just waiting on the ground and once I decorated her with ribbon, string, carvings, coloured paints, shells and feathers, once I'd blessed her with mama cacao, she became my wand - both fairy and witchy - beautifully

24

marked and imbued with whispered sacred words and secrets to the very essence of her being. Mildred is her name, such is the power of the wand.

When I'm floating off into a wonderful meditative bliss, I return, excited about sharing my experience with my sisters, knowing that they'll all be as excited as me such is the power of sisterhood!

True Power

'Where does this feminine power come from and where does it lie?' was my question. 'Inside me', I heard, 'I am the Power'.

So much I have learned in order to grasp and hold that feminine power.

So much unravelling.

So much unpicking.

So much UNDONE.

Gradually as I grew from child, to maiden, to woman and into crone, I see now that I had knitted a 'jumper of life' around myself, each stitch catching the memories left by life's situations both positive and negative.

As I finished each part of the 'jumper' I began to wear it. It became the very fabric of my existence. First the sleeves, not such a large body of space but enough to be able to slide my outstretched arms inside and to feel comfortable. Here I found myself begin to wrap these comforted covered arms about myself keeping myself safe, holding that part of me so vulnerable to outside influences.

Then comes the biggest metaphoric leap, placing my head through the neck and pulling that 'jumper' all the way down enveloping my entire body. 'Now I'm protected! Now I know only my own dogma'. Perfected for my own human journey!

But what happened when I started to awaken, my knowing, my coming home to myself? The unravelling began. It was like I found an end and I pulled it until I had unpicked that 'jumper', I was UNDONE.

And then I was free to choose everything. To see myself differently, that I belong only to myself, that I'm walking my own path. I was free to be!

And then I listened, I explored, I felt and I had trusted myself. When I sat in sister circle with ceremony and ritual, I began to draw intuitively what I needed. I felt what was right for me.

Meditation makes me still so I can hear. Plant medicine connects me to my home mama Gaia. I begin to attune my bodily senses, then attune my spiritual vibrational energy senses and gradually my growth was and still is exponential, limitless, infinite.

The smallest of things made a difference to me, the mundane and ordinary became magnificent, life changing even. I refer to my ritual with bathing. I say this because for me this really was life changing and something I had never considered before. As part of this immersion, we took a ritual shower.

How would I make a shower sacred? 'Trust and let go' is my absolute mantra now. Firstly, I found my music a piece that I loved, I knew this would carry me away to wherever I needed to go, I set this up in my bathroom and the acoustics were perfect. Then I cleared all the debris out of the room, debris that would bother me, things that would not serve me in that environment and space, perfect. I wanted my space to smell sweet, to have an aroma that would heighten my senses, this was quite easy as my incense sticks were all my favourite fragrances as were the candles which were strategically placed around my space. Next came that which I wanted and needed to clean and cleanse myself, oils, creams, natural sponges and soaps.

Finally, the flowers, the petals were strewn around the floor, up and over shelves, in the shower itself.

No one was in the house, I was alone, it was quiet, it was peaceful and as I began to prepare myself for this ritual there was a flutter of excitement in the pit of my stomach.

Slowly, I undressed, slowly I brushed my hair, slowly I observed myself in the mirror. I didn't care that I was looking at a body of a sixty-nine-year-old, I was looking at the woman that had travelled down through the ages, she knew about life, she saw life on her body, she saw her scars, her rounded sagging bits, the bits we so desperately want to change. I brought my hand slowly up to my face and laying it gently on my cheek with fingers apart, I touched the tears that were falling. Why was I weeping? I weep now at the very thought of those feelings, I was weeping for all the three aspects of myself and how far I'd come on this monumental journey they call life.

I gradually wrapped myself up in my cotton sarong and started towards the bathroom I stepped into my space and pressed the music play button. I turned the water on. As the water cascaded down hitting the petals they floated softly around, I placed my foot in amongst the petals and they playfully kissed both feet. I moved my body under the falling water, my hair, my arms, my legs, my body filled with a sensation of cleansing, the water moving down my body touched every nerve ending, all of my senses burst forth into ecstasy, the sounds, the smells, the visual sights of flowers but most of all my mind. The power of ritual had transported my mind from a practical, functional practice to an ecstatic almost out of body experience. It was one of the most beautiful yet simple changes I have ever been witnessed to or taken part in.

It is said that sister circles have always been the ancestral way for women to connect and feel protected by each other, I now know that no-one nurtures, loves or is as fierce in loyalty as we are, when in circle...such is the power of The Women who Gathered.

Jenni Hallam

64

Self nurture was her ritual,
her own wishes worshipped,
her most fantasized dreams imagined.
Boundaries protected,
respecting and protecting those of her sisters in return.
That's how she became an empress.

from 'A Woman's Blessing'

Finding her

I was afraid. When I thought about joining a sister circle, I felt the clutching fingers of fear around my heart and I prevaricated. I've been involved in deep personal change work for many years, so what on earth was it about this particular journey that created such apprehension in me?

The next morning, I woke before dawn. I curled into my favourite chair. It holds me like a velvety cocoon. I lit a candle and sat with this conundrum. As the candle flame glimmered in the darkness, I heard the quiet voice of the girl I used to be, the Jenni of more than half a century past, reminding me of long-ago pain, summoning me back over years to the agonies of rejection and bullying.

I have no blood sisters and I always longed to be part of a feminine closeness, the closeness I perceived would be found in sisterhood. In my first year of secondary school, I'd been accepted as part of a group of girls, 'the clever ones'. I was so grateful to be included, I felt validated, I believed I had found my sisterhood.

Then one tiny incident set in motion a nightmare that forced me into bitter isolation. One of these adored 'sisters' accused me of deliberately damaging her homework. As I protested my innocence, they gathered like ravening wolves 'You did it, you did it'. Relishing their power, they carried on for days, holding a mock trial where one after another they destroyed my character and broke my trusting heart. I was found guilty and sentenced to be ostracised for the rest of the year. For my twelve-year-old self, this caused soul destroying anguish and it changed me fundamentally.

It took me years to begin to recover and trust in relationships with other girls, other women again, to feel anything like safe and accepted. But I genuinely thought my deep held fear of rejection was by now, way in the past. I'd worked through it, I'd been a joyful participant in women's groups, my work is even with women and they are always beautiful and empowering experiences.

Still, I held back and at the very last minute, as I was about to opt out of joining this immersion, something shifted. Suddenly I felt electrified with excitement and in a blind surge of courage, I took the leap and confirmed my place. Hours before our first sister circle trepidation still lurked within. My heart pounded against my chest as my finger hovered over the Zoom link to join the opening ceremony. I felt the raw vulnerability of my twelve-year-old self.

Then there we were…a spectrum of womanhood, differentiated by decades and circumstance. I smiled as I looked at the radiant expectant faces in front of me and sensed a beautiful golden thread of connection and acceptance from the start. As we began our journey together a sense of tranquillity embraced me. Lighting our candles, drinking our cacao, sharing our thoughts, each element powerfully dispelling my tension and calming my heart. I was at last relaxed and able to be fully present. In our first guided meditation we were invited to travel back to meet the girl we used to be. To my surprise I was eager for this, my fear all flown. I was in my office which had become my sanctuary, my peaceful place. Slowly and with love, I prepared, lighting my favourite candles with scents of lavender and citrus. I sat with my cacao and allowed the guided meditation to gently lead me back in time.

As I excavated through the layers, I understood there was still so much to be mended. The closer I came to my young Jenni, the more I felt her acute pain. How she was lost in her difference, knowing she didn't fit in and yet not really understanding why. She felt out on a limb. Afraid to give rein to her true self in front of

31

others because that self, had previously been so despised and rejected. She had escaped into dreams and stories, living a rich life in her mind, becoming the characters she read about in her childhood books and those she created in her mind. She dreamt of being beautiful and beloved.

At last, I was able to truly reach her. I came to her bedroom, that so familiar place. In that chilly house without central heating, she sat huddled in front of the gas fire after an icy journey home from that school where she felt so alone. I sat by her and took her in my arms, holding her close as she longed to be held. Wordlessly giving her the gift of unbounded love. I felt myself - both something of the absent sister and of the gentler mother she needed so much.

We never spoke but I knew she understood. Time dissolved as I took her into my heart and finally accepted it was ok for her to be me and for me to be her. We no longer needed to be afraid of who we were. Our journeys of imagination, storytelling and creating were not and *are* not oddities but joyous beautiful gifts to be celebrated.

And I realised there are others like us, girls and women who embrace us and travel with us. At the next ceremony it was amazingly comfortable to share my thoughts and feelings with my sister circle. Knowing they too had been on this extraordinary adventure to meet their younger selves. Listening to their stories and insights, I felt a deep sense of peace as all those golden threads of connection wove us closer together in a glorious tapestry of womanhood. And from it flowed my creativity - in the rituals and ceremonies throughout that 22 day container, I drew and I painted as I haven't done for years! That little self who was always

32

drawing, always filling endless books with her picture stories and designs - she flowered in me.

Then came the letter. One of the rituals for the girls we used to be, was to write her a letter. A joy filled process - she loved words, I love words - and they flowed easily. I wrote ceremoniously, crafting each sentence and reviving my rusty calligraphy skills because I knew beauty gave her (and gives me) such pleasure. As I wrote, it was as if she and I morphed to become complete, as one being.

There was an unspoken process of forgiveness between us. I understood how, in a sense, I had been afraid of her, of being her and now the fear was dissolving as we blended. The reassurance, the understanding, the unconditional love I was expressing to her was for me, for us.

To us, I said 'You are loved and lovable now and always. There is no need to chase love, no need to sacrifice yourself, your values, your beliefs to gain love'. The words resonated through me, this was such an essential learning in my life. 'The person you need to give your love to more than anyone else is YOURSELF. Be gentle and kind to you, be proud of who you are, care deeply for yourself and live your life, not a life thrust upon you' I wrote.

The letter sits beside me now, decorated with a border of roses, a precious message to the girl I used to be, who is me and has always been. On many days since I wrote those words, I have lit a sweet-scented candle and as the flame flickers we talk together and cement the peace and understanding between us. Connecting with her and honouring her has strengthened me and enriched my life now. I am truly inspired to embrace and explore her gifts and power of imagination, which are still mine and to go on to facilitate this journey in others.

33

She will never feel lost and alone again.

Being a 'grown up'

'What is being 'grown up'?' This was the question that struck me as I travelled with my sisters on this journey of self-discovery into the present day. At what point, in the many years since my lonely schooldays, did I feel 'grown up'? Tall and well developed, I looked a woman from my early teens. I felt the simmering power of my sexuality, I loved yet hated my curvaceous shape.

My physicality seemed to be pushing me to face 'grown up' challenges far too soon. It summoned me into a visceral relationship with my body that has been a driving force in my subsequent experience of womanhood. Starving myself and exercising to excess in pursuit of an impossible ideal, I believed that if my body was 'right' then I would be accepted, wanted, loved. Slowly and painfully, I came to understand my delusion and in my second half century, I have learned to be kinder to myself, recognising more of my value and beauty beyond my physical frame.

As I sat in the safe feminine space of our sister circle, I sensed some of my uncertainties echoed in the words of my sisters, their rollercoaster stories of the vibrant peaks and troughs of youth and their challenging journeys towards the centred clarity of maturity. 'Where was I now?', 'Who was the woman I had become?'. She'd spent sixty-four years on earth, she'd been a daughter, a mother, she had loved and lost passionately, adventured and risked, been so brave and so very afraid.

After ten days in our sister circle I felt unrestrained, able to open my heart as never before and to explore immeasurable layers of myself. I felt ready to discover and fully embrace the woman I was now. Just as well, for we dived deep. It was as if every word that was spoken and every ritual we engaged in, had been created specifically to bring me face to face with those old demons who still raised their heads on dark days. Especially my body demons. I recognised them as manifesting in the present around the physicality of ageing.

Travelling in guided meditation, I touched my body, engaging with my physical being and feeling it's power in my breath. Visiting every bone, muscle and ligament, the framework that supports me, honouring the service it has given throughout my life. Allowing my awareness of the vast network of nerves, the magnificent mystery of connections that permit my sensory existence, the very joy of touch itself, of sight and taste and smell. Understanding intensely how deeply enmeshed are the body, mind and spirit.

This sumptuous journey left me feeling more at one with myself than I had in a long time. Contemplating the extraordinary functionality of your own human body, is both humbling and exhilarating. For me, this now often-repeated meditation, has become a source of self-love. It dispels occasional negative thoughts and feelings about my signs of ageing, helps me appreciate every line and wrinkle, saggy skin, even my varicose veins! They are all me, they are integral to the woman I am and who I am proud to be.

This meditation set me on the path to peace with my body. Then came the ritual that was for me the most intense of all we undertook on our immersion journey. The Ritual Bath. I waited

35

some days to do this, so I could be alone at home and have the time and space to create an experience that combined rich sensuous pleasure with sacred honouring or self.

I bought armfuls of roses, my favourites with the sunset petals that mingle vermillion, coral, apricot and pale gold. Lilies too, blush pink and glorious. I placed some in a vase in the hallway by a mirror where I would watch myself undress. I prepared petals to scatter in a pathway to the bathroom and to scatter in the bath. Lily heads and roses decorated the bathroom with rose and lavender scented candles.

Tealights were spread along the shelf by the bath and my favourite lavender bath oil swirled into the steaming water. Gentle music played as I walked from my bedroom. I wore my most beautiful underwear and a Kimono which I shed ceremoniously in front of a full-length mirror, taking time to gaze at every part of me and acknowledge it for everything it had given me.

I followed the petals to reach my bath, revelling in the glorious scent and subtle light, reverently lowering my body into the water and allowing every sensation to be slowly blissful.

I lay in this liquid paradise, lazily stroking my hands over my skin, cleansing myself with loving intention. As in our mediation, I focused on gratitude, appreciating every part of me for the amazing functionality that allowed me to do so much in my life. Gazing at my body, raising and stretching a leg or an arm from the flower strewn water, I was suddenly acutely aware of what my maturity meant to me. This body was, *is* magnificent! Not in the sense of the wand slender perfection that I'd craved for so long. It is magnificent in having lived and worked and served me for over sixty years. And it is unique because it is mine!

36

Accepting, loving and honouring myself, my physical, cerebral, emotional and spiritual self is what being 'grown up' means to me. The glorious ritual bath gave me certainty in that.

Does that mean I am now fully at peace with my body and honour and appreciate it every day? No. I am still on the journey of my womanhood. I've come a million miles from the punitive struggle and self-doubt of my youth and yet I still have times where my demons rise. The difference is, I know how to manage them. Even on the worst of days, I can connect back to how incredible it is to be a human being, a woman, experiencing and learning about her own life.

The woman I am yet to become

Writing this nearly a year on from my immersion experience and I have already travelled through two significant life changes, moving into a new home and becoming a grandmother. Both have created inner shifts that I did not anticipate. I feel more than ever that my future self will always be something of an enigma. She will inevitably grow in directions I do not yet comprehend.

When I embarked on the exploration of my future self, in the third week, fear again raised its head for me. Secret fear, for despite the deep trust I now felt within my sister circle, I resisted sharing. My fears were of ageing, loneliness, illness and death, of losing people, losing my mind, becoming invisible. They seemed inappropriate to share with those with much more time before them.

Entering this part of my journey with such reservations I was beautifully surprised by the playfulness of it. Our rituals were joyous explorations and made me feel free, re-engaged with my childhood self, creating ethereal dreamworlds, yet fundamentally in touch with my core being and aware of the depth of wisdom that has grown in me.

Two of these rituals brought me particular joy.

The first was making my 'holy water' in preparation for our final ceremony. As my container, I chose a cut glass vase that had belonged to my mother. This was a seemingly spontaneous choice but once made, I recognised it's significance. My mother and I had a challenging relationship marked by peaks and troughs. Even at its lowest ebb I admired her strength and never more did I admire her, than in her last days, when she showed incredible resilience and positivity, making everyone around her laugh. I recognised that the woman I want to become is as courageous and determined as her and like her, will never lose her sense of the ridiculous.

I collected beauty and love to add to my water. Scents of rose, lavender, vanilla and jasmine, fresh basil leaves, creamy flower petals, tiny white pebbles and pearly shells from an adored beach in Greece. I revelled in the process and was again reminded of how vital rich sensory experiences are to who I am and who I'm becoming. My life will always be enhanced by smell and touch and taste and sound and most of all by sight.

The second ritual was equally delightful. Sitting in tranquillity, pen in hand, inviting in words for my future self. Words for the essence of her, words for the life she lives and for what brings her joy and fulfilment. A cornucopia of delicious words flooded my mind, I discovered many were synonyms. Instinct guided me to select those I carefully scribed and embellished on my final list. Perhaps my wise woman instinct, leading me to create what is to come?

Reflection enlightened me to see how the words were and are, integral to my whole life, to my values and beliefs and to the learning gleaned from every experience way back to early childhood. Passion and sensuality were there. Freedom, Courage and Adventure. Joy and Abundance. And what mattered, was not the words but what those words meant for me. My adventure isn't about courting danger, my courage is not about bravado. As when I was a child, in the present and into the future, I know I will always be an adventurer of the mind.

Exploring each word on my list, I understood how the woman I am yet to become will always be me. She will see and know things beyond my present perception – the very pace of technological development ensures this, even within a relatively short time but she will experience them through the filters of my lifetime and the fundamentals of my personality.

The most exhilarating and terrifying realisation of the whole sister circle immersion was seeing how connected every part of my life has been, how there are spiral patterns of revisiting, relearning, renewing. I am all my selves; the lonely child, the wild rebellious girl, the risk taker and adventurer, the loving mother, the woman who has guided and mentored others for over forty years. In maturity, these elements are coming together and giving me the power to be more truly comfortably myself than ever before, which doesn't make it easy. I still have days when I don't feel 'grown up'!

And are my fears of ageing and mortality still with me? Yes and they were intensely emphasised as I held my four-day old grandson in my arms. But I have come to see that engaging with my fears in essential in my being and my becoming. These fears remind me to live in the moment and to take pleasure in the tiny things that make up the hours and days of my life. My fears remind me to cherish those close to me and reach out to people I haven't seen in a while, to stay in tune with my values and beliefs and to be true to the woman I am and to the woman I am yet to become.

Lesley Readman

45

When the time came to push for the light, oh she
would absolutely know.
And nothing would stop her.
It would seem like the most obvious move in the world.
So to pass the time, she just counted the stars, pushed
her seeds deep into the earth
and watered them with spells and medicine and smoke.
Whispers on the wind always found their way home.

from 'Sacred'

Grounding, raising vibration, honouring and loving the land

When I was drawn to honour myself by completing this sister circle, I did wonder what the purpose of it was for me. I discovered though that there are many aspects of this journey which held gifts for me, in fact, to be honest, all of it did.

One aspect however reigned supreme. The immersion brought me back to truly honouring and valuing the power of ritual. As I write these words, I feel my whole core is alive as I light my candle and create my cacao medicine.

My core being recognises these actions as a portal to my very deepest inner self and I drop into a deep meditative state quickly now. In the past I found it really difficult to be in this state...I was too yang...too much doing and not enough being. As I moved into my Wise Woman years, I was drawn to reconnect with mother earth and her rhythms and cycles, in the same way I had when I was much younger, in my early years – the girl I used to be.

Somewhere in the middle of my life, the business of life had taken over and I'd forgotten the grounding of mother nature. Through this sister circle however, I remembered once more and I began to walk in nature alone and at the liminal times of the day...dawn and dusk. Dawn and dusk are the times of day when magic happens. The veil to the other worlds is thinner.

I'm lucky enough to live by a beautiful wood which leads down to the ocean, so as I walk, I experience the wonder of forest bathing and the power of water. As I begin my walks, I drop down into a meditative state. My heart opens and I'm deep in a state of bliss. It's usually dawn when I take my daily ritual walk, the route is always empty of human activity. I'm able to be just me and raw with nature, waking up to the world. I am deeply in love with mother earth. I feel her as a mother, feeling the solidness of her body as she caresses me and makes me feel safe and loved. I feel oneness with all that resides on her, adoring the songs of the birds and the running water in the stream flowing down to the sea through the wood. I often want to dance on her surface. She has become sacred to me and I feel myself wanting to honour her more and more.

I love that I now make life decisions in order to tread lightly on her surface. She looks after me and sustains me, in exchange I look after her. As much as possible, I dance barefoot on her surface and feel the negative ions rising up through my body, resetting me for the day. In being in nature daily, I now honour all weather patterns and seasons. Honestly? I'm a warm weather sun lover but I now see the value in honouring the silence, rest and cold present in winter, the yin phase where mother earth rests and recuperates, everything is happening within, under the surface and deep inside both mother earth and in me.

I feel the seeds I've planted in this still time are being nurtured inside, ready to burst into being during the coming growth season.

One of my beautiful, beautiful memories of the girl I used to be, was going on a treasure hunt for flowers, discarded bird's nests, stones, sticks covered in moss and lichen. Anything actually that mother earth wanted to gift to me. We always had a nature table at school so I created one at home to reconnect me to this time.

In our sister circle immersion, there is a treasure hunt for the girls we used to be, my heart opened at this ritual, my face was wreathed in smiles. This was my very special activity when a girl and the one that made me skip with joy. I delighted in the simplest of things. I loved doing this wherever I was, so I was delighted to carry out a treasure hunt just for my little girl, it raised my vibration and grounded me at the same time!

These rituals of collecting, brought me to a lifelong dance with nature, to deeply love and honour our beautiful planet, to question always what is done to her and to live simply. I felt I needed to anchor into the earth and so making the decision to walk daily in nature helped me to do this. As I walked, I carried out a ritual where I would connect heaven and earth with my heart field being the central point.

I imagined a silver thread starting in my heart, travelling down through my chakras and out through the soles of my feet, down into the earth star chakra and the core of the earth. I remember bringing that energy back up to my heart field allowing it to rest there, the silver thread travelling up and out through my crown chakra into the cosmos to receive cosmic energy. I imagined cosmic energy coming down into my heart field to mingle with the earth energy.

I would visualise the energy of roses and connect deeply to them. This beautiful ritual of walking in nature and collecting things rekindled my love of her and changed my life. I've been able to bring in structure and be more balanced, to really work with my foundation which needed to be much more stable.

So, from a simple daily walk, in nature, I gained the ability to change my life for the better. I became like the trees in the wood, firmly rooted, with my branches reaching up right into the cosmos, truly bringing heaven down to earth in a beautiful and simplistic way.

When I do this, I notice that my beautiful heart attracts life experiences and people which resonate with the frequency emitted from it, so I look after it now by not exposing it to negativity, in order to attract my best possible life.

I've noticed that as I do my work, my health and life have improved and I've attracted amazing opportunities. As I continue to walk in nature, I feel myself improving in so many ways. I've learned that the earth emits a vibration equal to 7.83 hertz and I feel that receiving these frequencies in my own auric field makes me more relaxed, I heal.

I noticed that friends matching my old lower vibration fell away as I magnetised new friends on my new higher frequency. I began to attract awesome opportunities as I truly began to love myself as I am.

As I continued to work on myself through this ritual, I've been able to strip away the conditioning and ancestral patterns that were binding me and to see myself as a lighthouse shining from within.

My vibration feels higher and I believe in the doing of these rituals regularly and the continual work I do on myself, I receive so many rewarding experiences.

During this time of renewed connection to mother earth, I realised I felt called to certain lands. Almost as if the land was speaking to me and calling me to commune with it. I started to learn about dowsing and stone circles, ancient buildings and land energy.

The land beneath my feet speaks to me, allowing me to feel in my body (usually in my solar plexus) either positive or negative gut reactions. I have evolved this ritual now so I can visit significant points on the earth where there is heightened earth energy. I soak up this fabulous energy from whatever I happen to be visiting, I always feel energised and in tune with my beloved mother earth.

As I write these words, my heart is wide open in honour of the power of ritual in my life.

Lighting my candle

I always considered lighting a candle quite an ordinary act. However, doing this in ritual has become a doorway into my inner being. As I approach my altar, dedicated to honouring myself and my wellbeing, my heart stirs knowing that I'm entering sacred space.

As I approach the candle at the centre of this sacred space, I bow my head with reverence now before lighting it, drawing in a breath, loving its dance and feeling my heart fly open. I have become the dancer in the flame! I mirror its movements with my body temple. Moving meditation is my practice. Always in candlelight, I'm deeply grateful to create such ambience by lighting a candle. Candlelight has become a necessity in my life.

My altar is dedicated to me, not in an egotistical way but as a reminder to honour myself, to fill my cup up before serving others. As I perform this simple ritual, my body knows it's being honoured. Sometimes I add beautiful essential oils to the melting wax which gives off an intoxicating aroma and I slip into a meditative state easily.

When I move in meditation, I find ideas for beautiful self-care rituals arise and I feel so much love for myself. The daily ritual of lighting the candle, for me, is the key to beginning to really love and honour myself and that, in turn, led to a new life where I let go of things that no longer served me. I've begun to really look after my wellbeing.

I always used sugar and sweet foods to fill the gap created by one of my heart wounds – abandonment. However, in that very act, I was abandoning myself, I wasn't looking after myself physically or spiritually. The gaping hole inside me cried out for sweetness. I knew that before I could receive it from others, I had to give it to myself.

So, this honouring, the ritual of lighting the candle, has brought me much needed improvements to the way I live my life. I no longer crave sweet foods, instead, I feel truly blessed.

Throughout this immersion, I lit candles to honour the three aspects of myself and in ceremony, a candle is lit for each of us as we speak in turn, the eldest first. We also lit candles, in the most beautiful ceremony, to honour all the children we love and wish to remember. This ceremony was one of the most moving for me…two of my children are in the spirit world and I realised how beautiful it is to honour and send them my love in this way. My tears flowed. I realised I'd never fully grieved for them.

In the closing ceremony, we lit three candles to honour 'the girls we used to be', 'the women we are now' and 'the women we are yet to become'. Again, such a truly simple act, so deep and profound.

I grew up in a culture where women and children were seen and not heard. This conditioning directed my life choices for many years, causing me to stay small and not to embrace my gifts, so this ceremony of honouring and bringing attention to 'the girl I used to be' just released all that old cellular memory and stored emotion I'd been carrying around.

I truly love the flickering light of a candle now, even more so when my room is lit with many candles…my happy place is now dancing in my temple, with candlelight and cacao, the aroma of essential oils and flowers on my altar, honouring the three aspects of myself. Such a simple gift.

Sacred space and water

I listened to the flow of water cascading down into the tub and was immediately transported into my world of deep nurturing. The room was dimly lit with candles, my heart opened as I noticed the dancing candle flames. This sister circle ritual of bathing with intention and the darkness of my bathroom transported me into my nurturing womb space. I allowed the water to run over my hand and I noticed its warmth. I poured healing salts into the water, essential oils and rose petals. The aroma was divine and luxurious.

This room is my sacred place, my deep bath, my cauldron of transformation. I climb in and feel the warmth of the water enveloping and nurturing me. I remember lying back and inhaling the fragranced air, allowing me to go deep within. I communed with my guides and higher self, in my sanctuary, where I can be truly me.

Many years ago, when I was truly 'the girl I used to be' all young and open, I remember seeing an advert for a well-known chocolate bar where the lady eating the chocolate bar was relaxing in a beautiful roll top bath. I'd never seen one before and I remember the water spilling over the top of the bath as if there were an abundant supply bubbling up from the base. The idea of being in a vat of pure warm water, relaxing felt like a portal to another world to me, a portal to the ancient celts whom I feel a great affinity with. I feel they are my Scottish ancestors. Water is sacred and part of *their* way of connecting to the divine was going to the edge of the ocean or bathing in a sacred spring, well or waterfall.

So, as time went on, I installed roll top baths wherever I lived! My bathroom became my sanctuary. All I regarded as sacred was in this precious space. My candles on wall sconces, my deep cauldron of a bath and my ritual incense and oils. Once I was in this room, I could be alone, just me, to spend sacred time with myself.

I began to see bathing as far more than washing, the whole ritual became an honouring of myself, a chance to be with me, my real self. The ritual of oiling my body and sculpting the divine became a loving honouring of myself and I became more and more connected to myself, nature and I started to develop deep love for myself through this amazing ritual.

The act of stepping off the treadmill and allocating time to myself is essential in my wellbeing practice. As I allowed the experience to develop into a beautiful sacred practice rather than just a quick wash, I felt the need to create other practices which became sacred too. To this day, as far as I can, I live in a sacred way, very simply but with great reverence, honouring timelines, events and people, being fully present in life, honouring mother earth and nature, seeing the beauty in everything and everyone.

Slowing down and living, my cup is absolutely full.

Mikel Ann Hall

23

Planets did their thing,
the world spun in perfect harmony,
all she needed to do was meet her beautiful Self.

from 'HELD'

Self-forgiveness

Salty and sweet with a large dollop of comforting cream. That's the flavour I'm tasting right now. A familiar flavour I've tasted ever since I was a little girl. The salt of the tears pouring down my face mixed with the sweetness of swirled chocolate in the rich creaminess of my favourite ice cream. I can still hear the voices except they're no longer *their* voices. It's my own voice I hear. I sob even harder, my shoulders heaving as I listen to it, begging it to shut up. I feel weak, vulnerable and powerless like the little girl I used to be. It's here, as I reach the bottom of yet another pint of ice cream, that the anger sets in. It's been rising with each spoonful. The silent sharp rage turned inward onto myself, I've been desperately trying to stuff down and silence. Sitting in isolation, in a sea of shame, again, I ask myself, 'When will I ever learn?', I'm nearly 58!

I have many very sweet moments and memories of my childhood. Growing up, we spent a lot of time in Mexico with many other families camping and sailing, laughing until we had stitches in our sides. We played, wandered, explored and pretended. Oh the adventures we had! They were sweeter than *all* the flavours of ice cream in the whole wide world!

But it was behind closed doors, in the dark moments at home, the secrets that no-one knew, where things were scary and my childhood innocence was lost. It wasn't all the time, yet there were too many moments, too much repetition that it couldn't help but leave a deep searing pain and scar on my heart. The ugly yelling, raging untruths. Blame turned into so much shame. Home was unsafe for I never knew when, or for what, I would be blamed and all the malicious hurtful untruths would come raging out, burying me.

52

One moment I was happily playing, singing into my hairbrush, laughing and dancing with my bestie, the next I was alone sobbing, cowering, wishing upon a star that I was invisible, as the untruths that were hurled in screams of an angry rage, slicing my heart to the quick. 'You're not good enough. Who do you think you are? You're different from everyone else and will never fit in. If your friends really knew who you were, if they saw you now, they wouldn't like you. Look at you crying. They'd laugh at you and not invite you to play with them anymore'. And on and on it went.

Even as a little girl, I knew, I felt it deep in my heart that these lies were untrue. What about all the beautiful fun playful memories I had of Mexico? They gave me hope, promise and truth, for I had lived them. They were real and that's who I was. Happy, carefree, filled with laughter, a sense for adventure and zest for life!

My young mind divided life into good and bad. When I was good, I was heard, seen, loved and cherished. When I was alone, afraid, unheard and unworthy, that was the bad. I spoke up against the lies and untruths but my soft voice wasn't heard. Their voices got louder and louder until they became my voice. Their untruths were repeated over and over until they became my truth. The pain and chaos of the conflict became too much over the years and I disconnected from my heart. I started to pretend I was happy when I was crying inside. I became someone I wasn't, in order to please others, in the hopes of stopping the pain and the shame inside.

Conflict became my world. A judgemental world made up of good and bad. 'What if this was who I really was?' And so, I lived between two worlds which were both real, not knowing which one was the real me. At a young age I learned to live, and survive in a sea of untruths yet still dared to dream. When I grew up, I was going to be a mermaid and swim in the seas and travel to faraway places and foreign lands like my grandma. And that's what I did! I became a scuba instructor and dived in seas all over the world, sailed through the Caribbean and Europe, spent several years in French Polynesia, ran marathons, competed in triathlons, climbed to Mount Everest Base Camp, crossed the finish line of my 1st Ironman in New Zealand for my 50th birthday and I've spent the last four years traveling solo and living in South East Asia, never once celebrating myself for my accomplishments yet always looking for more. Something to fill the empty space within.

And through it all, I found the sweetest of sweetness, better than any flavour of ice cream or gelato I have ever tasted! Self-forgiveness. I sampled it many times over the years, yet it was a flavour that I had to grow into. I didn't like it right away; I'd even spit it out and wouldn't go near it for many years! Every now and then, travels would find me sampling it again, as I stumbled and fell into blame and shame traveling through foreign places, the deep dark scary shadows I'd suppressed, buried and lost myself in.

It wasn't until I turned 58, that I tasted the yummy flavours of self-compassion, self-acceptance, even true self-love...the sweetness of self-forgiveness became one of my favourite flavours! Self-forgiveness has been a life-long solo journey of discernment. Unlearning and remembering. Adventuring down dusty dirt roads, through foreign lands exploring who I am and who I am not. Living my best life and then taking a wrong turn into untruth, self-rejection, self-abuse and swimming in the depths of shame for it.

It became easier over the years to share my story and be heard by others. No-one was judging me. I was being seen for who I was and each woman carefully listened to my story. Women were gathering and I was invited to sit in circle with them and so, loving a new adventure, I did.

I found an amazing community of love and support. We were women of all ages from all over the world sitting together in circle, sipping ceremonial cacao, learning about rituals and self-honour. Today I am seen. I celebrate who I was, who I am and who I am becoming.

Self-love

As time went on in this gathering of women, I was falling in love and little by little, my life was changing. A deep inner peace was settling in and I'd found the sweetest love of all, self-love. Like love sometimes does, it snuck up on me. It found me actually, in rituals, which until now, were foreign and unfamiliar.

My favourite...sipping cacao in the early morning hours. The beautiful warm heart opening elixir, guiding me to clarity and truth. She grounds me in the true essence of who I am and who I am becoming. As we sit together, I can taste the sweetness of life as joy returns, gratitude and an acceptance, a sense of love and I experience a deep inner peace within.

I awakened with each new sunrise with a deeper sense of peace and self-acceptance. I honoured myself by lighting a candle. And each time I did, I watched the flame dance and change as it swayed in the wind. I saw myself. The soft gracefulness of changing beauty. Just like the tides ebb and flow in the sea, so does my life. Surrendering, I have realised, is a process of allowing and going with the ebb and flow. Sometimes I get pummelled as a huge wave of challenges crashes ruthlessly upon the shore of my heart and I fall, I forget about rituals and shrink back into the darkness and harshness of untruths and hurtful habits. It takes time for me to catch my breath, to find my truth again, yet I do.

During this process, I was being held by the tenderness of my sisters in circle. Each time we gathered; I was listened to. I was seen and I am no longer alone. As the days passed and my heart softened, with seeing myself as I am, one of my greatest moments of bravery came when I invited my little girl to sit next to me. We sipped cacao together as the sun rose. I'd lit two candles on this particular morning, one for her and the other for me - the woman I was. I invited her to bring the heavy bags of untruth she'd been carrying and all the words she had spoken that went unheard. Sitting in tenderness with her for days and allowing her to be heard with no judgement, our truth emerged.

She spoke about the darkness, the loneliness, the isolation and her fears which had become her prison and her reality. Bless her...she poured out her heart, the words and sobs tumbling out of her. With each day that passed, each candle that was lit and with every cup of cacao sipped, we explored. With a child's curiosity, we invited each untruth to sit with us. Together we looked at it, bringing it into the light. She cried and kept talking until there was no more. I found self-love in rituals, time does heal and for each day, I honoured myself with rituals, the truth of who I am grounded in my being.

I began to feel differently, to see things differently and the bounce in my step and sparkle in my eyes returned. It was becoming clear to me who I was and who I was not.

One evening during this immersion, as the sun began to set, I sat on the shore. The last golden rays dancing, sparkling like glitter on the sea, the waves tickling my toes, my feet in the sand, I tossed my untruths into the wind...speaking them one by one out loud.

'I never was and am not the emotional abuse I grew up with'

'I'm not responsible for other people's anger and unhappiness'

'I am not my tears or the sadness that I hid behind'

When there were no more words, tears filled my eyes as I opened them and I marvelled at my view...the golden glow of the clouds softening into a honey colour and then transforming and filling the sky with soft pale pastel pinks and purples.

Just as the sky had transformed and softened, so had my heart. Forever grateful in silence, solitude and stillness I was able to say good-bye to who I was not.

Choosing ritual, choosing me

I'm an elder now, wiser and I know that each tear I cried throughout the years taught me something. Like snowflakes, no two tears were ever the same. I'd been holding onto the pain because it was all I had left from all I thought I'd lost. The heaviness of it had become a part of my identity. Who I thought I was. It took time for me to listen to the sweet melody of truths stirring in my heart. They had always been there, yet had become faint whispers I'd been afraid to listen to. My truths now become crystal clear with each day I sit in ritual, listening to the silence found in solitude and honouring who I am.

Self-grace travels through me and soothes my soul like a sweet lullaby. I am no longer divided. I am whole and complete as I am. I am enough. I am beautiful and deeply loved by many. Grown wiser throughout my years, I am a respected woman who has many gifts to share with the world and a heart for service and support.

This is my truth.

At 59, I've been respected as the elder each time I've sat in a sister circle. I realised during this time, that we are all elders to the younger women in our lives, holding space and allowing them to journey into *their* truth as we walk beside them. Entering a new phase in life and thinking of myself as an elder hasn't been easy and came with a kaleidoscope of colourful emotions! It's been a rough and bumpy transition which, in all honesty, I'm still learning to embrace. My heart opens more with each sip of cacao, allowing the tears to flow. Releasing sadness eases the loneliness I've felt for having not been seen. I know the world needs to both see me and hear what I have to say, so I'm settling into a new role with a deeper sense of who I'm becoming. A woman who chooses to share her wisdom. A woman who is seen and no longer remains in the shadows. I'm my own heroine exploring and discovering a new way of living.

Spending so much of my childhood in Mexico, I grew up thinking I was open minded. Getting the first stamp in my passport taught me otherwise. I was only as open minded as my experiences. I've travelled and lived in foreign countries all over the world and have returned to the pure bliss of seeing life through a beginner's mind, always coming back to myself. To my mind, the relationship I have with myself is the most important relationship in my life. What if I loved myself fully? Loved the imperfections and learned with mindfulness to become the love I always sought?

I breathe and I listen to what's stirring within me, I trust myself and my visions for the future and I commit to the desires in my heart, the ones I've known were there and have been longing to be pursued. It's time for me to listen to that.

This new chapter is a new path, clearing out the old. It's bold and brighter than ever, for I'm dancing in courage and radiance. I'm active in women's circles, walking hand in hand with them, giggling as we walk, sharing my gifts and wisdom and receiving theirs. I'm embarking on a new and deeper journey of tenderness, the softness of the self-grace and compassion I've found in all the years I've lived. In the past, it's when I've avoided and denied this truth, that I've picked up the spoon for comfort, yet it's no longer comforting.

It's in rituals and honouring this new phase of life, that I'm finding a new sweetness. I have a choice now: to choose a spoon or ritual. And in being an elder, I know each time I pick up the spoon, I'm living in my untruth. I'm okay with not having all the answers and trusting that I'm more prepared for each new day than I feel. And when I feel low, all the confusion, doubt and fears from the past, marinating in self-pity, dragging me through the day, I have hope.

Sometimes hope is a radical act in itself for me, sometimes it's my second wind or the awareness of the beauty that surrounds me. Self-love is not something I 'feel', but rather something I 'do' each day. It's a sense of intimacy with my own Self. Breathing in joy, knowing I am simultaneously vulnerable and invincible. A deep sense of knowing I am safe in my own embrace. This is the essence of who I am.

I'm just a woman with a pen in one hand, sometimes a spoon in the other, who got tired of living lies, living in the shadows. I became curious and took a journey which led me on the magical discovery of who I really am. I choose now to celebrate life and this present moment: who I was, who I am and who I'm becoming by choosing what makes my spirit sing, what fills my heart with love, what makes my soul soar – and doing more of that!

Jennifer Levers

106

Feather earrings in honour of her soul sisters,
bare feet in honour of Pachamama,
incense in honour of her spirit,
cacao in honour of Source.
Tattoos in honour of her journey,
meditation in honour of her Self.

from 'A Woman's Blessing'

Speaking up

I feel the rocking, I sense the movement side to side. I open my eyes. I see a woman looking at me. I see her smile. It doesn't reach her eyes. I see the fear before she looks away quickly. 'You're in the back of an ambulance' she says. 'You are on your way to A&E. You passed out'.

It's August 2017 I've had a cancer diagnosis. Part of my treatment is a programme of high intensity radiotherapy. At a deep visceral level, I know this is not what I want for my body. It feels intuitively wrong to me. Barbaric even. My consultant tells me it's what's needed. Everyone agrees. It is the pathway of treatment. It's expected. It's the only course of action. I'm full of fear. Desperate to do anything that will rid my body of the cancer. And yet. I know. The core of my being knows this isn't right for me. I yearn for another way. I don't speak, though. I don't say 'no'. It just doesn't come.

At my first radiotherapy consultation, I'm strapped to the bed in readiness for the scan. Suddenly I'm very ill. We have to stop. I sit for a while breathing deeply. I want to say 'no more' but there's a restriction in my throat. I want to roar 'stop'. It doesn't come. Silence. The word remains unspoken. My voice is buried deep inside. I convince myself it's just nerves. It will be OK. I don't pay attention. I don't say 'no'. At the second visit, my right arm goes numb. The consultant straps my arm tightly in place. My body is saying 'no' for me. I don't hear. I don't say 'no'. I feel the panic as the machinery whirrs and clicks and moves around me. Stay calm. Stay calm. Breathe. Just breathe. I imagine rays of beautiful rainbow colours landing on my skin. Healing my cells. Protecting my skin. I don't speak. I don't say 'no'.

At my last radiotherapy session, I pass out. The bright lights of A&E. The noise. I sense the pain and fear of others. I'm numb. Nothing touches me. It's as if I'm watching it happening to someone else. I'm not really part of it. I'm left in a bed behind curtains. The pink and yellow flowers dance as the curtains sway with the movement of others. I lie back. I close my eyes. I sense a stirring. I breathe.

A breath as deep and wide as the ocean and it lasts forever. I feel the calmness wash over me. I know deep inside. I know the truth. This is the learning. This is what I needed to hear. This is what it has all been for. Deep wisdom whispers to me.

'You have stopped speaking your truth.'

'You have stopped listening.'

'It's time to find your voice'

'It's time to speak'

The tears come then. I'm dissolving in the saltiness. I'm melting in shame. The armour around my heart is cracking. Love pours out. I feel warmth as it surges through my body. It hurts profoundly and is beautiful all at the same time. The tears cleanse and wash away the hurt, the pain. The layers are falling away.

'Forgive me' I whisper.

That was then and this is now. As I sit in a sister circle, a gathering of women, it's clear that this has been a key part of my journey to authenticity, to the radiant and real me, to find my voice and encourage deeper knowing. Secret insights have been revealed in these circles, shared experiences, observations disclosed, wise words spoken. So often, I've heard what I needed to hear. Recently, as other women spoke, I felt the stirrings. I felt emotion rising from the depth of my knowing. I felt sensations surfacing. The memory of those times in hospital hit me with full force. The emotions welled up and nearly floored me. So strong. Profound meaning. The insights landed. The power of sister circle had worked its magic again.

This time;

I was paying attention.

I was listening.

I was speaking.

I knew I had to share. I knew it was time. That's why sister circle is so important for me. The space where I feel I can truly show up and be me. Other's experiences eliciting my own deep learning. Letting go of the pretence, the fear of not being accepted. There's no need to hide in sister circle, I can allow the layers to fall away and be witnessed in the becoming of the woman who pays attention, hears her own wisdom and speaks her knowledge with conviction.

It's a journey into 'Unbecoming'...

Unbecoming the woman I thought I had to pretend to be
Unbecoming the woman who thought she needed to please others
Unbecoming the woman who looked outside for love
Unbecoming the woman driven by fear or pain
Unbecoming the woman who hides her power and her voice
Unbecoming the woman who was seen and not heard
Unbecoming the woman who had forgotten how to love and honour herself

Becoming the speaker of my truth in sister circle. I love the deep pleasure in sister circle ritual. The importance of self-care and expressing love to myself. We light the candles. They shine for me.

Bright and beautiful. They light my way. I feel spacious and grounded with deep roots to my own nature. It's my time to share. I hold my special cacao mug to my heart. I breathe the earthy smell of love and nature. I feel the warmth against my skin and the spreading to my heart. I bless its goodness and the women with whom I share this experience. I feel it. Deep joy. Deep peace. I glance at the faces of the women around me. Luminous with love, shared wisdom, deep knowing. I feel safe. I speak. It starts as a whisper. It catches in the back of my throat. I cough. I stumble. I breathe.

A quiet voice hardly heard. It gathers its power. It grows and grows. I'm letting go. The words tumble. They are from a deep place. I'm speaking. I'm really speaking. I feel heard. There's a shift inside. The veil is lifting. I am showing myself, bearing all, no hiding. This is me. See me. Hear me. A powerful gift. The gift of sister circle. Embracing who I am. Reclaiming my life, starting with self-love. Sharing deeply. Feeling seen and heard.

Hearing my voice

I had prepared for sister circle. I had written some notes. A small share. A glimpse. Careful not to disclose too much of me. Comfortable and safe. Revealing a sliver of my week. That week. Yes, it had been tough…really tough!

But I didn't need to share all that. I had rehearsed my piece. I knew what I wanted to say. I knew what was within my comfort zone. I was ready, I was prepared. I had kept it light. I had kept it safe. Yes, it had been a tough week but I'd decided to preserve it. Hide it inside. I didn't want to burden anyone or disclose what had happened.

I had to appear happy. Happy Jenn. You could always count on Jenn to cheer you up. She's always so positive. It's what I'd become known for! I had a part to play. I remember waiting my turn. I started to speak. A controlled tone. My practiced words. It didn't feel right though. How constraining to stick to the words I'd written! But how restricting was the fear! It didn't feel right. It didn't feel real. It just wasn't me.

'Do you know what!' I heard myself say. 'These are words I've written to say to you. These are words I planned to say to you. They're not what I really want to say. I need to speak from my heart. I need to say something different. I need to share what has really happened this week!'

And I voiced it all!

I spoke from the heart. The core of me. I heard my voice full of emotion as I shared with these beautiful women my true week. These strangers that were so much more. They knew the core of me. They'd touched my soul. I shared it all. The pain I'd felt at the loss of a dear friend. The sadness I couldn't express. The tears that hadn't fallen. The fear that had gripped me. The shame that I'd survived and she had not. It all tumbled out. The fear of the cancer returning. I spoke for twenty minutes. The words had demanded to surface. They had been bubbling there and they had to be released. My emotions had found their voice. I finished speaking. I remember feeling bereft for a second. I had challenged my understanding of how it should be.

Then it was the sheer joy of sharing. The freedom of saying what I felt instead of what I thought others wanted to hear. The force of that experience. The potency of the words. Their deep magic. The spell was broken. I was being me. I was speaking my words. The release was profound. I remember sitting in stillness after my share. Hardly breathing. I felt somehow cleansed of the need to please. Purified of the game of pretence. I heard singing. It was my soul. YES! YES! YES!

What of the other women in our sister circle? What did I see reflected in their eyes? I looked at their faces. I felt trepidation. What had they thought? Had they been bored? Had they judged me? All I saw was love and compassion. All I heard were the words repeated,

'I hear you'

'I hear you'

'I hear you'

A'ho...

Feeling safe to speak from the heart. As I grew up, I learnt that oversharing (as it was called) was a bad thing. I remember the discomfort, the disdain and the criticism for those who'd shared too much emotion. It was a time for hiding feelings. Hiding hurt. Hiding tears. We just had to get on with it. It was convention. The cancer diagnosis changed that for me! I soon realised there was no way I could keep the emotions bottled up inside and squash them into non-existence, they were too raw, too frightening. At times overwhelming. I needed an outlet. I needed a safe space. I needed acceptance for all that I was feeling.

Sister circle was that space for me. I could speak. I could share. My voice could be heard without fear of judgement, disapproval or withdrawal of love. I'd become good at hiding myself emotionally. I was an A student at wearing the mask of convention. Yes, I would have a good cry alone and that would release the pressure. Speaking from the heart and sharing my deepest feelings and fears though was a very different matter. I wanted to be part of a group of women where there was no agenda, no narrative or back stories about me or who I had been. I needed to be seen as the woman I had become. Radiant, real me!

That was exactly what I found in sister circle. Sister circle is like an embrace of warmth and acceptance for me. When properly held, it feels safe. There's no judgement, only connection to other women. The other women who know nothing about my daily life, my partner, my job. They only know the deep profound me in that moment, at a level far beyond daily routine. It's a soul sharing connection. Everything is confidential. There is silence and space for all that needs to be expressed. No trying to fix each other because there is nothing wrong with us in the first place! Sister circle for me now is a space of allowing, of being whatever that means to me on that particular day, that particular hour, that particular moment.

Sister circle, ceremony and ritual support me in understanding what I bring to this world. I feel my value. I'm growing into my truth. All aspects of me. These are ancient ways of dealing with problems, with endings and beginnings. The creation of space to ask ourselves questions and hear the answers. The invitation to go deep, do meaningful work of exploration in a sacred space.

Speaking only my truth now

Speaking my truth within ceremony rites and sister circle helped me to reveal from within. For me speaking my truth means honouring the woman I am, it means honouring me, it means celebrating that I have much to say.

For me it's an acknowledgement of my voice. I can set it free; I can let my truth be heard. This sacred time provided insight and knowing where once there was numbness and protection. Ancient rites have touched me at a deep level. Self-realisation merged with unbecoming and becoming. Finding my own true voice. Now...well I can ONLY speak my truth. I am a courageous truth teller. That is the essence of me. Radiant and real.

And within that essence of me, I still find triggers and when I trace them back to the conventions and expectations I placed on myself, I see the fear I held of being different, of standing out but now I choose to celebrate my differences.

I give thanks to my heart for showing up and being open to receiving the insights that I'm meant to receive. I give thanks for the journey taking me further into the depths of my soul. I give thanks for feeling at home in my body, for finding my voice and speaking with pride. I bow in humble gratitude for the ritual that brings my sister tribe to me. Thank you for being a part of my journey, allowing me to sit in discomfort and still feel supported through my most difficult and vulnerable moments.

When I sit in sister circle, I feel honoured for who I am and what I say. Sharing the somewhat 'unhelpful' feelings I have inside of me with my tribe somehow releases their power over me.

Sitting in ceremony, lighting a candle just for me, drinking cacao with other women brings love to my heart. Self-realisation mixed with unbecoming and becoming. It's special. It's sacred. It takes me out of everyday living and into a new space, into the woman I am. I allow peace and clearness of my mind; I embody the tranquillity that is there beneath the turbulence of my daily thoughts. I find that connection and sharing helps let go of the noisiness of everyday living. The invitation to be vulnerable and let go of pretence, expectations and convention is daily devotion to me. I'm human, I'm real and while some days it's harder to master the quietness, I tell myself 'be still', 'do nothing other than shift your awareness inside Jenny'.

I enter my heart when I do that and that's where I speak from. The joy I feel from a gentle word of encouragement received or given, is powerful. I've made promises to myself and to my sisters and so now, there is a difference. As I speak, I feel the sharing rippling through me. A precious disclosure, sometimes profound, sometimes with learning and insight.

Sister Circle and ritual has created the space for me to emerge with a new awareness towards myself. Everything that happened to me including the pain and fear, created a deeper connection, a deeper wisdom and knowing of myself.

I am not growing older but growing wiser. My journey happened for a reason. Perhaps it's all been about taking me to my destiny of teaching and showing others what's possible, that there's a different way.

I've now established the patterns of ritual, the desire to give myself the space and focus on my own pleasure. It allowed honesty and truth to come out. I knew at a deep level that it was safe. It allowed me to know my truth and to speak my truth more clearly. The power of listening to other women is part of that journey of expansion for me too. What a wonderful experience to be heard and to hear others speak their truth.

I sit with others as they go on their journey with an ease and a beautiful flow. We journey together. I love to see the transformation, the light of insight and intelligence at a new level. I truly believe now that I have the capacity to understand what has meaning for me and to access my inner guidance in order to change my life. Being held in a safe space and following daily self-care rituals creates freedom for me, allowing connection to my inner wisdom.

I have a desire for other women also. I want every woman to find her voice, find her truth so that she can be a beacon for others. I feel a new confidence and have bigger dreams as a result of finding my voice. A dream where I share my knowledge and use my experience in order to guide.

I'm open to whatever comes my way now. This is a very different way of being. I feel no need to control. I'm open to this beautiful world of magic and mystery. Whatever the situation, I'm me and I'm clear on what and when I feel the need to speak my truth. The words come. And when some days I forget, I feel the change, I feel as if I'm a little unbalanced and everything is a little harder, so I go back to ritual, I go back to connection, I find my voice once more. I speak my truth. I'm radiant real me. Always.

Angela Pepperell

25

Standing in the crashing waves,
holding her drum to the gods of the oceans,
offering herself and her spells,
they took her breath away and replaced it with bliss.
Vital energy rushing through her veins, she hollered so they
could hear.
Every woman, calling them to gather, ancient DNA,
she'd held them a thousand times before
and today, they would remember.

from 'Sacred'

Finding peace

I'm sitting here on the beach having escaped for a few hours, the sun is setting and the waves are gently crashing onto the sand. The beach is almost empty apart from a few dog walkers and a couple of mad paragliders in the sea. It's so still and the setting sun is reflecting on the wet sand as the tide goes out. I'm wrapped up like an eskimo sitting on the sand with my laptop, nursing the warmth of my cacao. Do the people walking past wonder what I'm doing or do they just pass me by? I'm so grateful for the time I get to spend here in nature, watching the sea or walking in the woods with my dogs.

I'm looking after my 86-year-old mum at this point in my life and she has Vascular Dementia. Six years ago, with her declining health, I made the decision to give up my corporate career, let my house and move into her house with my two teenage boys. We all thought it would be a short-term thing as Mum had been so poorly and we didn't think it would be long. Later that first year she was diagnosed with the dementia and then her illnesses of the previous year began to make sense. It's been the most challenging and yet rewarding time in my life and I'm so grateful I'm having the opportunity to share these last years with her.

It was my Mums dream to live by the sea, so I bring her here when I can. She's immobile now and uses a wheelchair, she loves to be here but doesn't remember that she's been. This is my situation and its hard. Each day is a challenge. And so, within sister circle, I have found ritual has helped me to cope so much better.

74

Meditating has been one of the most important parts for me. I wanted and still want, to meditate daily. I find it difficult. It's difficult because I'm tired. I'm tired these days beyond anything that sleep alone can cure. Finding the motivation each day to look after myself as well as my Mum is easier said than done, so bringing meditation in and making it a part of my routine, just like cleaning my teeth, really does make the difference between surviving and thriving. When I do that, it gives me the opportunity to stop everything and I feel so much better.

Generally, during the day we spend our time in our conservatory, watching the birds and letting the dogs in and out. When she's calm or asleep, I can close my eyes and try to find a blank page in my head, fighting my thoughts away like a cat waiting for a mouse to pop out of a mouse hole. Sometimes the sun shines brightly straight through the windows and it's wonderful to relax and feel the sun on my face and the warmth wrapping itself over my body. This is when I can relax and feel new again. When I have carers at home, I love to disappear to my bedroom and put my headphones on, finding a guided meditation to take me away completely. I often find myself asleep at the end and don't know where the time went. Doing this at bedtime is a real joy too.

Meditation has been an amazing way for me to grab time out and to go within and focus on my breathing. When I close my eyes and drink cacao, I get to find some peace in what can be very stressful days. I've become more aware of my breathing, what exactly happens when I breath in and out. My favourite is to breath in for three seconds and out for six seconds, this really calms me and when something triggers me in Mums behaviour it is my go-to first step. Breathing in and giving a big sigh, letting my shoulders drop and feeling the warm breath come from my feet balances me to cope with whatever comes next.

I'm more aware of my breathing and of calming my breath. I also love listening to the waves crashing on the shore, they make me feel safe and held as only a woman can feel.

When I'm in the practice of meditating daily, I also sleep better but when I can't or lose the momentum to meditate, my head wizzes and it's difficult to get out of that cycle when it starts. It's so important for me to be ahead of that and make the time to switch off.

Meditating has brought me both 'me' time and more time. It makes me take care of myself, it's a ritual that can stop the anger and frustration of dealing with someone with dementia rising in my head, boiling its way to my mouth. There's nothing worse for me than feeling that I shouted at my mum for a bizarre behaviour or, yet again, for feeding raspberries to the dogs and getting them all over the floor.

Being calm, the feeling that meditation gives me, means that my days are less stressful and have more joy in them. I can appreciate the gratitude I have for this amazing opportunity to care for my mum. And when that becomes hard, I have to quickly remind myself of my rituals, of how much more I achieve each day when I'm calm and can see the gratitude in her heart too. She knows me still, I'm with her all the time and that's amazing. It brings tears to my eyes when she thanks me for everything that I do for her.

My life changed the moment I decided to look after her in so many ways and finding the peace of the rituals of a sister circle has been a huge part of that growth.

76

Lighting candles every day

Lighting my candles every day has given me a complete sense of space and peace. I wonder what's in the concept of lighting a candle, that it can bring such joy and self-love. A way of honouring myself – wow I hadn't expected that! Lighting a candle in my honour.

In the past, I've lit candles in church for my father who died thirteen years ago, I've lit candles for my friends who are poorly or who need some support too but it never occurred to me to light a candle for myself. It is said that in church, people light candles to allow the smoke to take our prayers to heaven to be heard and answered. I've happily lit candles for birthdays where I've blown the candles out, making wishes come true and in marriage, I've seen two candles being lit to celebrate the bringing together of two souls in unity. So many candles are lit in religion to celebrate festivals and rituals but to me it felt strange to light a candle for myself, like I was thinking 'What for? Why should I deserve to have a candle lit for myself? Is that not selfish and not what people do for themselves?'

This immersion showed such simple ways to take care of myself, building loving rituals into each day. That was a surprise. Now it's normal, to honour myself, to take the time to give back to myself. A simple easy to do and easy 'not' to do ritual that has actually changed the way I am each day.

It has given me a sense of peace and loving, allowing me to open up to being loved again. Sharing each wonderful day with my mum and my husband, extending that peace to my friends and family, allowing me the insight to appreciate everything I have around me.

It allows me to celebrate every day, the small things, the mundane without anger, to wear my special things, use the good glasses and find the joy in everything – it was in there somewhere and now it's visible. I used to get bogged down with weariness and resentment of life, the hamster wheel of surviving, the times when I just felt relief at the end of each day, now there is more.

As I sit lighting a candle for the girl I used to be, I ask 'What did she teach me?' as I sat beside her 'What wisdom did she bring to my life?'.

Lighting a candle for the woman I am now means stopping and taking time to appreciate all my past life, everything it taught me and showed me. I wouldn't be anywhere without her.

And lighting a candle for the woman I am yet to become is awesome. What great opportunities are there for me out there? Without the previous two candles and the feelings brought about by these rituals, I might not be looking forward to that prospect. Now I'm so excited as to what she's going to do and what she has to bring to life. My future, my love and the joy of expectation.

I cope so much better when I've taken the time to light my candles, I feel calm and full of self-love. Every day is a celebration of life now. I ponder sometimes 'how long do we have to make it better?'. Who knows! I recently lost a lovely friend to cancer, so young. She was full of positivity and joy, she showed people the way and it's so hard to see life without her now. So, what did I learn from her? That life is precious and ever-changing like the waves on the sand. Every time they crash on the beach, they're different from the last one. They have energy and determination to reach their goal. They don't wait till they're ready, they don't wait for anyone to approve, they just keep coming. Time after time after time, like the rituals that serve me when I take the time to do them,

I don't need anyone's approval, I can be different every day and I just keep walking.

Being the Elder

Not so long ago I was a young woman with my whole life ahead of me. In a flash I have three grown up children and more life behind me than ahead. The biggest impact on my life was being the elder of my sister circle.

I remember my Mum sobbing on her 50th birthday as her life was over, a woman who had dreaded growing old and had rejected any sense of beauty and wisdom in anything as she grew into her later years. She was and still is a very critical woman especially about herself and me. This led me to dread the growing old bit too. Being part of this sister circle had a huge impact on those thoughts and turned the whole thing on its head. The Elder with a purpose, who'd have thought!

Being elevated to the Elder of the group made me feel so special – to be included and asked for my opinion first and not left till the end was a wonderful feeling.

I changed my perception of 'the end is in sight' to 'there is so much still to do in my life'. I'm not giving up and accepting old age. Just because I'm a grandparent doesn't mean my life is over. There is still so much to do.

Within the group I felt cherished and proud to be the Elder. I really did feel that the others gave me the respect and the time to be heard. All the women there had experience of life, however to be honoured and cherished was a complete surprise.

In our society where the young and beautiful are sought after, the feelings I had as I grew older were not necessarily uplifting

79

ones, so this immersion gave me a different feeling about growing old. I am valued and I can still love me. I opened myself up to being loved again for who I am and the experience that I have in life. I felt so strong when I came together with likeminded women, to still have some value and be thought of as wise in my opinions.

Where has that lead me? I'm much more confident in myself and have so much more love for myself and others. There's still more I can give to the world. I'm fast approaching sixty with a true sense of achievement and confidence in myself now that I never had as a young woman! I can do anything I want and I don't care what other people think of me anymore. What I wear and where I go. I want them to think 'Oh no! What's she up to now!'.

The thoughts I had about growing old have changed. I've accepted myself... the scars, the lumps, the bumps that go along with all the wrinkles. I have a full mind of a life time of memories to cherish. I am blessed to be reaching the age I am and looking forward to the meeting the woman I am yet to become.

Lynette Marie Allen

81

She strode right into the roaring seas
until her thighs were drenched with wash.
Unsteady on her feet, trusting the movement, becoming one with
turmoil,
diving head first into the froth,
mermaid disappearing into crashing waves,
to re-emerge the sylph with the pearl
that everyone else only wished they'd found.

from 'A Woman's Blessing'

Deep gratitude

I sat in the space of security that only home can offer. A home I'd created through the finetuned skillset of my experience as an artist, builder and interior designer. The oversized sheep skin rug I sat on was plush and soft, as it rested on the solid foundation of my floor. The lustre in the plaster walls reflected the dance of the flame of my candles in the early morning darkness. The incense engulfed the room and soothed me. The music softly carried me to stillness. I held the intricately carved teak stick that I'd purchased on my climb to the peak of Nepal's Annapurna Trail several years before. The stick had been blessed during our 22 day immersion when I wrapped alpaca wool yarn around it, reminding me of healing, love and gratitude to the young woman I once was.

I now sat with the same sacred stick in hand, having taken my knife and carved three rings around the thickest part, honouring myself and the woman I am yet to become. I questioned, 'What qualities does the wise woman I am becoming have, that through my 56 years I've been in the process of embodying?'. As I surrendered into the sacredness of that moment, stick in hand, I smiled. I laughed. I cried.

Those emotions came from that deep place of gratitude when laughter and tears come simultaneously because of the ah-ha moment that has just occurred. I spoke out loud; 'I GET IT!' I knew exactly what my wise Self, the woman I am yet to become, has been guiding me to. She has utilized my life, with the wide variety of experiences including the challenging ones, the exhilarating ones and everything in between, to teach me a valuable character trait - the art of courageously leaning in, in a non-resistant state, allowing change to naturally have its way.

I've learned that my ego has an agenda; its 'job' is to protect me, in the human form. It's been an incredibly important part in the survival of my body. But I realise it doesn't have the capacity to access universal intelligence, creativity and the philosophy of the cosmos.

I notice when I'm in resistance and my ego is unwilling to change, it causes conflict and turmoil in my life, yet when I learned that change is a blessing and inevitable, I get into flow. And this flow is my authentic power.

For years, I lived in survival at all cost, which took me into immeasurable sorrow and pain. Yet I can see pivotal moments now where I was guided by a teacher and intelligence that was wiser than the 'me' I was then. This wiser aspect of myself was always by my side, infusing me with courage, wisdom and strength that was beyond my years and maturity. One such moment came when I was a young mother.

I had just dropped my three young sons, aged two, three and four at their grandmother's, my mother had called that morning offering to take them, allowing me time alone. I burned the candle at both ends back then, working at night and taking care of my children during the day.

As I drove away, my mind raced with excitement. What should I do first? The buzz of opportunity and options overwhelmed my circuitry. With a feeling of incredible lightness, I changed the music in my van from 'Wheels on the Bus' to Kenny Chesney's 'The Good Stuff'. That's when the call came.

It was my brother-in-law, Doug, a powerful mover and shaker in my community, with an air about him that dominated the rooms he entered without him uttering a word. He was the President of the bank my husband had his business accounts with. It was highly unusual for Doug to call me. In his intimidating, harsh manner he requested I come to his office immediately. My heart skipped a beat. I was living in a perpetual state of fight or flight. Of all the men I knew, the one I least trusted at that time was the man I was married to, the father of my three sons.

My nervous system flared up, I shook, I had stomach ache by the time I arrived.

I walked in and immediately saw Doug in his office, rocking in his chair behind his ostentatious over-sized, carved cherry desk, cigarette in hand, he motioned me to come in as he got up from the desk. No smile, no greeting, no hug.

He got directly to the point. My husband's business was in trouble. Unrecoverable trouble.

"Lynette, your husband's business is going under, you and your sons will be homeless within the years end if you don't have a game plan".

The next memory I have is sitting in my van crying uncontrollably. I'd had a childhood of turbulence, violence, alcoholism and harm. Frequent house moves, unemployment and poverty, I had raised myself up from that and became the first woman in generations to put herself through college, determined not to repeat the patterns of my ancestry and yet here I was.

I was confused, angry, horrified, frightened and lost. At that moment, clarity came over me that stopped time, I hit the steering wheel as I spoke out loud; 'Like hell will my children have the childhood I had!'

A flood of awareness and adrenalin washed over me like hot water. "I will start my own business and it starts today!"

I started my car, drove downtown to an interior design firm who knew I was an artist and told the two owners they needed to refer me as an artist to their clients, I was in business!

Nothing in me questioned that I wasn't going to figure this out. In that moment in the van, I realized change was my only option, a non-negotiable requirement.

That naïve, innocent, idealizing maiden and young mother I was, had to course correct. I was called to lean into change for the love, devotion and survival of my family.

With courage fuelled by the fierce love of a mother, I whole-heartedly walked into my next chapter and embraced change. I had in that moment experienced the conflict between the fears of my ego and the power of my spirit, I'd been teetering between the two for years actually and the wisdom of the woman I was yet to become guided me into growth - which was on the other side of embracing change.

This moment in my sacred space, called to be with sisters and given the opportunity to remember that time gave me deep gratitude for the girl I used to be.

Rite of passage

When I was 49 years old, a set of changes seemed to come out of nowhere in my life, impacting me like a tsunami with devastating force.

My twenty-two years in the role of mother were some of the most intense and gratifying years of my life. Years facilitating growth opportunities as I nurtured, protected and ultimately let them go, I consistently facilitated their education and healthy self-concept, exposing them to different cultures and cultivating their unique gifts.

The transition out of motherhood ushered me into another jolting shift of change. As I see it now, becoming a mother was a rite of passage. And now moving out of that phase, has called me to my next rite of passage, entering the 'crone years' and with it, came the tsunami of change.

I moved out of my dream family home on the mountain top, I'd raised my children there. I asked my husband for a divorce which was extremely difficult on all levels, I saw for the first time all the toxic relationships I'd been living with and knew I had to cut off from them and they were very, very dear to me. I'd also survived a near-death car accident and my injuries were so severe they ended my twenty-five-year shining career and I had to close down my business.

Every single thing had gone. And for the next year, I found myself living in an 1840's homestead, an isolated property surrounded by over one hundred graceful racehorses in Montana. After the storm of that tsunami came the quiet as I integrated what I now realised was my 'crone' rite of passage.

I spent that year in daily observation, learning about and allowing change. I'd wake up at 4:30 am every day and sit on the old creaky swing on the front porch, sipping coffee, witnessing natures change, the sun slowly coming up each morning illuminating the sky with a rainbow of colour as the moon graciously bowed down.

And yet, my human experience of change had been incredibly challenging with the desire to repel it and retreat to my comfort zone immense. I have realised though, that change is inevitable.

86

As I spent my days in hermitage in that cabin on the horse ranch, I seemed to be in a school of sorts, guided by some wisdom within that taught me the power of acceptance of change.

I learned to allow myself to flow in the river of life without resisting the current. I eventually learned to live in a state of consciousness that surrendered to the rhythms of life. It became as natural as breathing. One of the more helpful tools at my disposal for embracing change has been ritual, the act of ceremony allows me to consciously mark important transitional periods by offering a sense of structure to it.

I've been using ceremony and ritual every day now, both before and after our sister circle immersion, as a structure to offer myself during the tsunamis of change and through challenging rites of passage.

For me, rituals strip me of my original role and prepare me for the new, they enable me to connect with my deepest thoughts, hopes and fears so that I can be present in mindfully navigating the changes in my life.

Trust

I have now lived 56 years of life. That's 5,283 days as of today to be exact – I know this because it's one of the rituals in this sister circle – to look at how many days we have actually lived and breathed this life. And at this point in my life, I've gone through some of the most significant rites of passage through my 'maiden' and 'mother' years.

The girl I used to be has given me gifts of great price: namely experience and wisdom. The woman I am now gets to benefit from every single one of those 5,283 days. One of the qualities I've developed is the ability to not only accept changes in life but also to celebrate the fact that the magnificence of today, was brought about BECAUSE of those life changes.

I trust the Universe has my back. I trust that the changes the woman I am yet to become will experience will lead to and be full of, abundance, peace and beauty.

I've seen my yesterday, I enjoy my today and I trust my tomorrow now. I enter into ritual and ceremony in the body of the woman I am now, a body with the muscle tone, wrinkles and the effects of gravity that come with my age and change. I love the life I've carved out for myself and the place of abundance I feel I was guided to live in. I'm at peace now with who I am; mind, body and spirit, filled with gratitude for the vast array of experiences that crossed over the landscapes, seasons and emotions of my life.

Ceremony has become a central part of my regular practice. It is my acknowledgement of the gratitude I have for my life. It's an honouring of my ever-present desire to be in surrender and a regard of trust in the intelligent source of guidance for my tomorrow.

I have just wrapped up five months of overseas travel. The woman I was at the beginning of that mind-opening sojourn is not the woman I am today. Once more I've changed. In the back yard of my home, with the remnants of fallen leaves and pinecones littering my space, I pluck a fallen willow branch to create a makeshift broom. With each stroke of my broom, I sweep away the shrivelled leaves and greying pinecones that once were full of life on the tree above me.

Symbolic of the need to clear the space of yesterday, I am making space for the intentions of today, to prepare for my tomorrow. I light my bundle of sage, decorated with a cluster of lavender, clove and cedar and smudge with the intention of clearing energy for purity. I gather rocks, sticks and flowers to prepare my altar's mandala.

The candles I have selected are symbolic: one dark blue for the girl I used to be, one dark blue for the mother I once was, a dark red one for the courageous woman I am today.

I place a series of white candles around to symbolize the unknown collection of future opportunities currently a mystery to me but will manifest for the woman I am yet to become. I press play on my playlist as the sun sets in the west and the sky colours itself in with rainbows. I light my candles and settle myself at my altar.

Tears run down my face as my heart wells up with gratitude for the precious life I've been blessed with. I hold my cup of cacao, 'the food of the gods', as I intentionally give thanks for where I've been, the joy of where I am and the gift of being able to consciously enter into the realm of the woman I am yet to become.

I journal about the life I live, so FULL because of my ability now to go with the changes of life. I speak my Self Blessing as I close my ceremony:

> *To the girl I used to be, I give great thanks*
> *To the woman I am now, I give great thanks.*
> *To the woman I am yet to become, I give thanks.*

from 'A Woman's Blessing'

Andrea Jackson

26

It bewildered her really,
how magically everything appeared right in front of her,
to touch and hold
once she let go of the illusion of reality.

from 'A Woman's Blessing'

Finding sister circle

I didn't know I would be here now, in this place right now. My journey to get to this place I never expected to be. But yet here I am, fifty-four years old, now a wise elder with a new granddaughter just arrived and a whole life of experience behind me. Here I stand, a much older, wiser version of me.

I used to watch my Nan knitting, so present in the moment. Sitting with her I always felt so calm, so at home, so comforted. The clicking of the needles, her gentle presence, in her elder wisdom she always made time for rest.

Mum was a hairdresser, she lived her passion. I would watch her when I was young, I loved to see her teasing the hair to get it just in the right place, everything just perfect. Always tidy, always clean, always perfect, never resting. I followed in her footsteps. It wasn't really my passion but I did love the chatter of the Salon, the energy of women coming together, sharing their worries and hardships, sharing the personal stuff they'd often never speak of outside the hair salon.

I knew by just listening, it helped, it made a difference to them, it was their time to be pampered and also to be seen and heard. I learned to listen in those years, to communicate, to be the sounding post for these women. I didn't know it was leading me here to this moment, to this life I have now but I did know that women being together helped lift a burden.

I had a challenging existence at this time. I had two young children within a volatile relationship and most of the time it felt like a living hell, walking on eggshells, waiting for the next explosion, the next upset, the next place I would have to run to escape to until things calmed down.

In my moments of darkness, wanting to escape, to flee, to run, to find freedom somehow, I would go to friend's, sisters who saw me, who I'm sure got tired of hearing me but I knew when I shared, I would feel better. They would hold me, put me back together and it would be OK until eventually I would find the courage to leave, to walk away and to be free.

I stumbled upon Yoga, it helped. It soothed my battered nervous system, it was like a balm for my stressed body, my tight shoulders and clenched jaw. My body, mind and soul became strong again and I began to feel the first glimpses of freedom. I learned to sit and be quiet in the early hours of the morning, I learned how lighting a candle would remind me that my own hopes and dreams hadn't been totally extinguished. I remember the first night in my own house, the safety of those four walls, my little girl asleep at my side, both of us tucked up in bed, her sleeping. I dreamed of the life I have now.

Through those years I gained more inner knowledge, I would live in tune with the seasons and the cycles. I began to follow the moon, I began to feel alive. My passion grew. I followed my heart, I loved yoga, dance and the spiritual path that had healed me so well. I had found my way home, back to me, back to my heart and freedom.

Losing my Mum to cancer was such a pivotal point in my life. Mum had lived her life working hard to maintain perfection, keeping everything under her control until eventually it created dis-ease in her body. Her death left such a void in all of our lives, we missed our elder, our wise woman, our port in the storm.

Drawn deeper into my spiritual practices, they became my strength and backbone. I was guided to visit Glastonbury and the goddess became etched in my soul. I met mama cacao there and began a love affair with her, deepening my daily rituals, she healed my heart and led me to more love, more freedom.

I returned home with a song in my heart, the awakened goddess in me would guide me to create support for my sisters. Sister circles, over the years, have totally blown my mind. The healing, the wisdom, the support, the beauty of women in circle, it is such a calling to encourage expression, to write, to dance, to share, to love and accept myself to follow my dreams.

Sitting in circle has given me courage and support, it gifts me time to think, time to reflect and time to be. It gives me time to share my deepest pain and sorrow and my greatest passion and dreams. Connection with other women gives me a reflection of myself and allows me to see that I'm not alone. I am totally held.

I see life as a dance that we are all invited to join, to dance with life on our wonderful earth and shine in own individuality. I didn't know I would be here now, but I am so happy I am.

Loving her

It took a while to sit and write this part of my chapter. Who am I to write part of a book? Who am I to be seen, to be visible? I feel vulnerable and exposed yet this journey has been such a beautiful reflection on my life, an honouring of the courage and strength it has taken to get here. As I look back, I remember the stepping stones I've taken and how these rituals have been such a big part of my journey.

As I entered into the rituals for the girl I used to be, I remembered the bully at school. As I wrote a letter to my younger self, it felt so powerful to give myself the space to feel, to acknowledge those feelings I wasn't able to express at that time.

My life had, up until recently, felt like a series of mistakes, with men mainly. Looking back though and through the eyes of ritual, I can now see the patterns and where they took root.

The feelings of being small, of feeling disempowerment, unable to be my true self or express my feelings all stemmed back to those times. I understood during my reflection time why I loved to dance so much, it was to shake off the feeling of being crushed by the ones who were meant to keep me safe. I guess Dad thought he was doing that.

Seven years old was the first time I remember feeling the crush of disempowerment – a feeling of rage at being caged, like a bird unable to spread her wings.

'Get your hair out of your eyes, stupid girl!', he bellowed at the front of our house, pontificating over his new car, in front of all the village boys, I felt 2 inches tall! That was the first time I felt Dad's crushing energy over me. They laughed. I felt stupid and small.

Then my teacher. 'Stand on your chair!' he bellowed. 'Recite your 9 times tables!'. I struggled with maths so much. My teacher terrified me every day, ridiculing me in front of the whole class. He was so tall, his whole being scared the living daylights out of me.

And with his hands around my neck, the school bully 'Don't tell or I'll kill you' he said. It happened every lunch time, in the playground, just out of sight. A boy. Older than me, his grip around my throat terrified me. I had a constant knot in my stomach. I hated school, I hated the restriction I felt there, I seemed to be living my life in constant restriction, I couldn't wait to get away, to be free.

Looking back, I was always searching for freedom. To flee, became my natural state.

The girl I used to be grew into a teenager and still, what felt like crushing, continued. 'Don't speak until you are spoken to! You are a child, you know nothing! You are not going out of this house dressed like that! You'll amount to nothing! You'll end up working in a factory all your life!'

These became daily affirmations in our house, the fights with Dad continued. All I could feel was hatred for him with everything I had. I felt such rage, the feeling in my belly was crippling, I couldn't express it, there was nowhere to go with it! I wanted to scream, to punch, to hurt someone!

Let me be FREE! It was all I wanted.

By seventeen, I'd left home, on a mission, a rebel without a clue. I was searching for that familiar feeling of crush and flee, the constant knot in my belly. I created it over and over again. I didn't realise. I was just a girl, searching for the familiar, out in a big world.

Drugs, alcohol and partying felt good. Aggressive relationships fed the anger in my belly. I entered into the ultimate 'crush and flee' relationship, it fed all my feelings of unworthiness. Constant crush and flee, it had become an addiction.

I still danced and partied, fought and fled. It became a cycle of self-abuse.

My heart was broken, I was broken. How would I ever find the freedom that I craved so deeply?

When I looked at my younger self in meditation, I just wanted to hold her, to say, 'It's ok. You are a strong spirited girl and that's never something to be ashamed of, it's exactly how you are meant to be. You were so brave and I love all that you are and through this you will learn so much about yourself'.

I put so much love into our stick ritual for her, I tied beautiful ribbons representing her strength and beauty. We painted a lovely picture together, remembering how I always loved to paint houses, always cottages with trees and roses outside, just like where I live now.

All I ever wanted was to be accepted and loved and guided and yet, now, I wouldn't have my past any other way. My soul needed this moulding and I feel it was an actual moulding, a 'shaping' into the woman I am now. Something so beautiful about life's plan for me.

Freeing her

Oh my god, that first feeling of freedom. I have never let it go! Looking back, it has been such a journey, as I honoured the woman I am now, in sister circle. I could see that everything had happened exactly as it was meant to.

In moving into the rituals for the woman I am now, I made lists. I realised how far I'd actually come. Wow! I wish I'd known then that I really didn't need to have anything worked out, it was all there.

The woman I am now lives in a gorgeous cottage in the woods, I have a beautiful sacred space, life is a dream and it felt amazing in that ritual to really honour myself. I mean really, when do we ever give ourselves time and space to look back to see how far we have come? I was in awe.

From the angry, disempowered young girl I had been, I could clearly see that every step had so lovingly brought me to the now. I could see how I'd hated myself and loved myself back to life. Through love and acceptance, I have healed so much but I hadn't ever given myself the time to be still and reflect and honour my journey to get to this point.

I remembered my mum – as the perfectionist workaholic who never sat down, I was taught that giving yourself a break wasn't even an option! I pictured her always cleaning, working, dieting, avoiding. The sacred elder I lived with, my mum, was punishing herself, THAT was the teaching that weaved through my life, that a clean house, that working yourself into the ground in a thin body, validated a woman's existence and made them loveable.

'You are doing the best you can', my nan once told me and right there, in that moment, I dropped the feeling of having to be perfect. I gave myself guilt-free rest and I began to break the patterns I'd observed growing up.

Journaling is one of my daily rituals and such a powerful way to express how I'm feeling. I gained so much strength from the contemplation, just reading them out loud, I got so much power and acceptance.

'I am fifty-four years old' I wrote. 'I've been a wife, a mother, a daughter, a granddaughter, a sister and an addict. I've lived through abuse, eating disorders, disempowerment, homelessness, death, grief and I've survived. I've raised two beautifully spirited humans. I've lost the fear of rejection and what other people think about me. I've gained so much courage, strength and independence. I've started many things but most importantly I've started loving and accepting myself more every single day'.

Through beautiful self-massage, pleasure and bathing rituals I've accepted this sacred elder body I've been gifted. I never appreciated my body enough in my younger years. I apologized for all the times I treated her badly and all the times I starved her of food and of love. It felt so good to be in acceptance of my sacred elder body and for making it to my age! We really did make it!

All I've ever really needed to do, is to give myself a break and be kinder to myself, to follow my heart. And I had done, in a kind of rough and tumble way but now I've given myself permission to be imperfectly perfect exactly as I am.

Looking back to the last week of our beautiful rituals, I had no idea that becoming a grandmother was anywhere close. As we sat with the elder, wiser version of ourselves, I felt the strength of her, how could I ever have doubted myself? How could I ever have felt small and insignificant? The older, wiser me would always be there, she always was there, guiding me and giving me strength to take the next step. She already knew, she always knew and all I ever needed to do was to sit with her and call her in.

As we lit candles for our children, I remembered the child I lost, she was in the arms of my elder self. There was such wisdom within her. She invited me to step into the younger part of me, to play more, laugh more and not take life so seriously. 'What will be will be' was the reminder.

'Nothing is really under control' she laughed wanting the best for me, asking me to trust myself and my path.

As I put those final marks on my sacred stick, I felt a deep faith and trust in myself to confidently take the place of wise elder, to be empowered by my age and my wisdom, to be of strength and comfort to my lineage, just as my elders had been to me.

As I write, I have just become a grandmother to my first beautiful grandchild, Hallie Francesca Rose and what an absolute honour it is to take this seat as wise elder of our family lineage. I could literally feel the shift and it's taken a little while to integrate.

I felt my own grandmother, great aunt and mother close to me, they were always there, supporting me on this earth plane.

I was reminded they would never leave me and I had the strength of them all within my bones, within my blood. As we created our sacred water blessing, I remembered the waters of life that flow through me, as we blessed ourselves in our final ritual.

I felt such pride for the girl I used to be, for her strength and her sacred rebel nature.

I feel so proud of the woman I am now, for following her dreams and even in hard times, keeping her heart open.

And I cannot wait to embody the woman I am yet to become. She is so strong and wise and free and she knows it all works out and that I am always exactly where I are meant to be.

To the women behind me, before me and within me.
A'ho.

Mairi Taylor

128

'Listen' she heard, 'just observe'.
All clenching released so she could see
what was actually unfolding, away from the stories.
She laughed more than she should,
all blind folds and rose-tinted glasses put aside,
her higher Self holding the picture now
and with her blessing, she saw straight through the clouds.

from 'HELD'

Brave

They say that menopause is the time to go down to the basement and unpack the boxes. Boxes full of the emotions, stories, triggers and secrets never to be told, that you've been gathering, storing and carrying with you your whole life.

Twenty-five years ago my little sister invited my mum and I to unpack those boxes. She was dying and she asked us to sit together, discuss and unpack our family wounds. We didn't. We couldn't. We both very quickly said NO THANK YOU and that was it, the lid was on the Pandora's box of our family life and it was staying firmly shut thank you very much.

I continued to carry that box with me and even added a few more too as the years flew by. Having lived in a home with an often-absent alcoholic father, a mother who became dependent on pain killers (whilst trying to keep up appearances), debt and parents who screamed – well a mother who screamed – every night, we all simply walked around on egg shells, being good girls, so as not to trigger the rage.

My sister had always been ahead of her time but I was simply not brave enough to open the box when invited. Either that or I thought we knew better and that there was nothing to discuss. I now realise though, that I've also been carrying around guilt for denying her one of her dying wishes. She wanted us to sit down and bring into the light the so-called 'shame' of our family – to openly discuss it, to allow each of us to be seen, heard and held as we shared our pain, disappointment and sadness.

I now know that had I been brave enough to trust my sister and understand what she was trying to gift us, the following twenty-five years may have looked and felt very different. Whilst I thought I was soldiering on with life, keeping myself busy and giving myself away, I was actually trapped in feelings of worthlessness and 'not good enough'. I ran away from any kind of conflict that needed me to stand in my own power and I became passive aggressive as the anger, resentment, rage and rejection kept bubbling up. Rather than being brave enough to stop and look it straight in the eye, I ran faster until I just couldn't run anymore.

This was the story of my life, 'don't let anyone see the cracks', 'hide the shame', 'dress up and show up', 'get the good grades' and 'be successful. As my mum had once said to us 'keep your eyes closed and think of England!'.

So, I did just that. I kept my eyes closed, my heart protected and focused on being the good girl, getting the good grades, constantly looking for approval to be me and giving my wisdom away to those I believed held 'guru status'. I allowed myself to be disempowered. I protected my heart with a huge thorny bush and I ran and ran.

I wasn't brave enough to stop and I know why. I would have been left standing with my own thoughts and if I'd have stood in my own power, who would I have had to blame?

When cacao brought me to gather with women (for sister circle finds you, you don't find her), the cracking open of my heart started. It was when I felt truly brave enough to gather with a small group of women, with no place to hide and weekly accountability, that I was no longer able to simply skim over the surface.

As I sat in the first circle and I heard the heart felt plea of our elder, asking if this really *was* where she would finally be able to truly trust other women, I heard her call deep inside of me. In that moment I realised I too had struggled with trusting women. My own mother didn't trust me, or so I believed, so how could I believe anyone else could?

I was longing to trust other women to truly hold me. This was now where the story would be rewritten, if I could be brave enough to open up to this sister circle and share all aspects of me.

'Could I simply show up as me?', 'No attachment to outcome and simply do the work I was being called to do?'.

As I leant in and dove deep, actually allowing myself the opportunity to be brave enough to truly feel all the feels without fear of rejection, I walked around my story, studying it from every angle. Through daily rituals and journaling, I came to realise what a brave and likeable girl I was and always had been. I was always loved and both my parents were simply doing their best.

I wasn't responsible for my father's alcoholism, my sister's death or my mum's pain – none of it was mine. But I'd carried it all for so long, it had festered in me as rejection, anger, fear, guilt and shame. Finally, as I wrote the letters, set the intentions with my stick and listened (without judgement) to other women, I started to forgive myself for my feelings and emotions. I replaced them with love and compassion. I realised that if I could listen to these women without judgement then surely, I could listen to myself in the same way.

I celebrated and danced with her for the brave, tenacious being she was, oh how we danced! On day seven of our immersion, we were invited to revisit our seven-year-old selves. The first thing I did was look at the Top20 on my seventh birthday and create a playlist. Music had always played an important part in our family, as we would dance joyously together on Saturday nights or at family gatherings.

It was then that I heard the magic and secret whispers from my father, it was then he shone a light on this little girl. He knew I had the 'gift of the gab', trying so hard to protect her mother, whilst also raging inside against the injustice of not having a 'normal life', like everyone else - or so she thought.

For it was only in circle, where sister promises had been shared that I came to realise 'me too'. We are all simply looking for that place of connection and community, where we can be seen, heard and held without judgement or fear of rejection.

And so...I danced every morning with my cacao and candles, in my living room, in my pj's (aka a t-shirt and knickers), barefoot and blindfolded with a community of other women stomping, swaying, flowing and at times simply surrendering...lying down, letting the music wash over me.

I listened to music wherever I went - in the car, walking in the woods, at the supermarket, often breaking into a few groovy steps or belting out the words, allowing the tears to flow, making my face itchy and red. The forgiveness came. The appreciation for the boxes my parents had been carrying. Seeing the patterns being repeated and yet forgiving them. My smiles grew as my heart filled with love and my soul danced bravely back home to me.

Acceptance

It's almost one year ago I sat in that circle and the woman I am now, typing this, (listening to 'The Arrival of the Queen of Sheeba'), is a very different woman to the one who first arrived in that sacred space.

This one knows her worth now, I hold other women now from a place of humility and grace and others have commented on the shift in my energy – for the woman I am now is a kinder more compassionate woman to herself.

For me, the true magic and miracles of gathering with women, is what happens afterwards. I've had the courage to start advocating for myself, I've found magic and miracles in everyday life as I continue to hold the space for myself, creating my own daily rituals, honouring myself with daily anointment and seeing 'the work' as simply how I live my life.

I set and protect boundaries around my time, my health, my physical and mental wellbeing. I know I deserve to be nourished and I understand how daily rituals replenish me, so I have the resilience to be in command of the emotions and feelings that used to control me.

They're still there, those emotions and feelings but the environment in which they thrived has changed, my inner eco system is no longer fuelling them and the women I gather with now, no longer feed into my feelings of worthlessness.

It took a lot of courage for me to release (with love) those in my life who no longer served, supported or honoured me but I found that the lightness that came from letting them go, was worth those feelings of unease and fear.

I've stopped trying to influence others to see the light, I simply show up as me. There is no place now in my world for the hustle and grind I used to garner. Now I feel I can achieve all I need with ease and grace, a cup of cacao in one hand and women who truly have my back beside me.

The girl I used to be is now getting rest. I've thanked her for what she did to protect me and let her know that I've got this from now on and that I can be fearless and tenacious, exactly as I came here to be.

I wake up every day as the woman I am yet to become, thanking the girl I was yesterday and honouring the woman I am right here, right now in this very moment.

I still uphold my sister promises, to those women who travelled with me but for myself too. I allow those promises to ripple out to all those who continue to walk beside me, seeing them, hearing them and feeling them with a fresh new perspective, without judgement and knowing that none of us are broken or need fixing.

The sister promises have been a very powerful tool to take forwards as the woman I am yet to become. They've helped me to honour the woman I am now, the one I see in the mirror every morning.

I have found that sister circles can be found or created everywhere I need them. Many of my circles now overlap and dance with each other, some are bound by time, others are ever rippling out and flowing with life.

The peace and gratitude I found in sister circle has given me the courage to hold my own from a place of abundance and gratitude for my journey, because they're soul led rather than ego driven. They are a beautiful space for me to simply show up and BE.

Every morning when I sit with my cacao, I use my oracle deck to set my intentions and to hear the messages I need to hear. As I prepared to write these words, asking for guidance, the word 'acceptance' came up twice.

For me that meant 'acceptance' of self and 'acceptance' of season. The woman I am now has the courage to fully accept my season, my curves, my vitality and my wisdom, for that's what makes me, ME.

Through the awakening of gathering with women, I have found the courage to speak of things that I'd buried deep inside of me, bubbling up as the layers were peeled away.

I knew that to find true peace, I needed to find the safety and sanctuary of a sister I could trust to hold me, as I purged and released this deep-rooted shame and guilt.

Through this work and the continuation of my own work, I now talk of daily rituals, womb wisdom and sister circles. I didn't know her five years ago! But she's very much the woman I am now – courageously talking of cacao, candles, connection and of 'blending old worlds with new'.

There is a cacao prayer in the book 'A Woman's Blessing' – it says, 'for those who blend old worlds with new, please continue'. It deeply resonated with me.

I read them out loud and share them with others now as I've found the tenacity to release the hold of 'gurus' who proclaim to know more about me than I do.

I know there are women like me, secret sorcerers out there who are waiting to become the women they want to be, without fear of being judged. And it wasn't until I sat in a circle with sisters who were truly ready to welcome and honour the woman I am right here, right now that I found me. When I stepped into that circle, I had nothing to lose and I gained so much. My heart rejoiced in the magic we created and continue to create on our journey. The magic of being connected to self, to honouring self to being unashamedly self in all my glory, showing up so courageously.

Connected

When I stepped into this container of cacao, candles, words that were spells and movement that became dance, almost 18 months ago, I had no idea who I would become as a result of mistaken identity, synchronicity and finding my way home.

Those very things used to repel me; rituals, 'sister circles', talk of angels, ancestors, yoni's and womb wisdom. However, like many things in life, it's what we resist the most that we need the most.

I found this gathering of women at exactly the right time, at a time when I discovered that the woman I loved the most, who had hurt me the most, who I'd always sought approval from, whose approval I would never get again in this realm, was not who I thought she was.

Like me, she too had secrets, shame, guilt and stories I would never know. Forgiveness and compassion for all that had gone before, was the only way to find freedom and connection.

Each of the women I gathered with still flow through me each and every day as I recognise that I go to bed the woman I am now, I wake up as the woman I am yet to become, while the woman I was yesterday, has become the girl I used to be.

This constant state of flow has given me a greater connection to myself. And for her, as I light my candles, drink my cacao, read my passages and turn my oracle cards, I honour my story. The story I now have the power to write, rewrite and edit as I allow my wisdom and intuition to guide me.

When I stop the inner turmoil and allow the girl I used to be to rest, the woman I am now can shine. I speak the words that simply flow from her heart and soul. They show up in her truth, unashamedly dancing, showing off and being 'too much!'. The woman I am yet to become simply smiles and guides me rather than pointing and directing. She cheers me on, knowing that all of me is now connected and at peace with myself. Ritual and movement continue to connect me back to me.

I honour the wisdom I've gained over the years. For too long I sought approval through certificates, qualifications, promotions and pay rises but no matter how many I collected, it never felt enough. I needed to give myself approval.

Having spent too many years frozen, movement is now my medicine and I love being back in my physical body after taking time to make friends with my spiritual being.

I find the woman I am yet to become in circle, listening to elders, being the elder, sitting in sister promise without judgement, cheering other women on. I find her in tuning into my body wisdom through dance and by no longer seeking external validation in the aesthetics.

To become this woman, I needed to get uncomfortable, I needed to swing so far away from the girl I was, that it would be too uncomfortable to go back. So, I adorned myself with flower crowns and floaty dresses, changing how I looked, learning a new language and stopping the world for a while, so I could dance with this version of me.

I danced with her until I believed her. I started showing up for the ceremonies, the gatherings and the rituals, learning what was mine and what wasn't.

I allowed so much to fall away, my circles became smaller until I finally felt connected enough to the true essence of me that I could step out and simply be 'me'.

Julia Anastasiou

125

She realised sometime later that her
heart break was her initiation
and that initiations come in so many ways
and that if she had listened to Madre more deeply that night,
her human might have been spared such an arduous,
tumultuous, cutting and deeply lonely journey.
But, of course, that was the initiation, a rite of passage in itself.
And one must walk through those underground tunnels on their
own.
It's where the feminine goes to rise.
And rise she did.

from 'Sacred'

The Girl I Used to Be, 11 Candles

My journey with cacao began in an Ashram deep in the foothills of the Himalayan mountains. Under a starry indigo sky, lit by a voluptuous full grandmother moon, on this sacred evening, the aromatic wind blew eagerly along the banks of Ganga Ma.

Intoxicating incense wafted through the corridors, candlelight paved the way to the yoga hall, the room hushed in anticipation, altar adorned, one by one we were welcomed, smudged and anointed. The circle formed, invocations chanted, ancestors honoured, cardinal directions called in 'as above and so below, great spirit, be with us on this alchemical journey'. Intentions set, the ceremony was about to begin.

Plant medicine ceremonially poured, to the spirit of cacao, we sang her name, honoured mother earth, asked spirit to guide us 'Allow us to know our true selves, allow us to believe in ourselves, allow us to love ourselves. Allow. Allow. Allow'.

Intimately we merged, infused with intentions of our deepest heart's desires, with wild abandonment she entered my body. I could feel my heart beating, my breath slowed, ever so softly we became one. The journey into the dark, juicy and wanton space unfolded.

Hours passed and we slowly drifted back to our rooms. The familiar exotic sounds of India lulled me to sleep, grandmother moon shone her moonbeams into my humble ashram room, illuminating the pathway for ancient images to fill my dream state, whispers from beyond the thin veil of consciousness, heart cracked open wide, a yearning deep in my yoni. I floated through the sands of time, temple settings, swirling and dancing as a high priestess, Amazonian woman tending to the earth, deeper and deeper I travelled until I was one with the Light.

A cellular change took place that evening, I knew I had found my plant teacher, my guide and I re-membered this was not the first-time cacao had been my medicine. 'Welcome home my love, I have been waiting for you!'.

This was my initiation into the goddess of cacao…full moon to full moon…years rolled by, close by my side she remained, ever present, patiently waiting.

Fast forward five years, by happenstance I came across 'Held' by Lynette Allen. Captivated by her writing, I devoured her words as if they were nourishment for my soul, every page I read. It was towards the end of the book, a mysterious invitation…to be part of a circle, to connect with cacao, an opportunity to collaborate. The three c's in my cauldron of creativity!

And so, I gathered in circle. The connection of the heart awakens when invocations are spoken with devotion, when cacao sipped, senses aroused. One by one we took our turn, starting with the elder as is tradition in this circle. Attentively we listen to one another, holding space for the pain, loss, sorrow, grief, disappointment.

This circle gathering happened to be on November 11th and it was very close to 11am when my turn began, serendipitously I lit eleven candles for the girl I use to be …

For the time I was not seen,
the time I was not heard,
the time I was not loved,
the time I was not held,
the time I was not understood,
the time I was not appreciated,
the time I was not listened to,
the time I was judged,

113

the time I was ignored,

the time I was bullied,

the time I was violated …

Tears streamed down my face as I sat sobbing with all of these raw childhood memories of not being enough, not being loveable enough, not being popular enough, pretty enough, smart enough, witty enough, thin enough. I sat and cried salty tears for all the times I had felt that I was not enough. Waves of memories, heart aching, deep sadness flooded through me, the release was enormous!

Deeply buried, little poisonous seeds of self-doubt, self-loathing, self-judgement, waiting to sprout into my conscious mind at any given vulnerable moment. On that day I made a pledge to light a candle intentionally to myself for the rest of my life, to light her way, to heal her through the light, to let her see that she is never alone! To allow her to know that she is SO much more than enough, a brilliant light of luminosity, a light so bright that she can be a beacon on the path for many other girls.

That's what happened when I lit a candle for the girl I used to be.

The Woman I am Today, Sacred Bathing

The shower is my preferred daily cleansing method; it's practical, effective, quick; I can multitask - exfoliate my body while my hair absorbs the conditioner. On the other hand, bathing requires planning, time and space, a sacred act in my life usually set aside for full moons, new moons and honouring my sensuality. An opportunity to slow down, rest, soak, percolate, reflect, immerse.

So, this is what happened as I plunged into the waters of purification at the age of fifty-four.

Accoutrements gathered, oil for bathing and anointing, rose petals to remember my womanhood, Himalayan salt for purification, bubbles for the little girl within me, candles, incense, a large steaming cup of cacao, fresh nightwear, plus my favourite silk robe. Towels ready on the heated towel rail, journal close by and music playing softly in the background.

The sacred act of purification and honouring the divine sensual self, to the woman I am today, I crafted my intention, 'I honour and accept my body, as the sacred vessel that holds my inner light'.

The bathroom is smudged with incense. The first candle lit; I turned off the lights and preceded to light the other candles. The bathwater salted, oil dripped off my fingertips, bubbles swirled and rose petals scattered; I offered a prayer and invocation to release, cleanse, purify, heal and expand my awareness. As I slowly undressed, my body awakened to the chill in the air, steam began to rise; a warm glow filled the room, the scent of rose and cacao lay heavy all around.

I stepped into the bathtub and slid beneath the bubbles, disguising my breasts and curves...toes and fingers poking out in an attempt to prevent the dreaded wrinkling!

The moon's light softy graced the room. I spoke my intention out loud three times and began to sip the rich earthy medicine infused with salt and rosewater. As cacao tenderly entered my body, a familiar sensation aroused every part she intimately touched, luxuriating within the divineness. I closed my eyes and slid into the healing, all-encompassing, watery womb; the sounds of the outside world faded; all that I could hear was internal.

My body swayed gently beneath the aromatic water to the rhythm of my breath; the internal waves began to swell, to ebb and flow: an inner awakening, a connection to the divinity within. A cascade of emotions, my inner voice permitted these tears to flow, be one with the water, release and let go.

How long I lay beneath the water, I do not know. It was the chill of my body that brought me back to the present moment. I turned the hot tap and attempted to reheat, a futile offering.

A dramatic rebirth occurred within these womblike waters; it was time to rise out of the sea like Venus. I stepped out of the tub, wrapped myself in warm towels and sat for a moment to reflect on what had just happened.

I lifted the plug and watched the swirl release down the drain to end the ritual. To let go of all that no longer served me began to disappear before my very eyes. Oh, the power within these simple rituals is astonishing!

Slowly and sensitively, I caressed my body with balancing aromatic oils; I anointed my crown chakra, symbolising the divine connection, my third eye to awaken inner vision, insight and intuition. I massaged my neck and throat to openly speak my truth and express myself creatively. Anointing my heart centre, I paused to recognise the healing that had taken place. I massaged my breasts, formed in strength and beauty, sweeping down my arms and hands, acknowledging that my hands express my heart centre. They descended to my navel, honouring the luminous inner light of vitality, growth and transformation. A sensual sweeping symbol of infinity across my soft abdomen, awakening the creatrix Shakti energy deep within my yoni; an inner yearning, the flower of life radiating beyond my physical body, rising in waves of delight.

Finally, I touched my root, legs, and feet. 'Great Mother, may I tread so lightly upon your skin as I walk my soul's true path'.

Stepping into my fresh pyjamas and robe, I wrote all of these experiences into my journal by candlelight. Upon completion, the bath is mindfully cleaned, candles extinguished, bathroom returned to a semblance of normality.

This is what happened when I took a bath for the woman I am today.

The Woman I am Yet to Become, Metamorphosis

So, the cyclical journey of womanhood continues, as the moon, waxing and waning; in its darkness and fullest expression. Through the daily ritual of drinking cacao and being in circle, I have contemplated at great length the cadence of the girl I used to be, the woman I am today and the woman I am yet to become.

I imagined what a blessing it would be if we told our daughters that they would meet their blood power at menarche, their first bleed. As bleeding women, they would have the opportunity to practice that blood power for many, many, many moons. Then as they reach menopause, they will become that power, they will hold the inner wisdom of the blood. As I write, I feel the deep desire of such a blessing for all the daughters of the earth.

The woman I am yet to become stands at a precipice of metamorphic transformation, in a state of peri-menopause, a spiritual cocoon, a sacred holding, recognising there is no going back because transformation is a permanent state; while change is temporary.

Deep within my womb, there is currently an inner pause, a quiet stillness, a secure containment…I embody the sacred yoni vessel, the need for internal rest, the soft whispers from spirit, the anticipation of the unknown. Her active phase has come to an end, she graciously slipped away; she bled and effortlessly released with the phases of the moon for forty-two years. She grew two bonny babies, birthed two beautiful baby boys and she has experienced much pleasure and delight.

With honour and integrity, she has held the secrets of her bloodline, the herstory of her ancestors, the codes of her feminine lineage. I humbly recognise the sadness that she is the last, in a long line of strong northern women! Her particular female codes will die with her.

So, it is imperative that I listen closely to the inner oracle until the day I leave this earthly realm. Dare I believe that she whispers the truth, that the wisdom and all I am seeking is within me already? She has told me that she is ready to open the floodgates, to return the ancient wisdom, the ancestors' knowledge, for the circle of women who have gone before me to be complete!

There is a magnificent cycle, rhythm, phase ahead of me. One day I will share that too, until such a time it has been privilege to be held within this circle. It is through my steady daily practice of self-honouring that this formula has emerged, an outline I carry for living a life of clarity, connection and expansion.

My Body is The Altar

My Practice is The Ritual

My Life is The Ceremony

'My body is the altar' means to me regular self-care practice that has a physical, mental, emotional and spiritual impact on my life. That I treat my body with honour, respect and loving-kindness and that I adorn and dress my body to awaken my senses.

118

'My practice is the ritual', is for me, what it feels like to connect daily to the sacred through cacao, the power of yoga, meditation, divination as an individual practice and within a circle. The gifts of nature inside and around me, the signs and symbols, the messages and connections I see.

And 'my life is the ceremony' when I consciously live from the embodied altar and when I practice rituals – life does become the ceremony. It's when I alchemise the mundane into the magical, bringing magnificence into the forefront of awareness. It's when I cultivate a sense of my inner sovereignty, when I live from a higher level of expansion and rise above the trivial.

I recognise that this is a journey, a process; that I can shape my energy in any direction through intention and desire and that daily cacao, circle and rituals have facilitated this shift. Cacao has been the catalyst to a deep awakening within me and I find myself inspired, encouraged, engaged and elevated through working with her.

Through this sister circle, I saw and healed a part of the girl I used to be; I recognised the woman I am and currently preparing for the woman I am yet to become.

A'ho

Ali Hutchinson

134

Nothing emptied her full heart of a heavy load
faster than her spells.
The written word.
Promises on a page.
Notes to self and love pouring out of every cell.
So much love, so much love, so much love.

from 'Sacred'

The Girl I used to be

I found myself searching her face. The girl in the photograph. The girl in the green dress. I remembered that cotton dress so well, the familiar feel of the soft, over-washed fabric. The way it swirled around my legs when I twirled. The tiny mother of pearl buttons down the front. But oh, the anguish of looking back at that girl. The girl I used to be. The haunted look in her eyes, the dark circles underneath. The stick thin arms that sprouted from that green fabric. That photo was taken when I was happy. I thought back. Was I happy? I was teaching pointy toes to a class of tiny tots. I loved those classes. The freedom of tiny bodies throwing themselves around the dance studio in total abandon. The joy of finding I could help them express themselves. The joyous expressions on their faces when they understood what the music was saying to them. Their freedom. Their total freedom. When had I lost that freedom?

I recalled how I came to own that photo. The pianist accompanying me had snapped it without me knowing. She presented it to me later, not with a flourish but as a gesture of.... a gesture of what? No-one was speaking about it. The weight I'd lost. The lack of energy I had. The haunted look or how empty and lost I was. But that photo captured it all.

That photo changed everything. I saw the girl I was for who I was. I saw me for the first time in months. I saw how I had lost myself and what I needed to do to reclaim me. It was the beginning of my recovery.

I don't wear green. I haven't worn green for years and yet I love the colour green. The colour of nature, the myriad colours in the foliage on an evergreen hedge, the distinctive green of a freshly picked blade of grass, the bright highlights in my Pilea plants. And yet for over thirty years I've avoided wearing green.

This one picture, this one ritual, brought it back. Witnessing the growth of the girl I used to be – revisiting her in her time. Not simply looking back at my life but stepping into it. Time travelling. Energetically shifting my energy to witness hers.

Consciously noticing the journey I'd been on. The healing I'd done. Giving myself permission to buy a green dress. To wear it with pride and step into the energy of my younger self. To observe the girl I used to be in her happy place. Blessing her, praising her, sharing her strengths, her passions, her future. Showing her just who she would become. Expressing the myriad ways she would impact those around her. Allowing her to see how her independent spirit, the thing she didn't understand as a teen, would be the thing that ultimately defined her life.

In starting on this journey, gathering with these women in ceremony, building ritual into my daily life I had opened my Pandora's box. I had so much still to let go of but I had a framework that would support me, a group of inspirational women around me, a tribe of non-judgemental fellow truth seekers. I didn't appreciate how letting go would be so cathartic.

I let my daily rituals evolve in a way I would have played as a child. If the urge to go to the woods beckoned, I listened and followed it. I walked bare foot on the grass on dewy mornings and on frosty days. I took my cacao to the woods and shared it with the forest, reconnecting with all my senses. The smell of damp earth under my feet, the light creating dappled shade as the trees came into leaf, the touch of rough bark and the resinous smell of the pines, the taste of wild garlic and the bird song. I stopped and listened. I slowed down and let a shaft of sunlight catch up with me. I breathed it all in and I brought it into my ceremonies too. I added nature to my alter and allowed her to adorn my room. I had fun, I lived.

I visited the girl I used to be, that seven-year-old playing in the garden, her hair flying as she turned cartwheels on the grass. I shared experiences of how much she was loved, how happy she was, how her parents cherished her. And yet it was not this girl I was called to sit with. The girl that kept returning to me was my teenage self. She came to me energetically, she came to heal and in allowing me to witness her healing, she witnessed mine.

I allowed myself to celebrate her wins, the small successes she made in her life, her strength, her courage. I shared how her past had helped her, and others, to grow.

In reconnecting with her, I reconnected with myself and stepped into my power. I soared on angel wings, to rise up and look down on the amazing life I had created and to celebrate it. To seek forgiveness of myself. To realise that my healing has helped other women to mend and that this journey was simply a new beginning.

My childhood angst helped me relate to my relationship with food in a unique way. It had taken me until I reached my mid-forties to release the power that food had over me. In this first week of ritual, I came to understand this.

I came to accept that my teenage vulnerability and inner turmoil was my strength. It made me relatable and able to relate to others. I didn't need to judge myself anymore.

Meeting cacao and ritual

'What even was a cacao-dieta?' I asked myself. I found myself agreeing to drink ceremonial cacao every day for 22 days but I was questioning it. I'd worked with women who had yo-yo dieted for years, surely, I wasn't signing up to a diet of chocolate? I didn't even like chocolate. And yet the pull of adding this to my daily life was so strong, it just felt right. There was an aching within me to start this journey. That little inner voice, so quiet, yet so dominant was saying 'just begin, just begin'. I struggled to comply but I listened.

And with that first taste of ceremonial cacao, the bitter hit of chocolate, like nothing I had ever tasted before, I felt like I'd reached home. All my worries dropped away and I was transported to a place deep within. I breathed in the scent - dark, earthy, guttural. I held my breath then let it go and with each deep breath I realised the pain was a little less.

From that first day, I opened ritual in a way I hadn't ever done before. I'd read the personal development books, I had my miracle morning, my daily routine. I'd been getting up before the rest of the house even surfaced for years to find that solitude time for myself.

I did these things by rote. I meditated, exercised, journaled and drank my lemon and ginger.

But these rituals lacked feeling, there was no emotional connection. They were things I ticked off in my journal, the good girl dutifully following her mentor. But this was different. There was a visceral pull creating this connection between me and my morning cacao ritual. My mornings changed. I looked forward to the daily ritual, it became 'me time' in a way that all the other morning rituals had not been. It became a time for me to focus and connect with something deep within. It was therapeutic. I opened my heart and let the tears fall. I cried for me and for all the lost hours I'd missed while dutifully following 'the system'. I cried happy tears for all the time I still had left to enjoy this new ritual.

Lighting my candle, calling in the woman I was, witnessing her drawing near to me and honouring her presence was cathartic. I asked her to guide me, to sit with me, to hold me. 'With this light I call you' I whispered. And each day my whisper became a little stronger. My belief that she would hear me a little clearer. My inner knowing connected parts of me I had long forgotten. With this light I opened my heart to all that I'd been shielding myself from. I opened myself to new experiences, new connections, new opportunities.

I bought special candles, cherishing the time, choosing scents I could really relate to, knowing I didn't want chemical fragrances in my home.

Lighting my candle became a form of self-care, a way of showing myself some love.

I lit my bundle of sage and allowed release to come. 'With this smoke I release all that no longer serves me, I let go of all that has been holding me back, I step away from past hurts, pain and limited thinking'. Each day, I shed a new layer of skin, uncovering the fragile girl beneath and building her strength back up. Unearthing the woman I was now and calling in the woman I was yet to become. There were days when the smudge just drifted around me stagnant and painfully announcing its power. It would not disperse until I had let go. It lingered until, with a deep breath, I was ready to remove the blanket of whatever had a hold on me.

There were days when it burned brightly and floated away on a shaft of light, the sunlight illuminating it and drawing it heavenward. With that smoke I let go. I slowed down and released all my schedules. All my over thinking and timelines. I connected with who I really was at my deep core and I felt myself crack open. And with each sip of cacao, I felt her bind me back together, healing me, filling in all the tiny fissures where life had knocked me, created a tear or dimmed my light. She filled me with her soft gentle love. The warm trickle of her slipping down my throat with that first daily sip, the way she coated every taste bud and announced her presence with such gentle force. She gifted me this time to breathe. To look inward and to find me again. I found that girl in the green dress in my cacao cup. I emptied myself of all fear of ever healing her. I let her rock me into peace.

The girl who still cared what her peers thought of her, the woman who still wanted the good opinion of the school gate mums was still inside me. I was still playing it safe. My transition from corporate life to landscape and interior designer was safe. It covered for the fact that motherhood wasn't my life's calling. I loved being a mum but I couldn't just be a mum. It would break me and so I stepped into a well-chosen career that fitted in around family and still allowed me my freedom of expression. It was a recognised career move and my change into the health field was similar. It allowed more of me to show but it never really unlocked my full potential. I tried to conform. But mama cacao had other ideas. She had a hold on me and was not going to continue to let me play small. She kept putting ideas in my path. Synchronicities appeared, the moon kept revolving and with each new and full moon my confidence grew. My faith that I could pivot my career and find a new path that was not only fulfilling to me but allowed others to shine too was growing.

127

I found that photo of the girl in the green dress when we were moving house. She'd been a memory until then but in the clearing of a life's collecting, I unearthed her. I was working to create a compelling future for myself and it involved travelling, the freedom of not being tied to one location and so the exercise of letting go of the stuff I had accumulated over half a lifetime began. And with each box I unloaded to the charity shop or recycling centre I released more and more of the things that had been tying me down. I looked at all the things I'd achieved in life and celebrated my successes in a way I hadn't done before.

I'd been hard on myself, never thinking I was good enough, bright enough, popular enough but I saw in the letters I re-read from friends and family, from old work colleagues and even in the congratulation cards from my wedding day that I was loved, oh so loved. Surely this was more than anyone could ever ask of life. And with the shredding of those letters and cards, the tears and the laughter, I rebuilt the girl I used to be, filling in the parts of me that brought me joy and created the woman I am now, the life I now live.

Becoming me

And yet in all this letting go I was still stuck, I still had my feet firmly planted in the past, in past expectations of who I was, of meeting other's expectations of me, of not disappointing anyone. I mustn't be too bright, too loud, too much. I was still playing small. I knew the life I was living was not fulfilling me but I wasn't quite ready to let it all go.

How did I let any of it go? It had been what defined me for so long but I felt I was ready to jump ship. And so, I gradually started to ease out the guy ropes. I released a little at a time. Perhaps I should have thrown it all in, set sail on a new course immediately but I remembered that amazing quote about when the wind did not blow in the direction of her dreams, how she adjusted her sails. I was adjusting my sails rather than jumping ship and it felt right. I wasn't ready to let the sails down altogether but I was changing course. I embraced trainings and used moon energy to guide and support me. I centred each ceremony around release and letting go, finding an inner voice and leaning into my own guidance. I learnt to listen to my own inner voice and I trusted that she knew where we were going. I understood how powerful she was.

And so little by little I took charge and started to listen to the music within me. I began to dance to my own tune. I stepped back from the things that no longer ignited a passion in me. Yes, I felt guilty, I even had what the teenagers called FOMO (fear of missing out). But I did it, I said no to invitations and opportunities. And I smiled and danced because if it wasn't a 'hell yeah', from now on, it was a 'no'.

For so long I'd held myself back from making lasting connection with female friends. I had a close-knit group of friends but when I looked back on them, I'd made almost all of them in my early twenties. I had no real friends from my working life. Why hadn't I made lasting connections with women in those places? Why had I held myself back? I realised that in gathering with these women, I had found the tribe I'd been looking for, for many years. We were all so different, yet we were the same. We craved connection, we listened to our inner voice and we spoke of what we wanted from our lives rather than criticising what was wrong with our lives or those around us. We all had pain but we didn't have time for gossip, we were too busy being ourselves to care what others thought.

At each cacao ceremony, more and more women shared unique experiences. Their healing became my healing as I saw myself in and through them. I dropped the mask. The shroud of perfection I'd hidden behind for years and let myself be seen.

I meditated on how I could let go. I sat with mama cacao and asked for her guidance. I sat and listened. I watched the flicker of my candle, connected with my breath, breathed into that place deep within me that knew all the answers. And I heard her cry. Why such hurry? Take it gently. Take a step, don't throw it all away. You can step into who you are without trampling on what you were. Be gentle on yourself. I saw that girl in the green dress smile at me – her blue eyes shone and I remembered how she had taught those tiny tots to listen to the music and interpret it their own way. And I danced. She was thinking of me.

'You are exactly where you are meant to be. Your journey has been as unique as you are, there is no right or wrong here. Learn more, evolve more, be more - you will never be complete. You may be calling in the woman you are yet to become but your journey with her will never be finished. Even on her death bed she will be learning new dances, opening herself to new experiences and sharing her life'.

So, each day I light my candle, I sip my cacao, I smudge my space and I ask for guidance. I allow myself to take up my space in the universe – a space the universe has created especially for me. It's a space that's as unique as I am, as unique as we all are.

Stevie Jane Foster

134

And she sat in stillness,
Open to hearing whispers from above, below, behind and in
front.
Smiling guides and mentors flocked to her side,
So pleased to have been acknowledged.
Unseen wisdom just a breath away.
She was never alone.

from 'A Woman's Blessing'

Finding my stick

One warm and sunny early spring morning, I went for a walk. Walking in nature has been really important to me for years, drinking cacao before I go, has also been really important to me. It's my ritual. I noticed long ago how drinking cacao actually changed the way I experienced and interacted with nature on those walks. Colours became more vibrant; bird song became more harmonious. My whole body, over the years, had become more attuned to the sights, sounds and smells of nature, I had become so much more aware of the energy in the air and I felt deeply connected to it all.

That particular day, the warmth of the sun felt so soothing that I decided to sit for a while to soak it up. As I sat, I felt a warm wave of relaxation flow through me. That warmth penetrated right to the marrow of my bones. My heart seemed to expand, I felt so peaceful. There was nowhere to go and nothing to do. I felt I could sit all day in this companionable silence, watching the birds, the families around me and their dogs playing and running about.

As I looked around, drinking in this blissful scene, my eyes fell upon a stick. It looked like it had been there for decades being bleached by the sun. There it was, seemingly just waiting for me!

I wasn't looking for a stick, yet I was inexplicably drawn to it. When I picked it up, its weight felt good in my hands. I ran my hands over it and felt the smoothness, the knots, the secret nooks and the crannies. Something inside me whispered 'You'll need this stick, take it home and keep it safe!'.

I remembered all the times my children had found sticks and natural objects. They'd insisted on bringing them home. My pockets, the car and the garden were always full of precious treasures from our many walks in nature. I felt a bit silly carrying my stick home, with no children or a dog to blame but I did it anyway. When I got home, I put it in a safe place in the garden and more or less forgot about it.

A couple of weeks later, I found myself contemplating a sister circle. At the age of 53, I had decided to sit in ceremony with a circle of women. I'd never done anything like that before but I felt drawn to it, I wanted to know more about cacao and myself. As soon as the decision was made, I felt a childlike excitement rise up in me. It felt like something very special was going to happen.

Just a few days later and I realised I needed to find a stick! It was the first ritual of this sacred sister circle. I sat just stunned by the beautiful synchronicities that had led me to find my stick, when I didn't even know I needed one! I immediately brought it in from the garden and gave it pride of place next to my altar.

Sister circle at this point, was a bit of a leap of faith for me but it opened a kind of magic portal to new possibilities. This combined with ceremonial cacao, my love of nature and now my stick, I felt like I was in the right place at the right time. The right place to be able to receive some very precious gifts indeed.

Changing the past

At the beginning of this immersion, back in time, invited to meet the girl I used to be, I sat with cacao. I settled myself on my favourite meditation cushion, lit a candle and slowly and deliberately drank my cacao savouring every delicious and healing mouthful.

I let the cacao flow through my body taking me deeper into a meditative space, a place I know well, a place that connects me with my heart and the ground beneath me. I felt the familiar tingles and fizzes, then that glorious glow in my chest as my heart gently unfurls. I travelled back in time to the girl I used to be. I found myself with my younger self at about seven years of age. I could see her so clearly. She was in her school sports kit, long blonde hair in ponytails, in the car on the way to school. I felt she was both excited and a little bit nervous. After weeks of missing out on the fun of new sports activities (because of a broken arm) she was finally allowed to join her classmates. She was going ice skating!

I could feel her excitement and nerves, the fluttery butterflies in her tummy and I reached out and held her hand. I don't know if she felt me but for me, it felt like the air crackled and there was a definite shift in the energy around her. The radio was on in the car and a weird old song came on that really caught her attention. It was so catchy and fun that she was soon singing along. I remembered this moment so well; I loved this song and it comes back to me often. I sang with her in the back of the car and I imagined she could feel my enthusiasm and encouragement.

Instantly, we were both magically transported slightly forward in time, to the moment just before she stepped onto the ice for the very first time. I placed my hand on her heart knowing this to be a pivotal moment in her life. I told her I loved her and that she could do anything she put her mind to. Then off she went, singing that song loudly, without a shred of fear, she just got on the ice and skated!

And there I was in my room, on my meditation cushion, forty-six years later, sobbing at the sight of her. She could skate without fear or hesitation. She trusted her body, she trusted that she'd know what to do. What she didn't know, was that she would go on to be an actual ice dancer! She would learn to jump and spin and move so gracefully. She would learn to trust her skating partner to lift her, support her and bring her safely back down again.

This was so poignant for me because that little girl had been so ill as a baby and as a toddler. She hadn't been expected to live. As a result, her parents had cocooned her, she hadn't been allowed to do anything risky. They'd been told that she was fragile and weak. Until that moment, she'd been taught that her body was not to be trusted, that it could let her down at any moment, yet here she was, skating on thin ice with so much trust and grace, already!

At seven years of age, one of the most significant ages in a child's life, where they learn about their own independence and competencies, she discovered that her body was amazing!

It takes an incredible amount of physical strength and stamina to be a good ice skater. Strength and stamina she'd been told she didn't possess. It also takes a lot of courage to jump high enough to execute a spin and trust that you'll land on a thin piece of metal, on a very slippery surface! And there she was starting that process; there she was doing it.

Going back to this precise moment in the meditation touched me so very deeply. I cried because I'd never given it a moment's thought, yet this experience changed my life direction forever. How different my life might have been if I hadn't been spotted by a coach and told I had talent? Not because I went on to be an internationally famous ice dancer, that certainly didn't happen! But what did happen, as I whizzed around those ice-rinks, is that I gained an innocent freedom I'd never experienced before. I remember the wind in my hair, the power in my legs and time away from the claustrophobic care of my parents.

I have a sense that this act of getting on the ice, with no fear and an innocent trust, actually saved my life. As a teenager, I disliked my body. Part of me knew it was amazing and I know that thought and knowing had stopped me from being more extreme in my self-harming inclinations. However, I also knew that when I went back in time, in that meditation, I was not just a passive observer of my past.

There is a version of history and of science where there is no time, where there is no past or future and that energetically speaking it's possible to go back in time. I was really present in that moment and my actions then were able to alter my past.

The love and support I feel for my younger self and my devotion to her well-being, has allowed me to alter my timeline. I believe she felt that love and the confidence I had in her.

I believe she felt my presence and heard my voice and it gave her the courage she needed. As I sat on my meditation cushion observing and reflecting, crying and laughing, I felt I entered a magic portal of sacred, powerful, transformative energy.

My past, present and future had merged. All of this was possible because I was learning to honour myself on such a deep level. This was sacred act of self-love and radical self-care in action. I was moved beyond words by the gift I'd given myself and forever changed by this beautiful deep honouring.

Living in ritual

Before sitting down to write this chapter, I had an overwhelming desire to clean my meditation space and altar. I rearranged it and made it so beautiful and inviting, I had to sit at it with my cacao and spend a few moments in meditation before starting. Far from being an exercise in procrastination, this was essential for me to tune into what I wanted to say.

Daily rituals and meditations have paved the way to meeting the woman I am yet to become and so it seemed fitting to create a ritual before writing my thoughts.

I've had a meditation practice for many years. When I was fifteen, I read a book on transcendental meditation and I've been experimenting with different forms ever since. It helps me to deal with the stresses and strains of everyday life. It gives me a 'still' point in my day which is just for me. Joining a sister circle enhanced this meditation practice, it encouraged me to add beautiful rituals to my already grounding practices. Lighting my candles, cleansing my space, making and blessing my cacao, dedicating this time and space to myself and all the other women in the circle has very much changed my experience of meditation. It became much more magical.

To my mind, lighting candles, opens an energetic portal to different dimensions and timelines. Placing special found objects from nature on my altar magically transports me to the places in nature I love the most. Doing this, knowing that my sisters are also practising their rituals, gives me a sense of community and connection.

In the week I met the woman I am yet to become for the first time, I did some beautiful, deep and nurturing rituals with my sisters. And once again, I was invited into meditation to meet her. Each time I did, I gained more and more insight into the woman I am yet to become and the choices I am currently making to get there.

I had some exquisitely colourful and powerful dreams which took my breath away with their detail and intimacy. I prepared some holy water with my favourite flowers and essential oils, I placed it on my altar and added to it as the week progressed. I wrote messages from her to my present self and tied them to my stick, blessing them with cacao. I whispered secrets to her that only she would understand and one morning, after enjoying my magical rituals and meditation, with the power of it all still swirling around me and within me, I went for my early morning walk.

This was a particularly special moment. It was pre-dawn, still dark and time seemed to stand still. With the promise of a new day gently felt on the breeze and heard in the bird song, I was aware of the moon setting ahead of me. The tinge of pink signalling dawn arriving. I walked the familiar paths filled with magic and sparkles and starlight. I felt the cacao in my heart and the words of the meditation dancing around me filling me with expectation and excitement. I came to a dark straight path surrounded by bushes on each side, forming a kind of tunnel. The air was full of magic, the anticipation made my senses tingle. I stepped onto the path and felt the energy shift immediately. There was a stilling, a calmness around me. She was there, standing next to me in all her beauty and wisdom.

My big sister, my mother, my crone, the woman I am yet to become. She took my hand and walked with me, smiling at me and filling me with her love. As we neared the end of the path, with the sky gradually lightening behind us, our auras merged and she stepped behind me and into me, integrating herself with me.

We became one. Just as we have always been and always will be.

She whispered to me 'You are not and never will be alone, I love you and I am listening'. Filled with so much awe and wonder at this incredible moment, knowing that I am never alone, has been so powerful to me. Every day, in meditation, I put my hand on my heart and say 'I love you and I am listening'. She never fails me with her wisdom and her love.

Angie Gifford

41

Something healed inside her that day,
as she sat on her mat, floating,
Aware that her heart had just been flung open
and washed with fresh air.
Her wiser Self, had offered the most beautiful of blessings
and she was eternally grateful.

from 'Sacred'

Changing my story

Most of my life, I have felt unworthy, not worthy of love. My mother was a teenager when I was born. She didn't know how to care for herself, let alone a baby. Her mother, my grandmother, was not a physically demonstrative person, she rarely showed affection, so my mother learned from her mother: the generational cycle.

I don't remember feeling comforted or loved. My childhood was scattered, fragmented: I spent the first six or seven years moving with my mother or living with my grandmother and my auntie. As an adult looking back, I always felt scared. My mom went to night school to learn secretarial duties to make a better life for us but we were broke all the time. Life was difficult. I always felt like it was my fault that her life was so hard. I was told I shouldn't have been born. OUCH. Fucking brutal.

Looking back, I know she didn't mean to hurt me but I took those words literally, to my heart. They stayed with me through two marriages. I developed a tough exterior and kept most people at a distance. I learned early to protect my heart. Inside, I always felt like I was a soft, ooey-gooey marshmallow. I wanted to be seen as such but my inner lack of confidence and hard shell (developed and cultivated through many decades) prevented that.

Years of therapy, studying yoga philosophy, seeking release through everything from mediation, exercise and alcohol, I sought answers to fix myself. I was in a job I abhorred – it literally sucked my soul. I couldn't quit; I had a mortgage. The early years of childhood instilled in me a deep fear of financial insecurity.

I embarked on a journey with this sister circle to help release me from my past and guide me toward my future. What I found was something much deeper. Something much more profound.

I found a group of brilliant and talented women: all of us seeking answers. We shared two hours together every week for a month and became sacred sisters. We created a safe space to share our deepest, darkest fears, knowing we wouldn't be judged but held, lifted up, and supported by each other. I'm an only child and for the reasons above and more, I don't trust easily. These five special women held space for me, listened to me cry and supported me. I let my guard down. They didn't criticize me. They didn't judge me. They saw my soft, gooey insides and loved me. I felt like I'd come home – home to myself. I was able to breath. Full breaths. Deep breaths.

Through conversation, ritual, support and mother cacao, I found answers inside of me. I knew I held the key and the answers but this time, everything landed as it was supposed to, I had a major paradigm shift.

Studying yoga, I intellectually know everything and everyone is connected, however, I didn't FEEL it until sister circle. Listening to women across the world struggle with the same fears, shame, guilt that I had, drove home the notion that I am them and they are me. I am not alone. What a glorious feeling. I was not alone. I have always felt alone. Even in my marriages, it was me against the world.

Adding glorious mother cacao to my morning meditations increased my openness to share my story and my deepest secret, something I had never, ever told anyone. I truly believe, the 'food of the gods', cacao released the grip on my heart, allowing me to step fully into the circle. I created a morning cacao ritual: chopping the brick, boiling the water, adding the spices and thanking Gaia for sharing her gift of sacred cacao with me. Long after my journey finished, my cacao ritual remained. It's an integral part of my life.

Our first ritual was to focus on the girl I used to be, I remembered her vividly. All my life, I've felt that I was cheated out of a childhood. My life wasn't like my friends. At age six, I walked home from school, opened cans of spaghetti and cooked them on the stove, waiting for my mom to get home. I learned to be independent and self-sufficient. There was no room for being scared. I had to grow up fast.

Between kindergarten and first grade, I went to three schools in three different states. I had to learn to make friends quickly if I wanted to fit in. As an adult, I played the victim of a 'less-than-idyllic' childhood. I don't know where that idea came from or how or when I began to believe it but I told anyone who wanted to hear that I had a childhood of misery and despair; the more I told that story, the more I believed it. I used that excuse to behave rather poorly toward the ones I loved and who loved me the most.

As I sat in circle with my sisters, as I meditated, and dove deep into the rituals of those 22 days, my heart and mind began to change and soften.

The most profound experiences for me were the daily rituals of that first part of the week – the rituals of finding play again and going back in time to spend time with my little girl in meditation.

As I prepared myself and my space for meditation, I could not have imagined what ultimately shifted. I lit my candle, took three deep cleansing breaths, sipped my cacao and put in my headphones. In the meditation, I pictured myself at age six. At first, all the memories were negative, heavy and sad; that's my story, right? More deep breaths and the scene shifted to a holiday family dinner at my grandmother's house. It was loud. All my cousins were there. Everyone was happy. Where did that memory come from? That's not my story.

144

During the meditation, I was guided to place my hand on her back. I let her know I was with her. I told her that she was going to be alright; no matter what happens in the future, she is a survivor. As I spent more time with my child that week, the negative feelings fell away and I began to understand that she was a happy little girl who loved to laugh, had many friends and was courageous. Silliness filled my heart when I pictured her with her too-big front teeth and blonde pigtails. Rituals of finger painting and scavenger hunting rekindled my creativity and brought a new sense of joy to my heart. I couldn't remember the last time I finger painted! I loved the feel of the paints on my hands, cold and squishy. I don't think of myself as creative so getting started was a challenge but finally, I jumped in with both hands. Of course, I was harsh with criticism. 'What on earth am I going to learn from this?' The more I painted, the more I laughed. Who cared what it looked like? I was being silly. I am never silly. I was playing!

The ritual of scavenger hunting proved to be a treasure trove. I hunted and dug in my back yard. I found a blue, plastic army man, a rusted kickstand from a bike, a toy police car and a beautiful piece of green glass. I've lived in this house for almost ten years and had no idea those riches lay hidden in my gardens.

I laughed at myself with my hands covered in dirt from digging in my yard – digging for fun! More playing! I felt lighter. At the age of 53, I was playing, painting, digging in the dirt, having the time of my life. The intense grip I had on my 'story' began to change. Yes, there were difficult times, yet I let those negative experiences take over. I wallowed in them. I wrapped them around me like a security blanket. The lessons I learned from that week were life altering, a seismic transformation.

Soft things melt hard things. She melted me. She melted my heart. I loved her. I cherished her. I stand today on that little girl's courage, strength, endurance. She was smart, creative, clever and funny. She provides my strength, courage, intuition, and instinct. Until that week, I'd never celebrated her, honoured her, thanked her. 'Thank you, sweet, precious child. I adore you'. Her laughter, sense of humour and intelligence gave me the foundation I thrive on today and that will carry me through to the woman I am yet to become.

The woman I am now

In the past, I lived in fear. Fear of not having enough. Fear of lack. Fear of not being enough. Two divorces and a job that had no meaning to me left me seeking answers: 'How do I create my best life?', 'How do I heal?', 'What in the hell happened to me?'.

One of the coolest things I have ever done is a ritual to recognise what I truly am. This opened my eyes to what an extraordinary life I've lived. When I viewed my life from a different lens, when I viewed it as a whole, I was literally gobsmacked.

I've been...a daughter, a mother, a niece, a wife, a friend, a teacher, a mentor, a creator, a student, a bitch, angry, a workout instructor, a yoga teacher, a personal trainer, an employee, a landscaper, a lover...the list goes on.

I've lived through...childhood, two marriages, two divorces, writing my own divorce papers, giving birth, bad jobs, being a single mother and broke, going back to graduate school at the age of 40, a pandemic, fear, shame, guilt, a ten-hour bus ride through the mountains of Costa Rica, freaking out in a river cave in Belize, learning to ride a motorcycle, my mother's second husband, my grandmother's death.

I have lived through MENOPAUSE!

I've lost my mind! I've lost my confidence, friends, lovers, weight, dogs, jobs and expensive sunglasses.

I've raised myself, my son, my mother, dogs, my temper, my voice, my hand in rage.

I've gained weight, wisdom, knowledge, a group of friends, trust in myself, a daughter-in-law, a granddaughter, FREEDOM to do as I damn well please.

I've started new lives: marriage, divorce, being single and owning a business.

I've started new jobs, books, seeds, meditations and drinking cacao and I've started to heal, to know myself, to love myself.

The lesson learned: I am not a number, not an age. I am me. I now look at everything I have encountered, endured, created, let go of and lost. Taken as a whole, I can see my life as a journey. Each step to be celebrated. What an incredible life lived. What a blessing. I've embraced challenges and created opportunities. The most significant, eye-popping takeaway was I realized I have always been ok. Maybe not right in the middle of a storm but I've always come out the other side. We all do. That's a seismic transformation!

Seismic transformations

When I said, 'I stand on the foundation that my sweet, gorgeous, six-year-old gave me', words cannot express the depth of the shift in my consciousness.

The awakening I experienced with my child, created space in my head and led me to one the most life altering decisions I've ever made – RETIREMENT. I let go of financial security, the crux of my entire existence. Where did that courage come from? My little girl. I am 53 years old and I retired! Society tells me I'm supposed to stay in my soul-sucking job at least until my mid 60's. Friends asked me 'How will you feel valuable if you don't work?'…assuming I felt valuable at work of course…I categorically did not!

I have a Master's degree and was relegated to answering the telephone. One particularly close friend asked me if I felt invisible. She kindly informed me that women over fifty rarely get hired. I think I gave her a sarcastic retort along the lines of 'who fucking cares!'. I was finished living someone else's life (my parents, my friends, society's). Living their fears. I knew I had to JUMP. And jump I did. I now live on sixty percent of what I made. I pay all my bills, I own my house. Who in the hell do I think I am? Going through this sister circle gave me the answer.

I am FIERCE.

I am WILD.

I am a FORCE.

I am free from the constructs of what and how others think.

I believe I should live my life.

I am courage.

That is my biggest take away from this time with these women. The experience of looking at my life from different lenses: from the eyes of my pure, innocent, strong and independent child; from the perception of my current middle years; and looking into the future of the woman I am yet to become, has given me perspective I had never considered.

I do not need to cling, grasp or claw my way through life. Fighting life, fighting my body, fighting for Lord knows what...I was always fighting. Trying to get respect from people who could not give two shakes about me. Always trying to please. Always trying to put on a happy face. That pretend, fake, happy face was killing me inside.

The experience of sitting with women in circle, listening to their stories and sharing mine gave me courage to change the illusions I clung to from the past. My perceptions were permanently altered – I seismically transformed my life.

Finally, I saw myself as a whole person. I could feel deep in my belly how I wanted to grow into the next stage of my life. I found my courage, my voice, and the strength to shed all the ties that had kept me bound to an unhappy childhood and an unfulfilling life.

When I sit in silence in the mornings with my cacao now, in the soft glow of my candles and the scent of sandalwood incense, I relish in the calm and slow pace of my days. I sit in wonderment at how I got here. I have to thank a close friend for urging me to be part of a sister circle. She is a teacher, healer, mentor, and friend. She understood my need to break free, to let my light shine, to reveal my real Self to 'my' self.

I used to gauge everything by how much it cost. Living in fear, lack and always being afraid of not having enough money. I almost didn't take this journey, the Gather the Women journey, the journey that saved me – from myself. My deepest gratitude to the six women who shared my sister circle.

In grace and gratitude, this is my offering.

Aho.

Ann Ball

16

Heady yet grounded.

Spinny yet centered.

Overcome with deliciousness yet completely still.

Moments like these spun her to her balance, her strongest point,

her sweet spot.

from 'HELD'

I was the presence

Such a strange mix of emotions when you try and convey to your younger self that life will turn out well, when you try to give them a snapshot into the future.

Throughout my childhood I was aware of presences. I thought they were ghosts, things to frighten me, taunt me and cause me to jump in the night. Whispers heard, strokes like being touched by cobwebs, I now know that presence was me...visiting my younger self...from me in the future and done in kindness and love.

I was a jumpy, skittish child, seeing movement in the shadows and knowing that it was more than a shadow. Funnily enough I now work in a haunted location and muddle on fine for most of it but I'm still aware of shadows and movements in the corner of my eye. I amuse myself by wondering if this is my future self again, coming for a peek to see how I am getting on now?

It was in this sister circle, when we visited our younger selves that I realised, 'I' had been that presence in my room as a child, that I was visiting my younger self and that I was there out of love and to pass messages of encouragement to her.

As I sat with the younger version of me, conveying love to her, reassuring her, I felt a deep sense of calmness. Those were such powerful moments. I remember a big slow smile spreading over my face as I looked at my seven-year-old self. She was a sorry sight for sure. She felt misunderstood, she didn't get much attention in that busy household especially with a new baby and I remember one instance, as I endured enforced babysitting duties, that opposite feeling, a mixture of both love and resentment. And then there was that familiar space of my pink bedroom. Where I visited myself sleeping, reaching out to tenderly stroke her face. What a shame my younger self would wake in fear, unaware it was in fact me, her older self.

I like myself now, I liked myself then. 'Successful me' looking back, against the odds of being told that I wasn't going to amount to anything. I was told not to expect too much, not set the bar too high for myself.

I was a stubborn child; thankfully. And it's this attribute that helped make me the woman I am today. I took the not unkind advice that I shouldn't expect too much of myself and raised the bar, I made it my goal to do exactly that. I don't think I ever lost that childlike imagination of being able to do anything I wished when I grew up.

I lived in the moment, I was excited for life and I didn't worry unduly. I set standards for myself, I rewrote someone else's ideals for me, they weren't mine.

Meditation

I find meditation easy as I drift off into a daydream, in particular guided visualisations, they draw me in deeper each time I listen. My muscle memory strengthens with repetition and time and I have a very visual brain, so when words invite me to visit a place or a time, I'm pulled through time – like a whoosh sucked through space – floating particles to reassemble in another space, a moment to re-adjust, to settle in to wherever I am visiting.

Meditating to take me back in time to revisit my younger self, feels as real to me as turning over a page in a photo album but in 4D. Bubbling sensations of excitement and nervous anticipation, as I arrive. I allow the scenes to settle in my vision, knowing I am home. The pink wallpaper of my childhood bedroom, the gold flock paper in the living room and the backs of the heads of my dear ones. They look so young, I feel a moment of connection with my mum, as I'm now a mother, marvelling at how she coped with four kids, all vying for attention, asking questions, wanting answers.

I want to reach out and touch her, send her a message, that I know now, that I understand her more - solidarity, mother, woman to woman. What an honour to be able to view the past. The meditations soothe me; ease me into the sense of letting go, relaxing into it. The sentences form an invitation to take a few minutes to myself, like an 'already heard' bedtime story.

It's time to meditate, the house settled and silent, just me, calling in my time. I've been on call for the family for years and now, this is my moment. I don't feel guilty for taking this time out. The strike of the match to light the candle beside my bed signals the commencement of my relaxation. As the wick ignites, I feel my muscles loosening, my eyes flicker with heaviness and I'm ready for this.

I get a real sense of comfort from these meditations; certain words almost linger and form in mid-air to punctuate the meaning. I welcome that feeling of numbing sedation as I don't have to be anywhere or be anything for anyone. Sinking lower into the bed, body imprinted, going deeper into the visualisation, I feel the familiar release of acceptance. I find the rhythmic words work in tandem with my breath. Calm breathing, a balm for the senses, no space to overthink - how freeing is that?

And the destination, a sense of wonder, as until I arrive, I don't know where I'll end up. As I revisit my childhood living room, my eyes settle and get used to the layout. Not just a visual feast but those senses of actually being there, a rush of emotion as I'm back in that seven-year-old body. I'm slumped and annoyed, a tad

154

resentful of the unwanted job of babysitting my baby sister foisted on me. 'Why me?' I think. I could be doing something else but my sense of duty overrides my yearning to play, watch TV or read.

As I stand in the doorway, tears form in my eyes, I'm filled with pure love, of wonderment. An inner smile to myself, as I take it all in. 'Oh Ann, look at you, do you know the magnificence of yourself? Do you know that you are wonderful just the way you are? You are your own person'.

In that short moment of standing there, I try and bridge the gap, to download a ton of information to benefit the seven-year-old me, to give her wisdom beyond her years, so she can put all that unnecessary questioning and countless mental arguments aside so she could enjoy her childhood more. But even as I do this, I know this is part of life's lessons and really there's no shortcut to life.

One thing I've learnt in cacao ceremonies, is that the young are our teachers. 'So, for now, dearest Ann, be you, live and learn for me'.

What an honour it is to have this chance to revisit time, to look back and reflect. An opportunity to heal past hurts, to see the situation from wise eyes. As part of the meditation, we are invited to gift ourselves something. I gift myself a white rose, with some white feathers, to symbolise purity, perfection, beauty and nature's magnificence. The feathers are also for lightness, for innocence and a bridge between those who have passed and those who are here. I want the young me to have love and support from our dearly missed loved ones too.

Rituals, candles and cacao

Even the word 'ritual' draws me in, evoking so much potential, deep in meaning.

Growing up I would have scoffed at the importance of ritual. I'd have pictured myself donning a white robe, prancing around on a dark hill in a circle with other delusional women, uttering undistinguishable but scary-sounding chants in an invocation, an obligatory full moon shining down, with a sense of hushed secrecy.

But I've learnt that a ritual can be as simple as setting aside some time to do something with intention. For me, it begins with the lighting of a candle and then the drinking of ceremonial cacao. The lighting of the candle is my signal…the sipping of the cacao is my switching-on of the senses, saying 'I am ready'.

I've found that ceremonial cacao, my plant medicine of choice, opens my heart, it asks me for presence, I don't use it as an everyday slug-it-down drink, where I chat on with friends, read the paper or flick through channels on the TV. I recognise that it's worthy of my full attention, deserving of my respect.

It invites me in, to savour the texture, the flavour and the warmth, an internal hug as I recognise it as a heart opener, a perfect marriage for my meditations.

I heard that the lighting of a candle is like picking up the phone to spirit - an immediate connection. I liked that. It made sense to me.

Over the past years I've developed my meditation skills, I've journeyed to other dimensions, connected with loved ones long gone and respect the tenuous cord of communication. Sometimes it's strong, other times weak, it's something I work on, dedicate my time to, learn and practice.

The lighting of a candle holds so much potential I feel. I'm pulled in, magnetically, easing me into my relaxed state with an invitation to visit other realms. I feel calm, soothed, open, willing, curious, hopeful and a little like I'm living on the edge, my adrenaline kicks in, the familiar jumping of butterflies, after all who knows what I will encounter! It's exciting.

I feel safe, I have the opportunity to convey love, converse with ancestors, educate myself along the way. The lighting of my candle sparks not just light but illumination of me! Such a powerful link to other dimensions, to be able to time-shift. I relish the opportunity to meet myself again, to commune, to infuse love into the atmosphere, sprinkling love like glitter in a snow globe.

Drinking cacao is such a part of my life now, from cup to lips, an experience. As I prepare my cacao, I do so with intention, I sing to the cacao or speak to it with intention, love and meaning.

I have a little routine. I use the same utensils. Measure it out, stir it, add it like I am making a magical potion. A sprinkle of salt, a pinch of chilli, yummy. Stirring it in my special jug pan, each stir a strengthening of intention of meaning. The anticipation of making something for myself.

And then the drinking of the elixir. Not just drinking it but giving it my full attention, usually with a 'thank you' to those who look after cacao, to honour the journey of it into my home from some exotic far flung location, for the history of it.

As the warm fluid settles in my stomach, I feel that connection strengthening. As it warms me from inside, I allow it to open me on a vibrational level. I sense that I'm guided to drink by many medicine women of the past.

It makes me feel loved and connected, like a lifeline, an umbilical cord of connection to a long line of like-minded women.

A feeling of acceptance, that I'm part of the fabric of life. Alive. Pulsing, buzzing, happy, inquisitive, open, willing to learn. 'Teach me, show me, I am here'.

Circles are new to me. Ritual with other women, sitting in circle is so much more than sitting by myself. Being with women versus being by myself in my own home, away from my family, my sisters and my school friends, I miss them.

Attending women's circles has filled that gaping hole. I have shifted. I'm trying to be a better person, less judgemental, more open. Not always succeeding but striving for action not perfection.

I would not have been that woman attracted to the poetry or the reading of the books, the meetings, the on-line circles but with enforced lockdowns, another world has opened up to me, it has rescued me from my loneliness, my yearning, my need for female company. It seems to be that many other people's perspectives might have shifted too, our own goalposts moved.

Now I know I am just a fingertip pressure away from another woman. For me, being in circles allows me to slowly open up, like a flower. I often don't feel the need to speak, just being in their company is enough. It makes me 'feel' myself. My presence as important as the next. To be held, supported and listened to, to have space.

I'm a social being, although I enjoy my own company too but lately it's been too much. That solitude can sometimes be too loud, too busy for me, so to be in the company of others quietens the discordance of it all.

I witness the 'unfiltered version' of other women, their richness, their rawness, their flaws and primal feelings. It's been a deep dive into how someone else is feeling without censorship, without the hushing, for them to be heard, to be witnessed.

My tears sometimes flow – no rush to soothe, the strength is in the rawness, the tears, the open snot-fest filled moments, without interruption, without well-meaning, no empty hugs. No need to fix or be fixed. Speaking my words in this space can be enough, expressing my true feelings, insecurities and vulnerabilities.

I feel connected to the women in my circle, through vibration, like the plants have mycelium, an underworld of lines connecting, roots, veins, source, sap, life force. I'm drawn to like-minded women, to find my tribe, to emit a pheromone of openness, to be a beacon of welcome light and to be present for others.

Emily Madghachian

32

Burn the candle.
Smoke the sage.
Whisper your blessings.
Breathe out your fears.
This moment is yours.

from 'A Woman's Blessing'

Cacao and the girl I used to be

I can hardly believe I will turn 53 next month…a ripple of shock moves through my body as it awakens all aspects of my being as I type that. 'Where have I been all this time, who have I been and what has brought me to this moment of such profound gratitude and awareness?'

So much of my life had been defined by people's expectations of me that six years ago, I found myself emotionally on my knees literally praying and begging for something…anything please God to break free from this crippling sensation in my chest that was ready to wind me forever. I was utterly exhausted and yet, being a 'good girl' I kept going, in automatic mode. As the expatriate child of multicultural parents, I have been unconsciously driven to find safety in meeting everyone's expectations of me all my life: parents, friends, partners, teachers, bosses, clients. Everyone. I am *so* good at finding creative ways to please and help people, to make myself useful, needed, important and special, to create a sense of feeling love and belonging.

In 2015 while on holiday in Bali and in conversation with my teenage daughter Skye, a voice in my right ear whispered that I needed to move us to Bali, now. I had never heard this voice before but I understood somehow, that this was my prayer being answered, so I packed up our lives, left my company in the hands of a stranger and within a year we were based in the jungle. Over the five years we lived there, I found myself uncoiling through some wonderful women's circles, retreats, workshops and a wondrous conscious community but the truth was, I was still striving to belong. The unconscious belief that I had no worth if I didn't do so, was so strong, it kept me tethered and exhausted, even right there on the blissful Island of the Gods.

162

Back then, I had no idea how to access the capacity I have to be the most authentic version of my SELF. Until in January 2021, I discovered ceremonial cacao. A local Medicine Woman sent me three warm bottles of cacao freshly made, especially for me. As it made its way across rice fields to me by motorbike courier, I received a message on my phone: a meditation to listen to as I prepared to sip this plant medicine for the first time.

I was guided to light candles and to feel the depth and nourishment of this heart-opening dark velvety elixir. And so, I did. I sat alone in the dark, with candles burning, legs crossed and felt my torso warm and awaken. A clear vision of my torso as a drought-baked riverbed appeared before my eyes, cracked and barren. As the Cacao travelled down my throat through the centre of my body, it became the replenishing river that caused bright flowers to blossom on either side of my chest. I literally felt myself coming back alive. As they naturally softened, I realised that my shoulders had been up by my ears, my belly had been held tightly in and my breath was stuck in short sharp loop at the top of my chest.

I took a deep breath in, watching it cause waves of breeze over the fields of flowers that were my revitalising body. This gentle awareness of my body had me fully present and in wonder. It was simply beautiful, that I sat in tears and gently wept. How long had my body been this coiled? I quietly wept for the years I hadn't connected to this wondrous and intelligent body of mine and had instead been a slave to my limiting beliefs. So, I wept some more. How many versions of myself had I ignored while I strived to please?

From that moment, I couldn't wait to sit on my mat every morning, to light a candle, set intentions and sip while bonding to the grounding sensation of the earth through mama Cacao. I listened to the meditation, I gave thanks and, in my body, I found a voice. MY voice. And my voice said YES, yes to me, yes to my dreams, yes to my desires. It shocked and unnerved me but ultimately FREED me.

Nine months later, now living in the UK, upending my life once again, I joined an intimate group of women to gather and discover different aspects of ourselves through rituals and cacao. What wasn't to love?

For a week, I lit a candle for the girl I used to be every morning. On day one, with my eyes closed and cacao warming my insides, I found myself journeying back to be with my six-year-old self in her classroom in Egypt, where she's trying so hard to please the Arabic teacher. She isn't actually supposed to be learning this language because her father doesn't want it. But she so wants to. She is small and blonde, in a sea of Mediterranean complexions and she very much wants to belong here. She's sat up eagerly and yet simultaneously tense and frightened not to get the new language wrong but also to not upset her father in the desire to learn it.

When I sit next to her on the wooden school bench, she suddenly softens and I feel her melt into my love. I, sitting on my bolster, cry the tears that her tense and courageous little form is holding on to. As my cheeks moisten, she pulls out some pencils from her pencil case and we sit and draw together at this old wooden desk in a school on the outskirts of Cairo. She unwinds and relaxes even more. And I remember myself in her: creative and full of wondrous imagination, as she scratches her pencils into beautiful shapes. She breathes deeper, just like I do, as I prepare my ritual space: my candles and crystals all in loving patterns that still my mind and heart. Through space and time, I see how this creativity has served me my whole life. This little girl had an innate sense that her creativity could calm her and return her to her peaceful heart and I, as an adult, made it my superpower. I smiled in awe at her young wisdom and gave her a squeeze of loving gratitude. Was this one of the first times I had intentionally loved the little girl I once was? I gently opened my eyes and felt my body on the bolster lighter, as though the squeeze had changed something fundamentally in real time. Wow.

On another morning, I had just finished sipping my cacao, my breath was deep and my heart wide open, when suddenly three-year-old me appeared. There she stood, in a corner of the family living room in Montreal watching her parents lovingly welcome her new born baby sister. I felt into her heart gently as she stood there, lost in this new experience of no longer being the only child and knew immediately that I was experiencing the beginning of the wound that had held me in fear all my life: 'I am not important' said the wound.

I picked up my pen and wrote furiously to halt it forming in its tracks, as if I really could save her (us) from it, the words being screamed inside my head as I did: 'You ARE important, you NEVER weren't important! Your parents loved you then and they love you NOW! There is NOTHING you need to do to earn that love, it just is!'.

I desperately scrawled in large untidy letters, writing as fast as my hand could, not wanting another moment of that little girl to cement this belief that she had suddenly become irrelevant. I wrote to reverse time, to reverse belief, to reverse all the moments and times that I'd been a slave to the mistaken meaning I had created of my parent's natural love for their second born child, when I had been so young myself. And then I opened my eyes and wept, exhausted as I relived the pain of all the efforts I'd made in my life to feel significant, wanted and loved by anyone. The blessing of such a powerfully cathartic moment has been the awareness that is now mine and the washing away of the permanence of that wound. It no longer governs my intentions and I am free.

I took the girl I used to be for a walk in nature the next day and I almost expected her to be sad again. But as we walked together through the autumnal forest in Hampshire, I found myself looking at everything through her eyes. She was nine years old and her eyes were wide with wonder at every thing she saw: I felt into her curiosity as she bent to pick up leaves, sticks and feathers. She saw beauty in all of it, brought it back to a table and promptly made art out of it. I was struck by the joy and presence in her heart. Every piece she picked up seemed to speak to me through her of our resilience. Somehow by the age of nine, she had already found a way to overcome the hurt in her heart. It didn't rule her, she hadn't created a story around it. She was present and embraced life with curiosity and playfulness. And so, I realised, did I for a long time.

Autumn, cacao and the woman I am today

As we walked back through the woods, our pockets full of Autumnal gifts, I was struck by the idea of my ritual daily walks reconnecting me to aspects of my Self that had been buried for decades.

Having been based in the Middle East and then Bali for the past 27 years, I hadn't experienced Autumn and the stunning colours that transform the tree crowns in person for a long time. Suddenly she was revealing herself to be so much more than the thing of visual beauty that I'd taken for granted AND advantage of all my life. On this day I didn't only see it, I FELT it.

As I opened up to the energy of the forest, something about communing with mother earth was allowing me to be reflected in her greatness. Here she was, in the steady and slow decline of her vitality as she prepared for winter, leaves gently falling to earth for the ground to absorb and be nourished by in a cycle of regeneration. I stood and watched in real time as she was taking what would be her past and creating a new future with it. 'Wow...and not a manual in sight', I thought, no-one to guide or teach or show her the way.

That was the moment I became truly awe-struck at nature's innate intelligence and power to create and connect. I breathed in deeply and felt that take hold. My body expanded to meet the thought and again, I felt it come alive through the awareness that this conscious ritual allowed. Again, I found myself weeping with gentle gratitude at what was being revealed to me: 'my body is made of the same elements as this tree and the ground I walk on. I too have innate intelligence and power to create and connect.'

When I opened my eyes, they fell on a small wooden stick. A slow blink, another breath in. As I wiped my tears, I picked it up and brought it home as a reminder of that moment of profound understanding of the benevolent, loving and powerful nature of the universe that runs through all things. The stick is now with me when I sit in daily ritual and continues to play a part in keeping me connected to my innate nature.

As we continued gathering in sister circle, we flowed into honouring the women we are today. Being invited to write a wish list of our heart's desires, was something I'd previously found so deeply uncomfortable, that I'd abandoned every attempt to allow myself any such thing. But while sitting on my bolster, with my candle lit and cacao warming my belly, I set the intention. And still I struggled, the well-known voices of my conditioned brain awake and spewing the usual scorn and doubt.

So again, I intentionally re-focussed. I connected to my breath, inhaled deeply and in the space that breath provided, I found myself intuitively reaching for my stick - the stick that would once have been 'just a silly stick' - and then magically connecting in, past the voices and into my innate creative nature.

I remembered the leaves under my feet in the forest - regenerating into something new. Wondrously, the voices dimmed. In their place, visions of what I may never have said out loud before for fear of being 'too much' or 'unrealistic' or because I'd actually never been aware of my deepest desires. 'How is that possible' I thought, 'how could I not know what I really want? How long and how far buried had my desires been? And how much power did those voices have over me?'.

This time, instead of being sad at the dawning of the realisation, I acknowledged the thought and with eyes still closed, physically turned my head away from the painful thought and chose to look in a different direction to see those desires as seeds under the ground: seeds that simply needed some loving attention and some wetting. With my negative belief literally behind me, I put my stick on my lap, picked up my pen and I wrote my Authentic Self's list unapologetically and without a voice in my head telling me otherwise. This time I didn't weep, I started to grow.

There is no doubt in my heart that cacao is the connector, the fertiliser and the enhancer of the emerging expression of my greatness. There is nothing special about me when I say this. I understand it, each one of us has greatness within, it is our creative

168

spirit, communicated through our innate intuitive wisdom, that flows through us all and allows us to create any outcome our hearts' desire. Exactly how the seed of an Oak tree mysteriously and magically emerges from the regenerative dark wet soil as a shoot that reaches for the sky, so can the seeds of our desires transform into reality.

I found my ritual itself beginning to unfold and stretch. The power of sitting down every morning with intention to honour myself by lighting a candle, sipping cacao, and connecting to my heart, now expanded to reflect the beauty of Autumn's regenerating power. As I focussed on allowing my heart's desires to materialise in my future, I called my ancestral lineage to join me in ritual. Like the falling leaves in the woods turning to mulch and feeding the seeds, my ancestors' wisdom, courage, resilience, intuition, joy and love all feed my blood and make me who I am today.

Cacao, wintering and ancestral healing

[It is with permission from my beautiful daughter that I can tell a little of her story from my perspective, in order to reveal for me, my journey as a mother]

I looked back to the girl I used to be and how I dreamed of being a mum. I was never a girly girl with dolls but an innate wish to 'mother' was rooted deep within me. By the age of fourteen, I was given the nickname of Mother Hen at boarding school and often I would be serenaded with people clucking and flapping their arms around as I walked by.

Giving birth to my daughter, awakened the desire to be an exceptional mum for real. I left her father when she was two months old, so it was up to me to be the best provider and fixer I could. As Mother Hen, I delighted in the role and went at it with all I had. I worked hard, started two businesses, earned good money quickly, took us on wondrous holidays and created lovely homes for us in Dubai and then later in Bali. I attended every sports match, drove her to and from school and after school activities every day, created lavish birthday parties and provided her with all that she needed and more. We bonded over movies, music, cooking, art projects and finding new coffee shops to try out. I loved surprising her at every opportunity and was grateful for the laughter and connection we shared, even as the turbulence of teenage-hood arrived.

On the eve of her seventeenth birthday, we received the sudden news of her father's tragic death. I watched powerless as she withdrew from me, desperately unable to ease her enormous and explosive private pain. As grief settled into our home like an unwanted guest overstaying its welcome, the devastating landscape of loss forced a disconnection and something fundamental came away.

Two years later, as I sat in sister circle and was now welcoming in the woman I was yet to become, I couldn't remember ever connecting into this part of my Self, let alone acknowledging her. Up until this point, I kept my head down, busied myself with whatever project I could and ignored the realities of aging. Growing older was something that confirmed my vanity and which I feared - gently but definitely.

At the same time, I found myself distracted from the group as I focused on holding space for my daughter's deteriorating mental health. I was lost in guilt and doubt stemming from my earlier choices. Should I have tried harder to make my marriage work? Should I have remarried? Was moving her to Bali my best mama decision? Perhaps I should have played safe and stayed put, unhappily running my business in Dubai.

A robotic, unconscious standard of being able to take care of all this alone reasserted itself with a familiar anxious grip on my heart, squeezing me back into the torture of my brain and wounded beliefs: 'Unless you can save her, you will never be considered important'. Round and round I went striving to find solutions, a cure, anything.

Until one day I was asked, 'How are you? How is this week with the rituals?'. Instantly, I stopped spinning.

I was three days behind on the rituals as part of the group, yet, in the energy of that communication also came the sweet reminder that I could choose to ask the woman I am yet to become for guidance. Who could possibly know me better than the woman that I am yet to become?

Somewhat excited and no longer feeling alone, I got back on my bolster, crossed my legs and took a deep nourishing breath. In her honour, I lit a candle, sipped my heart opening cacao and smiled when I pulled the 'Heart Guardian' card from my oracle deck and placed it in front of the candle. I felt my body soften as I called for her. Beautiful.

She arrived. With a long silver plait down over a shoulder, so calm, grounded and solid. We found ourselves on a bench tucked away in my heart, me, exhausted with my head on her shoulder and her with one arm around me and a hand on my heart. She whispered in my ear, she told me of her gratitude for me; for all my choices and efforts, even and especially those ones I'd spent too much time berating myself for. All of these, she said, made her the woman she was.

She felt into the part of me that was currently feeling so small and powerless. I sensed her breathe all of our capacity through space and time into me. She reminded me that what I saw in her, was indeed MY strength and capacity and that it influences not only the women that will come after me but also those that came before. I sat quite still. And very much in awe of her.

No wait... of ME.

It was impossible to ignore the emerging vibration emanating from my heart. Connecting to my future Self revitalised my seeds instantly by infusing them with my innate but buried confidence and wisdom. In that moment, my ancestral women joined the woman I am yet to become to create the pathway forward and away from the wound of the girl I used to be. BEAUTIFUL!

My fire was stoked. I sat so still for a long while. In utter mind bending, heart pounding awe of it all: the power of universal love and the unending potential and possibility that it creates. Why aren't we taught this at school I wondered? But not for long... because the magnificence called me to simply sit and bask in it.

So, I basked in the magnificence of it ALL.

I'd been curled up in a ball just the previous day despairing at all my failures as a mother, partner, ex-wife, businesswoman, daughter, sister and here I was opening my eyes, with a gentle smile and warmth pulsing outwards from my bursting heart.

I instinctively reached for the book 'HELD' and closing my eyes opened it to page 83:

She gathered all the parts of her.
From all the random places
that she had scattered her precious Self.
Gently placing them ceremonially in her heart.
Her place of calm, rivers of gold painted over the cracks.
Breathing on purpose, bringing all of her parts together,
gathering her power.

I can't tell you how long I sat there drinking all this wondrous magic in and when I stood up, I took the strength, love, courage and resilience of the woman I am yet to become and wore it like a cloak as I went into my day. A day that could have been described as a 'hard day' ahead supporting my girl.

'That's just a thought', I told myself. 'It's not true. It's NOT hard and I am not alone'.

'You are not alone' chimed the women I used to be and am yet to become.

'You are important, you are ready,' they said, 'ready to be the creator of your heart's desires'.

Wow.

And yet. The energy to jump into action, transform or activate just wasn't available. In its place was a powerful, subtle longing to withdraw and nourish in this newfound understanding tugging at my soul. A desire to 'winter', to let these words sink deeply into my cells. I saw myself curled up in the foetal position under a tree, pulling a blanket of moss and grass over me, allowing myself to deeply rest. So, I did. I withdrew and chose very carefully who I shared my time with. I consciously kept my seeds wetted in my mind knowing that my rituals and my visualisations would trigger them to germinate in the spring. My breath deepened, short sharp breaths at the top of my lungs were a thing of the past; my shoulders rarely found my ears. The gift of allowing and receiving was born out of the added daily practice of speaking my gratitudes out loud ahead of taking my first sip of mama cacao.

When I peered out of my quiet haven, connections were magically being made around me - and none of it was whimsical, more these were clearly the dependable results of returning to my mat and bolster every morning to bow in ritual. A ritual from which I can open my eyes to see a broader, clearer version of my life, a bird's eye view that spans time and leaves the twisted details born of fear behind.

Wintering had also withdrawn me from the space where I tried to fix everything for my daughter. With me now resting and nurturing myself and in daily connection with the women I had gathered, my girl has begun to step into the new space of seeking me out.

These days I listen more and reflect back. I witness her drawing on her own resources and the curiosity of her future blossoming as she wills the fog to clear instead of letting its weight force her back under the cover of her own darkness. It has occurred to me how our experiences are mirrored. She is accessing her own strength, courage and resilience in dealing with the challenging situations that have been sent her way all at once and wondrously, I see that she's letting go of the need to do things both exceptionally well and alone.

And as I drink cacao, she even talks of finding her own plant medicine too. Then another dawning follows: my ancestors are working their magic in my life and I feel the new vibrations altering those of our future women...my daughter among them.

Oh. My. God. Of course! The full power of my capacity to create my highest desires in spite of my deepest fears, became obvious. It was as though nature, my ancestors, the girl I used to be, the woman I am yet to become and the wonders of cacao's medicinal mix were holding up a huge banner saying 'Hurrah!"

I see it now. Nothing is impossible when I intend to connect deeply to all the women that I am, to my heart and to receiving the end results of the choices I make daily. Through the power of self-honouring daily rituals, I choose to align with my heart for the greatest good of all through space and time. Sure, my ego rears its head from time to time but now I choose to re-focus on what's real and what is true: I am important, I have gifts to share and I am ready.

Mykela McAlpine

8

She felt blessed to know she could soothe herself.
She felt blessed to understand how to make herself happy.
Most of all, she felt blessed enough to rely on her intuition.

from 'A Woman's Blessing'

For my beautiful mum Susan Hanson, who taught me so much, to believe in myself and question everything.

Drinking cacao and healing my heart

Over eighteen months ago I went to a Goddess retreat, this was where I tasted my first drop of cacao and it was delicious. The cacao back then was mixed with plant milk, water, rose water and cacao butter. I was hooked on the whole ritual of the cacao ceremony, the dancing and connecting with other women as soul sisters. I hadn't felt connections like this since I had left homeopathy college almost twenty years before!

Now, each morning when I wake up, I head into the kitchen, I gather my cacao, a sharp knife and my very special chopping board only ever used to chop my cacao and I take them all to my sacred space to cleanse them before my ritual.

Soft chanting music is playing in the background and I begin to gently shave cacao from the block, I sometimes join in with the chanting music whilst I'm making my cacao and I always make sure my mind is full of loving thoughts so I fill my cacao with good intentions. I boil the water, let it sit for a few minutes and pour onto my cacao, stir and its ready for my daily ritual.

I've had my own little journey getting to know mama cacao, initially I made her with plant milk, maple syrup and a dash of rose water, gradually I no longer added the maple syrup and then missed out the rose water. Finally, she is pure, I don't feel the need to add anything else. She is just raw plant medicine now and it feels good. I feel like I've finished my apprenticeship and this is where the real learning and magic begins.

Following my time in sister circle in that ever-deepening immersion, I start each morning with cacao and I light three candles - for the girl I used to be, the woman I am now and the woman I am yet to become. I smudge my space and bless my cacao thanking all the ancestors and mother earth for producing such an amazing plant medicine. I smell the aroma of the cacao as I sip and feel into the energy of these three aspects and cacao. I sit with them all in the stillness of the morning, in silence. It's in these precious moments that the wisdom of mamma cacao ignites my own and my feelings rise up and out.

I was so happy that cacao was such a founding part of our sister circle, for it's been throughout my journey with her that she gently guided me back to a traumatic part of my life – a part that needed healing. This sister circle took part in that space too. It was when my marriage was breaking down and I was losing my beautiful mum to the cruellest disease imaginable, Alzheimer's, that I closed the door of my business because I couldn't cope. I never said that to anyone at the time but that's what was happening.

I told people I just didn't have the time to run a business and look after my family, when the real truth was that I felt lost and alone. I couldn't cope with anything else, so instead I just threw myself into looking after my girls, making sure they were both okay and trying to keep a roof over our heads, secretly hoping my mum would suddenly get better.

My darling mum became a victim to this most horrendous disease when she was just fifty-eight years old. She knew she had it and used to cry all time she had so much sadness inside her. Each day seeing her decline, broke my heart. I didn't want to accept it and I couldn't cope with this along with the breakdown of my marriage and a failed business.

When I say I lost my mum, I mean, the mum I knew is no longer here. Her body is here physically but her soul and spirit have long since left. In the beginning we could see glimpses of her, the sparkle in her eyes, especially when we played music or danced with her. But that time has passed and the occasional spark has gone out, when I look into her eyes now, I see only darkness.

I was incredibly lucky that I had such a wonderful mum, she was very level headed, so caring kind and compassionate. Very family orientated, she would do anything for anyone. She was the listening ear for her friends and family, everyone gravitated to her to spill out their problems.

Mum gave so much of herself to others and when I look back at everything she did for me and my family, I wish she'd been a bit more selfish and taken more care of her own wants and needs. This, to me, is one of life's valuable lessons and something I was able to ponder on in our sister circle...the need for me to take care of my own needs, as the woman I am now, as a priority.

Losing my mum has been the hardest. I used to speak to my mum everyday about anything and everything, she was always there, she always had my back. She was the person who believed in me and gave me the strength and courage when I needed it. I was losing my wonderful mum when I needed her the most, when my marriage was falling apart, my heart was broken in pieces and I'd lost all sense of direction.

Grieving for someone who is still physically on the same planet is very strange and never ending, each time I visited her, the whole process started again. Continuing to drink cacao each morning has taken me back to a place in me that needed to be healed. As I continue working with her daily, I can feel my heart healing and opening up once again, to enable me to give and receive love.

As a woman working with this plant medicine daily, I can feel her energy opening up my heart, connecting with my intuition and awakening my creativity. I can feel her nutrients nourishing my body and helping to balance my hormones...I am ever grateful to that first introduction to cacao and the sister circles in which we drink together.

Feminine connection and working on the woman I am now

I've never really been bothered about growing old. My mantra to friends who talked about it was 'if you don't get old, you die young'. For me, this is the harsh reality and so I feel very blessed to be here at the age of fifty-three.

During the process of our sister circle, working on the woman I am right now really had an impact in healing hurts, bringing all the grief to the surface to be healed.

I've struggled with my weight for a long time. I haven't felt good about my body, I've hidden myself by avoiding social events because I didn't feel good. I didn't want to go to gym or go swimming because I didn't want people looking at me. Of course, I realise that actually nobody is going to be looking at me because most women have body issues of their own, whether big or small, I've never met a woman who doesn't dislike some part of her body, I know I'm not alone.

In my late thirties, I felt I needed to get back to the gym again but this time because I was struggling so much, I got a personal trainer. I worked out with her once a week and did other gym sessions on my own, yoga and swimming and still couldn't shift the weight. I would get home from a session and be completely wiped out, to the point where I actually needed to go to bed. After working with her for a few months nothing was shifting, she was questioning what I as eating, you could see by the look on her face she didn't believe that I wasn't overeating. I would go home from my sessions feeling sad and hopeless because my weight hadn't shifted, just feeling exhausted all the time. Finally, I found out I had an underactive thyroid.

I took it in my power to treat myself holistically with homeopathy and nutrition and although my thyroid isn't perfectly balanced, it has definitely improved. I became a vegetarian and stopped eating dairy and I've been working on the grief I still feel for my mum – I learned that grief gets stuck in the throat chakra, which can cause an imbalance in the thyroid gland, this is all still very much a work in progress but I'm making big shifts.

The woman I am now works on loving and forgiving myself and through drinking cacao and allowing my mind to drift back over my life, it's like watching a home movie. Certain parts of my life are highlighted and those morning rituals with my sisters gave me an opportunity to reflect, so I can transition into my wild, wise warrior goddess!

Gradually, I opened up my creative side, dancing, journaling and connecting with other women on their spiritual journeys, sharing our experiences. This has made me realise how important this is, that I've needed these connections since puberty and throughout my life. I needed and found deep feminine connections to help me grow and learn from my elders, such a powerful part of sister circle.

Bathing with intent

The power of taking a bath in ritual! Wow, I resisted this ritual! Who would have thought that taking a bath could be so powerful?

Usually I love having a bath, so I couldn't really understand why I resisted this ritual so much. Now I understand. It meant spending time being in-the-moment with my body. It meant tenderly taking the time to notice every part of my body, lovingly cleansing it and going through a whole process! And so yes, it was me trying to avoid going back to that uncomfortable place.

This is exactly what I needed to do though, to learn how to love and appreciate all of my body including my wobbly bits. And I do this ritual regularly now and feel genuine love and appreciation for my body.

Each bath I prepare is different. I've made up four special jars of epsom salts packed full of minerals. I've added only natural ingredients and each jar has an affirmation wrapped around it as a loving reminder to myself.

My 'post exercise' ritual jar contains epsom salts, arnica bath milk and some fresh rosemary. My 'energizing' jar contains citrus bath milk, epsom salts, beautiful orange and lemon peel. My 'sleep' ritual jar contains epsom salts, lavender bath milk and fresh lavender. And my 'sensual' ritual jar contains epsom salts, ylang ylang and fresh rose petals.

My ritual starts when I enter the bathroom, I fill the bath with warm water and add two cups of beautiful ritual salts of my choice. I light my three candles for the girl I used to be, the woman I am now and the woman I am yet to become. These lovingly filled jars with natural ingredients are kind to my skin and the environment, so I'm looking after myself and the planet. After my bath I fill up a container, go outside and water my garden with these precious nutrients.

I dry body brush before I plunge, gently brushing my skin from the tips of my toes upward towards the heart to help the flow of lymph and help detoxify.

I immerse myself in my bath, enjoying the soak and taking care when washing my body. When I get out of the bath, I dry myself with a snuggly warm towel and begin the process of self-massage.

I take great care and attention when I gently caress nourishing oils into my body, noticing every blemish, every wrinkle and every scar. The areas of my body that I spend the most time on are the parts that I struggle to love.

I've always been conscious of my tummy, its full of stretch marks, rather like a road map. Each time I do this ritual though, I feel like I'm honouring, learning to love and accept this beautiful part of my body. I give it great thanks, it's not only carried me through life but it's carried and nourished two beautiful babies.

After each bath I feel every muscle and every cell in my body has released and let go of any tension or negative energy I was holding, I always feel like a new woman after my bathing ritual.

For me, this ritual is about learning to love and embrace every inch of my being, to love, honour and take care of myself. I feel like when I'm nourishing myself, I'm also showing my sisters, daughters and granddaughters the way to be their true authentic selves, to have confidence and belief in themselves, to nurture themselves and help them to realise there is no competition, we all have our own qualities and can learn so much from one another.

Katie (KaT) Thomas

135

Walkways of ancient wood, candles and lights and fire so bright,
bare feet being called by that drum.
Medicine women and guides and fairies
and elderly witches with kind watery eyes,
ushered them silently into her sacred place
to sit and to breathe and to drink.
Oh Medicine. Medicine. Medicine.

from 'Sacred'

Dedicated to the inspiration in my heart, my grandma Hilda Thomas, who wrote stories and poetry all her life but didn't get a chance to have them published. This is for you and all those women who will read your name and understand.

Time travelling

I felt like there was a change coming, a change that would alter many parts of my life, including the way I looked at myself, my role, the way I felt...I felt like there was something big just waiting around the corner.

And so, I reached out my arms, widely with cupped hands...and my very being, mind body and soul followed willingly.

I have a strong love and connection to mother Gaia. I communicate with all living things as well as those who are passed or dormant. I work my magic understanding energy and only use natural things. I've always known myself to be this way, since I gradually became more aware of myself around the age of six. I began to notice that I sensed more than other children and that only some of the adults knew what I was trying to convey, which lead me to understand what my Grandma told me. She said this was a special gift and that one day, when I was older, I would meet others like myself, others that were kindred spirits...and I have.

To write this chapter, I went back into quite a delicious overwhelm of my time in this 22 day immersion. I got lost in reading all the messages on our group chat between the amazing women I shared that beautiful sacred and held space with. It was immensely special and the group is still live and active to this very day.

Through carefully collected daily ritual, I was carried back to the girl I used to be. I can taste the salt of my tears now from another time, when I was a little girl aged six or seven.

During the guided meditation, I could feel myself drifting away. I saw the shift in my thoughts and memory being pulled back. The intensity of the draw, as I travelled back in time to find the young, vibrant, bright and beautiful child I was. My heart was singing along with her little voice, my whole body feeling the flutter from all of her excited childlike thoughts, her creative brain pulsed inside my mind. I actually became that child again. I was meeting myself as a little girl. This was a complete revelation to me, a dream I hadn't even thought could come true, was happening.

I sat with her, gave her a cuddle, I stroked her hair and told her how beautiful she was. I told her that everything was going to be ok. I spoke to her, she looked up at me and spoke back, we had an actual conversation, she knew I was there. It felt like a beautiful profound moment of connection.

And then, as soon as I came out of meditation, I remembered. That moment had actually happened in real life! I'd been playing in the front garden at my Grandma's house when a lady I hadn't seen before came to the garden. The sun was blazing behind her, so much so that I had to squint my eyes and hold my hand up to see her. She asked me my name, then she spoke to me so tenderly. She told me how beautiful I was, she stroked my hair and said something like 'everything turns out alright, you don't need to worry'. After she spoke to me, I went into the house and asked my Grandma if she'd seen that lady before. Grandma asked if she was still outside, so I ran after her, down the path, through the gate and around the cul-de-sac to the snicket but she'd gone. It turns out my Grandma had never seen the woman I described.

Right there, after meditation, was the moment I realised I could time travel, that time traveling is real. My world has changed since that day. Everything began to seem more vivid, my senses felt like they'd increased, like something had been switched on from deep inside me.

Releasing anxiety

During that first week, I continued to relive the dreams of playtime as a child. So many wonderful colours, my creative brain, along with my heart was wide open. I saw and felt so attached to everything around me, everything sparkled and shone again.

I picked wildflowers and beautiful weeds for the girl I used to be. I noticed the difference in the seeded grasses again and how bright the buttercups and the dandelions shone, like the very sun in the clearest of skies that I'd ever seen, remembering doing this as a child. I'd go out aged seven, with bib and brace shorts, dirty knees, standing in my white mucky socks and red sandals.

I'd pick wild grasses for my grandma around her garden and she'd display them in the jam jars I insisted she kept for such occasions.

My poor Grandma was long suffering and ever so patient when I think back. I inundated her with so many wild weeds and bluebells, protecting the bulbs at the roots. I laughed to myself, remembering what the other kids on the street said to me...'if you pick dandelions, it's bad luck' but I picked them anyway.

Each morning, through the sister circle immersion, I looked forward to my next daily ritual. I would go to bed elated at the day I'd just had, snuggling under the covers with the biggest smile on my face, holding the perfect memories of each experience, thinking it couldn't get any better but it did.

I'd suffered from anxiety for some time and yet through the immersion experience with daily ritual, I realised I was able to control my anxiety more and more each day. The delightful surge of confidence and love I felt pulsated deep within me, like an immense joy with a tickle that expanded my heart.

My confidence was increasing more and more with every sunrise. I learned to dive deeper and deeper into my soul through ritual, to drop my consciousness from my head into my heart, to really feel into the woman I am now.

Every day, becoming closer to the women in this sacred circle, I witnessed and listened so carefully to their accounts and experiences. I felt closer to them, like real sisters, hearing every inflection of the agonies and the exquisite emotions that assisted us all to share.

I found myself blending deeply into each daily ritual, my senses so alert, I saw so much more detail than before. I immersed myself into this beautifully woven thread of daydreaming on a regular and daily basis. And I found another lost key...that I should write.

Becoming sacred

Every single day of those three weeks, I spent more time with nature and time travelling through my innermost memories. Synchronicity at play, I could witness it all for myself.

Each day I grew stronger, became more creative, allowed myself to dream wider and bigger. I communicated with each tiny element of what I was thinking so I could begin to write. I wrote the most beautiful words.

Draining the dark water from the gaping hole in my heart was the next important part for me. I realised that, in order to protect myself over the years, I had a pool of murky water within me where I'd had past hurts. I felt by now that I had all the tools to drain that away, heal the wounds for the girl I used to be and the woman I am now. And in doing so, I was actually healing myself to be ready for the woman I am yet to become and writing was the key.

After years of pushing myself down, deeper and deeper inside hollow holes, my now healing heart was releasing me through writing and daily ritual.

Suddenly I was buying myself the most beautiful flowers, dancing around my bedroom in delight at my feminine, in bright, colourful new caftans and summer dresses I had long forgotten about at the back of my wardrobe.

I found myself putting my hair up for Tai Chi classes, instead of dressing myself as the sporty Tomboy I'd always hidden behind.

I was dressing my body now in jewellery, bathing myself in lush handmade, fragrant water, smoothing my skin in velvety natural beauty creams, lotions and potions and having the most sensual self-massages, gifting myself nothing but utter pleasure.

I was feeling into my sacredness, organically, with my tired yet tender hands, touching, awakening the Witch and Goddess deep inside me, remembering who I was and I knew just where to find me...in lavish rose petal and lavender baths, with scattered bluebells, free again to breath, so loving and soft, then falling into freshly changed clean sheets on my bed. It was like I was enchanted, a being from Avalon. I found myself wanting to coax her out, to play again with life, to explore, discover and to play.

So many of my wishes and dreams began to come true. I noticed everything I was manifesting from the cosmos and I began to change my own luck as my confidence surged. I could speak clearer, communicate with ease, I was full of creative ideas, witnessing and calling in the spirits, creating space for the deities to visit if they wished.

I unfolded like a lotus flower after it's long and arduous journey through dark waters and thick mud. Expanding, becoming, cleaning up the obstacles that were in my way. I began to fully understand why I was on this journey. The 'woman I am yet to become' was waiting for me, she was given to me during a beautiful ritual.

When I saw her, she looked like dynamite, so calm, she really understood herself. Strong, focused yet serene and really self-assured, I could hear the mix of faint music in the background, all of my favourites, their voices moving and weaving in joyful memories all around me, Stevie Nicks, Robert Plant, Kate Bush, Siouxie Soux, almost like a combination of lullabies in the background I recognised the woman I am yet to become.

She glowed, she looked and smelled just like me, full of life, vital in energy, faint sweet scents of honeysuckle, lavender and patchouli. Sandalwood, sweet musk and bluebells in the air. There she was, singing her heart wide open to the melodic vibrations that I could clearly see in sparkling fractals floating all around her, like nobody was ever watching...and yet...what really stood out to me, when she finally noticed me looking at her so lovingly, was that she recognised me, she'd been expecting me!

During that ritual, I looked deep into her beautiful brown sparkling eyes, her reassuring, warm and loving gaze told me that she'd finally worked out how to really be happy and I'm sure I

191

heard her say 'it's ok, everything turns out alright, you don't need to worry'.

Louise Edwards

10

Her altar, her sanctuary,
Her place of self-worship,
her peace and her piece of the earth.
Held with resect,
gifts, finds, stones and feathers
to remind her that light shines and that life continues.

from 'HELD'

Healing the heart of the girl I used to be

The warm rays of the winter sun feel good upon my skin, the sweet shrill of tiny birds in nearby hedgerows are music to my ears and as the words of the Gayatri mantra resonate deep within my being and the rich intense flavours of cacao linger inside my mouth, I am in wonder myself at the woman I am now!

The woman who, every morning (almost), is up before dawn, sitting at her altar in contemplation of the day that lies ahead. She lights candles, cleanses her sacred space with smoke from a tightly wrapped bundle of white sage and chants ancient mantras before mindfully drinking her cacao, her daily plant medicine and settling into her meditation and journaling practice.

Just one year ago it was all I could do to get out of bed. A knot of anxiety dwelt deep in the pit of my stomach, present from the moment I awoke and accompanied by a lingering sense of dread as to how I would get through yet another day. Plagued by incessant self-critical thoughts, guilt and shame for not being able to show up for myself and my family in the way I so desperately wanted to, I could see no way out of the dark place I was in.

My childhood hadn't been a happy one and consequently negative patterns of behaviour and some serious self-sabotage played out into my adult life. In an attempt to 'fix myself', I'd attended countless self-development workshops and had shelves lined with 'how to fix yourself' books. Various forms of therapy had gone some way to helping me understand the nature of my recurring bouts of low mood and depression and yet, I still felt trapped inside those deeply hurt and sad parts of me, in the old sad stories that held me back and had me disliking myself so much!

That was until one afternoon when I found myself sitting in sister circle. I had a knowing that being part of a sister circle could show me ways to rediscover, heal, accept and even begin to love the parts of myself I'd discarded.

Going back to visit the girl I used to be, I knew would be difficult. I'd always avoided any form of inner child work in the past but there was so much of that little girl that I deeply missed. Her joy for life, love of family, creative spirit, connection with the natural world and her sense of humour, fun and adventure. As family life had become more dysfunctional, heavy layers of sadness, fear, hurt, rejection, disappointment and frustration had weighed heavily upon my young heart and without me even noticing, I stopped identifying with those happier elements of myself.

I became desperate to fit in, to be liked, I changed my identity depending on who I was with, yet so often, I felt like I was on the outside.

So, it came as no surprise that the floodgates opened during the very first meditation. Initially, panic and anxiety flooded my body, as I remembered painful memories, however, the connection I made with my younger self, was filled with empathy as I sensed into her sadness and confusion. Lying on my tear-soaked pillow, emotionally and physically wrung out, I felt something new begin to stir inside.

A small speck of light, a glimmer of hope and even pride was growing as I acknowledged the courage I was summoning to take these brave steps! There was a deepening sense of trust, that I was exactly where I needed to be, with sisters who would support me in facing my past, so I could build a happier future for myself.

The more time I spent with my younger self, the more I remembered her inherent, beautiful qualities. Her strength, courage, her resilience. Her forgiving nature, independence and compassion for others. I shifted from seeing her as a victim of circumstances, to a brave soul whose heart light continued to shine.

One early morning, as I sat in the silent darkness and stillness of the house, candle lit and a photo of myself aged four, a realisation hit me so hard it felt like a punch to the stomach. 'How could I have been so incredibly mean to myself for all these years? How could I have so consistently beat up on myself the way I did?'.

I looked into little Louise's eyes and saw only love, compassion, curiosity and childlike innocence…these were the very same eyes that were now filled with tears. I no longer felt disconnected from the little girl in the photo, I felt fiercely protective of her.

I wanted her to know how much I loved and admired her for everything she'd come through in her life. The blankness of my mind was suddenly awash with words that I had to get onto paper, all the things I wanted to tell her, all the amazing things she had gone on to achieve. My pen didn't leave the paper until five pages and half a box of tissues later!

An outpouring of heartfelt compassion sent to this precious part of myself. To complete that day's ritual, I took this love letter to my sacred spot outside, a place where I regularly go to sit beneath the boughs of my favourite tree. The early morning dew soaked through my pyjamas as I got down on my knees, dug a small hole and buried my letter, blessing it with the remains of my morning cacao.

This was certainly some journey we were taking together, as I slowly began to see that I had something worthwhile to offer her in these visits. Through these rituals I could go back as the woman I am now and show her all of her strengths, shower her with the love she needed then and tell her what an amazing person she was.

196

This shift was so profound. I was finally able to tell her that all of the hardships and suffering she had endured were for a reason, that nothing she had gone through was a wasted experience. I was able to thank her for getting me to this point in my life, for never giving up and for always believing and trusting in the purity of her own heart.

The unexpected but delightful bonus is now I no longer default to the sad times when I look back on my childhood. I can recall truly happy times too, riding my bike at breakneck speed down the lanes, hitting a ball against the shed wall for what seemed like hours on end, lying in a field on a hot summer's day looking up at the clouds passing by.

To experience this level of deep contentment was in sharp contrast to the absolute pain that reflecting back on my childhood used to cause. I was finally ready to let go of the stick I'd been holding on to for so long, the one I used to regularly beat myself up with. Now the only stick that matters, is the magical mystical one I treasure, the one I whisper my dreams to, the one I tie my wishes onto and mark with cacao and fire. I remember and treasure these sacred moments.

Seeing the woman I am now through new eyes

It's fascinating to me that having never done much more than light a candle as part of my yoga practice, I so quickly became immersed in daily self-care rituals, not only the ones in the sister circle immersion but also in rituals of my own creation afterwards.

Some of the rituals from this gathering felt gentle and nurturing, like warm familiar hugs, whilst others had a power of their own that took me to completely unexpected places! A ritual shower was one such experience and the journey it took me on was sublime! What goes on inside my bathroom isn't something I usually share with close friends, let alone strangers, yet here I am about to do just that!

I had no expectation that day as I gathered together candles, cacao, incense, body oil and my phone to play music on. All I knew, was that I was ready and willing to fully embrace the experience, to immerse myself in a sacred self-honouring and see what happened. I couldn't have known then how differently I would perceive myself just a short while later.

I waited until a time in the day when there was nobody else home so that I wouldn't be disturbed. I lit my candles and incense, warmed a beautiful body oil, added geranium to massage my body afterwards and put on our playlist. Instead of quickly undressing and jumping in the shower as I usually would, I heeded the guidance to undress slowly, drinking a little of my cacao as the music played, the beat and rhythm finding its way beneath my skin.

I began to move and sway, before I knew it, I was dancing, eyes closed, conscious of the soles of my bare feet touching the cold tile floor and the freshness of the air glancing over my naked body. It took no time at all for me to shift out of my head and into this connection with my physical body and my heart. I continued to mindfully sip my cacao, savouring every mouthful of the ceremonial dose, the flavour so rich and intense. A heightened sense of appreciation and gratitude growing in me for this heart-opening plant medicine that has played such a significant part in my healing.

As I got closer to the bottom of my cup, I discovered the cacao was so deliciously thick, it was impossible to drink her...and this is when inspiration came. I was going to use what was left and paint her onto my body with my fingertips.

I stood and faced myself in the mirror. Like a lot of women, I'm not someone who's overly comfortable with looking at myself any further than the neck upwards but this felt somehow different.

I started at my head and painted a spiral of cacao onto my third eye, then onto my cheeks. Reflected back to me I saw a brave warrioress as I painted bold stripes across my cheekbones. I gradually moved down the rest of my body, painting the remaining cacao onto each of my chakra points, acknowledging and thanking these parts of me for their unique energy and the wisdom that resides there.

What an incredibly empowering and beautiful honouring of myself, of my body, my soul and spirit.

As I continued to dance and twirl in front of the mirror, I was struck by something previously unseen in my eyes. I paused and looked deeply into these windows to my soul, into a part of me that is all-knowing and wise. The woman I saw looking back at me most definitely wasn't the same woman that had walked into the bathroom that day. She was a strong, powerful, courageous, sensual being. This woman was a version of myself I had never witnessed before!

I don't remember how long I stood there staring at myself but the more I looked into my eyes and then down the length of my whole body, the more I loved what and who I saw.

I'd never looked at myself that way, I'd never loved the me that was reflected back in the mirror. There have been times of course when I've had a nice haircut and thought to myself, 'ooh I like my hair' or when I've caught the sun and acknowledged that I love the deeply tanned colour on my skin. But I'd never looked at my whole body and seen deeply into my soul and really wholeheartedly loved who I saw.

I took this feeling with me as I stepped into the shower and washed the cacao from my skin, bathing in the beauty and the magnificence of who I am.

It was just divine, simply divine. When I eventually stepped out of the shower, the music was still playing, the body oil had warmed and to complete the ritual, I massaged my whole being from head to toe. It wasn't just a fleeting stroke here and there, I allowed my hands to linger on my skin, to get into every crease and fold and to feel into all the muscles and joints of my body. By the time this ritual was complete, I can honestly say that I felt like a completely new Louise!

I'm learning, not a moment too soon, that self-care rituals are seriously powerful! Oh, how my life is changing as I see them as an essential and integral part of my life.

Using ritual to visualise the woman I am yet to become

As a little girl I remember how easy it was to have big, bold, exciting dreams for my future self. Two of my uncles loved travel and exploration and they inspired me to adventure to far-off destinations. I went backpacking for three months to Australia, New Zealand and Thailand and later, I travelled to Peru and walked The Inca Trail.

This was 'the' dream come true for the twelve-year-old me who'd watched with wide-eyes my uncle's slideshow of a canoeing expedition to Peru and the then relatively unknown Machu Picchu. I wonder now…did the trust and inner knowing of that younger me already know that twenty years later I'd be standing on that same ancient sacred site, looking down onto the great Urubamba River, the same river he had canoed in the 1980s?

I'm not really sure when I ceased to have those exciting dreams but little me would have been so sad, upset and disappointed to think that she would stop dreaming and trusting in her big bold ideas. I can see so clearly now that as I grew up, I became caught up in the 'too many' dramas of my life, I was worried about how my future would pan out.

All I can say is 'Thank Goddess' for this sister circle! Visiting the girl I used to be and focusing on the woman I am now, the daily rituals of remembering, revisiting and honouring myself then and now, turned out to be the best gift I could ever have given myself! These rituals gave back to me the ability to dream again, to see a brighter, more audacious future for myself.

The day I invited in 'the woman I am yet to become' in meditation, I'd strolled barefoot down into the wildflower meadow, my wicker basket in hand, now a firm friend, each day carrying my cacao, cup, white sage, mala beads, journal and copy of 'Held'. As I close my eyes now, I can recall the firmness of the wooden bench I sat upon, the soft warm earth underfoot and the sounds of distant tractors and horses munching grass just beyond the fence. With my cup of warm cacao between my palms and held firmly against my heart, I breathed my intention to connect with the woman I am yet to become into this deeply nourishing and nurturing plant medicine with me.

As I did, a tiny, almost imperceptible ripple of excitement and anticipation pulsed through me, perhaps my intuition preparing me, reminding me that it was safe now to let go and trust. With the sweet rich taste of mama cacao lingering in my mouth, I put on my headphones and allowed myself to be lulled into that safe cocoon, that warm, nurturing space where words and imagery combined, to bring forth my future self.

She came and sat down right next to me with an air of grace and confidence. This vibrant, beautiful, free-spirited woman with a long flowing cloak of midnight blue around her shoulders, her hair was long and white, she had clear skin and fresh eyes...so warm, gentle and welcoming. There was such comfort in her presence and a deep sense of contentment and peace washed over me as I felt my trust, my knowing and ability to dream returning.

I loved this woman! I loved everything about her but I especially loved her serenity. Oh! To show up in my life like this! Free of all the worry, the anxiety, the 'shoulds' and 'coulds'. To be this version of myself, who knew that she truly was, exactly where she was meant to be, in every moment of her life. What a vision!

The beauty of all this, is that now, whenever I feel those pesky niggly doubts creeping in, I can revisit her anytime I choose. I call on her wisdom and her 'unflappability'. I'm not sure that's even a real word but to me it sums her up so perfectly.

I know this future version of myself couldn't have shown up in that way without me journeying back to visit the girl I used to be and rediscovering her strengths and all the things she used to enjoy. It was these discoveries, that enabled the woman I am now, to feel so much more at peace with herself, to trust her intuition and grow in confidence.

A huge weight was lifted from my shoulders that day, in fact from my whole being, as I no longer dragged around my old wounded self. I honour every day the girl I used to be and the woman I am now, for giving me this dream, this divine future version of me, to grow and bloom into.

Throughout these journeys, I knew without doubt, I was 100% held by the other sisters in my circle. Being able to show up in front of them in any shape or form made the 22 day journey feel so safe. One moment in particular will stay with me for the rest of my life. I had started to share some of my deeply painful experiences and realisations to the group and I was crying so much that I couldn't speak. As I looked up, feeling so desperately sad and embarrassed at my emotional state, all I could see were the kind, loving faces of these six beautiful women, women I'd never met before, women from America, Bali and the UK.

Until that moment I hadn't thought it was possible to feel so held and so loved and supported by a group of women I'd only ever met on a screen! I was learning in this moment, the importance of trusting other women, women who are choosing to do the work, who choose to sit in circle, to bare their all, to be vulnerable and brave – they are some of the most powerful, beautiful, deeply compassionate women on the planet and I forever bless the time I now get to spend in these safe spaces. I feel so excited now for the future me and the new possibilities opening up for other women to experience more of their own power and heart connection. Women holding space for other women...sometimes that's all we need, just a safe sacred space to show up, to be heard and to be held.

Francesca Yogini

115

If she remembers herself at her core, who she is, what she needs,
Her visions and her greatest dreams, then she has unlimited
power.

from 'A Woman's Blessing'

I've been, I've lost, I've found…

Today, as I light my candles to honour myself and sit quietly with cacao, as I do every morning, I am 18,499 days old. To really take in the number of days I have been alive on this planet has made an impact on me. And so, every morning, when I wake up, I think about my sacred me-time and about honouring myself. It's become such an important part of my life, it's become part of me.

It's not a routine, it's ritual. I bring intention into it, pure thoughts and questions… 'How do I want to feel?', 'What energy do I want to send out into the world today?'.

And with those questions, I make my cacao, with love, intentions and whispered prayers. I have a special cacao cup, I pour her in and walk down the garden to my sacred space.

As the fresh air of outside touches my face, I breathe in. I've learned in those 18,499 days to appreciate the nature around me, the fresh green grass, the pink sky, it all makes me smile. I sit on my meditation cushion on the floor, in my special spot and light three candles for my three aspects, for the little girl I used to be, the woman I am right here, right now and for the woman I am yet to become.

I light palo santo, I cleanse and bless myself, my cacao and the space around me.

I hold my cacao to my heart as I say aloud my affirmations, giving thanks, love and the deepest reverence to Ixcacao- the cacao goddess, the ancient tribes and communities who kept this sacred feminine heart opening plant medicine safe and alive. I invite her in. With the very first sip I feel her. Warming and nourishing every part of me she touches. The sacred warming river of cacao. I take a deep breath and feel the space in my body, my shoulders soften, my mind slows, my heart opens. I am home. Deep gratitude and so much love fills my heart as I feel held by the loving embrace of mamma cacao.

Tears, happy tears, run down my face as I think of how I got to this place, how I found myself and came home to me.

I come back to the thought, to the 18,499 days I have been alive. In those thousands of days, I've been a daughter, a little insecure girl who wasn't quite sure where she fitted in. A little girl who always believed in magic, who knitted scarves for fairies and picked flowers to make magical potions. A little girl who loved going on treasure hunts searching for four leaf clovers to make wishes on, daisies to make crowns and watching with wonder and excitement as caterpillars turned into butterflies. I would snuggle in my bed at night, under the duvet escaping into the enchanted worlds of the stories in my books.

I've been a wife. A mother to two beautiful daughters who have been and continue to be my greatest joy. To bring life into this world...twice, is my greatest gift, my life purpose and what I was put on this earth for. They are part of me and I am part of them. Forever connected, forever their mum. My Earth Angels. To give them all my love and support as they spread their wings, feeling free to fly and soar. I'm here to celebrate their successes and comfort them when they need me. I listen, give advice and cuddle, love them unconditionally.

I've been a student and a teacher. Forever learning, I shine as I share my passion, I light up.

I've lost my mummy, my greatest loss. I held her as she left her body and my heart was broken. She brought me into this world and was my best friend. She left this world way too soon, she had so much more to give. The only lesson from this, is compassion and to know this loss.

I've lost my wisdom teeth, my tonsils and a lot of blood! I've lost my womb, my sacred portal and the bringer of life...yet she is still here energetically holding space. I've lost my cervix, my fallopian tubes and a lot more blood!

I've lost a husband. I released him with love, compassion and forgiveness. Gratitude for many happy memories and for giving me our two gorgeous girls.

Ritual to remember how old I am, ritual to invite in the notion of Sacred Eldership is one of the biggest gifts from this sister circle gathering. As I consider these thousands of days I've been on earth, I notice I'm proud of my age! I'm proud to have been the elder in some of the circles I've been in. I wouldn't have liked it before but now, to write a tribute to myself in this way, gives me so much pride in myself and everything I've overcome, achieved, found and lost.

I've found my passion, my way and my rituals, I do what I love and my heart could burst I feel so overcome and full of emotion as I write these words. With cacao by my side and running through me as I write about ritual, in ritual, I am so fully present.

I broke to rise stronger

As my world crumbled around me, I knew there was a reason, I knew this was transformation. I knew my whole life had to fall apart and I had to break down to put myself back together from a place of love. To be the woman I am now. Compassionate and with a depth of understanding that I didn't have before. I wouldn't be the woman I am now if I hadn't been through what I have.

As I sit in guided meditation in the sister circle, appreciating the woman I am now, I feel so full of love and gratitude for myself

I could burst. I am overcome with emotion, tears of joy fall down my face, as I lovingly touch and caress every single part of me with such deep appreciation.

Through these last years and this immersion, I have found a new love, appreciation and acceptance for all of me. My shape, my curves, my scars. Every wrinkle and hair on my head, sacred portals.

I've never felt more at home in my body. Everything she's been through, everything my heart has been through...the heartbreak and tears, the birth and death, has all brought me to this moment.

I have come home to myself.

I know in this moment, I am the strongest I have ever been. I have found an inner strength and resilience deep inside myself. I know I can survive. I trust myself and have learnt to listen to the whispers of my heart and my soul, the nudges, signs and synchronicities, the feathers, butterflies and number sequences that always make me smile are there just for me.

They are messages to let me know I'm on the right path. My deep inner knowing. I know, I feel. When I come to this quiet, sacred me-time, when I drop out of my head and into my heart and I breathe, all of the answers I seek are right here inside of me.

I weave the sacred into every day. From the moment I wake up and adorn myself with my crystal rings and bracelets which mean so much to me, I make my cacao for my morning ritual. My daily walks in nature are about being present and looking for the beauty and the magic. I collect special things for my altar, offerings for spirit and sticks to become wands. I dry herbs and make them into bundles for burning and space clearing. I use flowers to make potent moon water and sprinkle drops into my healing baths.

I feel moss under my feet, soft enough for fairies to dance on and I notice acorn cups for them to drink from and to wear as hats. There truly is magic everywhere!

My life is candles and cacao, crystals, love and magic.

I love sharing this passion, I light up when I speak about ritual and ceremony, I feel like a lighthouse, magic happening when I gather with women.

With my hands on my heart, I close my eyes now and say 'I love me, I love me, I love me'. Breathing into my heart space, my heart beating under my hands, I feel my life force.

I feel love.

Sacred Eldership

Inviting in the woman I am yet to become, as I consider my thoughts for this book, I am overcome with the strongest feelings in my heart, so overwhelming and powerful, it consumes my whole body. Future me, the crone who is here with me now, needs me to write about the importance of Sacred Eldership.

THE most important gift I received from this gathering of women is the respect of the elder. For the elder in me, the woman I am yet to become, I see her, she sees me, she holds my hands and she looks deep into my eyes, she knows me. Wearing the lines of years of smiles. There's a mischievous sparkle in my/her eyes, deep inner knowing and love radiating from my/her heart. I feel her. I feel her hands on me, one hand on the front of my heart, one on the back of my heart. And in this moment right here, right now, I know that whatever happens I have the tools and I know myself well enough to come home to me. I can ride this rollercoaster called life.

I can't articulate how important this is to me, how life changing.

Before this gathering of women, before I heard about Sacred Eldership, I didn't like the thought of getting old, in fact, I had a fear in my tummy about it. Since understanding and appreciating age, wisdom and the depth of the elder, I now see becoming older as a privilege and honour.

The deep respect and admiration I have for the elders in our sister circle and how they inspired me, has stayed with me in my heart. And since that gathering, when I've been in circle with other women, I've been the eldest and I've loved it!

I feel it's now my turn to inspire. To show the way, to share the knowledge, the wisdom that comes with age. To show that I can still have fun, why on earth did we ever lose this reverence for the elders? How did we lose the instinct to listen?

I'm excited now and looking forward to aging. I see myself bare foot, dancing on the earth, the sun on my face and the wind in my hair. I feel the confidence, the self-assurance that comes from all the experiences I've been through, the life lessons, the perfectly imperfect, the messy and the down-right glorious!

And so, she holds my hand, the sacred elder in me, the woman I am yet to become, so tenderly and I feel safe, held, loved. She walks with me as my life path gently unfolds before me. We step forward together and I walk in trust.

Kirsten 'Kimama' Lapping

7

When one look said it all
and she opened her arms for her sister,
for tears to fall on her shoulder.
That silence was the most precious thing in the world.
When everything else was complicated.
She was the one who remained still.
Still by her side, unquestionable truth.
She had the ability to make everything ok.

from 'A Woman's Blessing'

An imperfectly perfect gift of freedom

I was ready to drive my youngest daughter to Glastonbury. It was a journey that would take around eight hours and I had just connected in meditation to my eight-year-old self! This was time for us, mother and daughter, time to connect and 'be'.

I actually never dreamed I would have this time. I didn't know such opportunities existed. I didn't know I would ever have the wonderful family I have, a supportive loving husband and two wonderful daughters, my loving family, something I yearned to have been part of as a child and being part of a wonderful community of women through our family run shop. I didn't know I'd get to be a mum and a wife. I'd seen too much pain within my family to think that I could ever be a part of this, a beautiful family, this path that I walk every day, being fully connected and committed through my work and daily connection.

We were running on time that day, so I had time to do my ritual, I had time to paint. I found myself deep in thought, ready to create a painting for my younger self. I prepared it in my mind's eye. An image I'd drawn so many times around the age of eight.

It was a picture of what I saw as being the perfect home. I caught myself tracing it on my hand. 'Yes!' I thought, I would recreate that picture for the girl I used to be, intending to make it even more perfect, more vibrant and more beautiful than I had ever done. I thought about the house I would carefully draw, of the perfect windows, with curtains, blocking out the view of the inside, trying to stay within the lines. The perfect path with neat flowers either side, the image on the outside, of perfection. As a child, I never drew anything of the inside of the house. I never knew 'perfect' or even anything close to what I longed for...love and nurturing. This ritual, this piece of art, I decided would take pride of place on the altar I'd created for the girl I used to be.

I would spend many hours daydreaming, creating faraway lands, seeing mesmerising images in my mind. I could never recreate what I envisioned in the way I desired, yet I still loved the connection of these worlds. I would revel in ideas; I would love to design and create. I had so many ideas, sometimes a spark of inspiration would come and I'd be captivated. Never the artist I once hoped to have been, paints were too messy in our house, I wasn't allowed to make a mess. So, through this process of making art for my younger self, I was also able to acknowledge some of the ideas I'd had, some of the inspirations and designs I'd achieved and that I could create now.

As time ticked by to leave for our journey ahead, I reached for the perfect colours, ready to prepare the perfect surface. As I squeeze the first colour on the palette, nothing came. I squeezed harder. Paint splattered everywhere. A rush of panic filled my body, taken straight back to the time where I wasn't allowed to make a mess, when I had to be perfect, neat, tidy, seen and not heard. The sight of the splattered, part watery/part dry paint filled me with the fear I used to have then when I made any kind of mess. I tried to clean it as though I was that little girl once more.

The paints I was trying to use were completely dry. Each colour the same. I went to another box filled with paints...beautiful, neglected sets and nothing! They were all dry.

In a house filled with more craft supplies than any craft superstore I knew, why was finding useable paint, a blank canvas or watercolour paper or anything in fact for this project becoming impossible!

Thoughts of my picture-perfect image faded. Dread and panic consumed me. I felt fear of letting my teacher down, fear of letting my daughter down, the same fear and dread which I used to feel whenever I was a child, only this time I was also scared to let HER down, the girl I used to be.

I wanted to create something beautiful for her, something to honour her. I suddenly felt the urge to go up to my bedroom, to see the altar space and look at that space for inspiration, as if somehow the picture would magically appear. My sacred stick was already packed, ready to take on my journey and it reminded me of the things I'd left behind each time we'd had to flee from our house. I saw in that moment how the things I could carry, became my memories and my future.

Absorbed in that memory I turned and caught a glimpse of a single torn page on my bedroom floor, completely out of place, it was from a book which was not in my room. Wondering where the page came from, I picked it up. My eyes jumped over the image and words. I rushed back downstairs to another cupboard and right there, was a pack of unopened children's pastel colours. They weren't quite the bright artist paints I'd imagined and there was no paint brush in sight, so I squeezed paints onto my fingers.

I had to complete this for her before I left, I had no time to create the lines, never mind keep within them. Swirling my fingers across the page, I smiled. She would have loved getting her fingers dirty, she would have loved this moment of freedom. I honoured her in that moment, I gave thanks to her and gifted her with the imperfectly perfect gift of freedom and messy paint filled fingers.

I was so often lost in my own magical world, so as to escape from the world I lived in, the words on that torn page were from Alice in Wonderlands story! Now I was gifting the girl I used to be with the love, nurturing and hope she'd yearned for. Behind the curtains of my own home now are memories of my own children's paint filled fingers, laughter and love. This process had been a journey in itself, one that peeled back so many layers from my childhood, I felt so many emotions stirring within my soul, ones I thought I'd 'done the work' to help heal. Whispers of them it seemed had remained and today, dry paint had created a pathway to make a mess - so much poignancy, so much depth and feeling.

Washes of colour from a torn page, I knew this had been a perfect alignment.

Repeating patterns, rewoven

Patterns repeated in art, woven into fabric, these patterns can be mesmerising. I can get lost in them, finding the hidden depth in their beauty. I can also get lost in patterns of behaviour that don't serve me. These patterns are not so beautiful or at least that's what I used to think, when I would berate myself. These are the patterns I believed were ingrained, woven into the fabric of my soul. One of those patterns is feeling that I've let people down.

I felt this strongly during the second part of the immersion when we focused on 'the woman I am now'. 'I'm at peace with me' I thought, I'd done so much to be there, to connect in with the 'now' in gratitude.

And yet, I was to find threads of these patterns still within me. The week of the woman I am now, I was in Glastonbury and I became ill. My time there changed, instead of the training I'd planned to attend, I had to stay in bed for most of the time, with a hospital stay added in for good measure. I had become too ill to even sit up in bed, I couldn't attend the circle for our session or open the daily rituals. I could only imagine the treasures that would unfold in those rituals, I didn't have the strength to partake. Standing on the side lines, watching in from the outside, feeling as though I'd be unable to catch up, I thought I wouldn't be able to bring anything to the table of value.

Thoughts raced through my head, I was letting my sisters down, I was letting my guide down. I reflected upon the times when I'd felt like I hadn't fitted in, the times I'd joined a school halfway through a year for instance, the outsider looking in, a whole new area, having to tick boxes, to fit in, others' expectations and perceptions of what was expected. I tried to tick, I tried to fit, I felt like I was the wrong shape, like I needed to bend a little more, 'too soft' they said, maybe I needed to create edges, I already felt like a square peg in a round hole back then, so maybe a different shape?

I saw the light within each of them however I couldn't see my own. In the dark tunnels I faced, I couldn't see my true shape. In thinking I'd let everyone down and hearing their disappointment in my mind, it was like my own shape got lost, like I was losing myself. My own fabric was being imprinted with someone else's ideals, my repeated patterns of how I wasn't good enough, beating myself with a stick, had me thread bare and all out of whatever shape I'd become.

At 48, a journey with Jaguar from the Peruvian medicine wheel and the plant medicine Ayahuasca, helped me see more clearly. It was time to face that which I knew would be the biggest challenge, to face myself, to face my fear, to meet with mighty Otorongo (Jaguar) to help me face my shadows.

Not long after I sat with Ayahuasca for the first time, through the depths of darkness and despair in that journey, I found myself wrapped in the layers of other people's stories woven through time. Those layers peeled back. I found myself, I saw why I felt unworthy and in facing and meeting myself, I found my worth. My childhood played out through clearer eyes, showed the hurt people who in turn hurt other people, their pain rippled out and when it came to me, it felt like a tsunami.

I used this time in our immersion to allow all of this to wash over me, as if it could cleanse the thread-bare patterned fabric my heart and soul were wrapped in. I saw Metatron's cube, all shapes existing within. I'm a multi-dimensional, multi layered, multi-faceted human being, I saw how I'm made up of every element, how unique I am, how I've woven a different story, with a different perception.

Transcended into darkness in the midst of this time of illness, I felt like I was taken to the edge where I was at peace with the woman I was and if it were my time, I knew my family knew they were loved, I could leave knowing this. Deep in this conversation felt like an Ayahuasca trip and it was not my time to leave.

And so, as I sat for the first time in days, I was able to connect with some of the rituals in our sister circle. One of those rituals was to create sacred water. In the simplicity of that ritual, the water and the tying of the string with intention around my sacred stick, I was reminded of the tsunami I felt I'd faced and I allowed it to wash over me, to soothe me again.

The string felt like the fabric I'd woven, it felt like the patterns I'd created and as I closed my eyes, I saw the beauty of those patterns. I took in all the shapes, they were all there, for each challenge I'd faced, it was woven. It also gave me something more. I saw the patterns in others, empathised with their journeys, saw the beauty they'd woven in their own fabrics and I knew that if only 'they' could step back to see those patterns, they'd see there was more, a bigger picture. It was as if I could see the light within them glowing more, illuminating their patterns to see the bigger picture more clearly.

I felt like this time of darkness during the sister circle, the fact that I'd worried about so much, had actually illuminated my own threads for me so I could see the patterns more clearly. I now had a choice. I could either become consumed by them once more or I could step back and see the bigger picture. Thoughts of letting anyone down, I realised, had been patterns from my past, a reflection of others pain, a reflection of my own pain and nothing had given me any indication that this had happened.

'This is not mine' I told myself, 'It's not a true story of this time'.

I looked at our group's messages, it was filled with loving, kind words, wishing me well, I felt 'held'. Upon my return to the next session, still weary and not fully well, I felt their love and kindness once more, I felt held once more. I have so often felt this feeling within the sacred circle of sisters and so that old story I'd created in my mind, that old reappearing pattern has faded into the background, it's no longer the centre piece.

Honouring the elders

I am not a writer. I recognise that somewhere deep within my soul I am, however, right now, my words are stacked in journals, long forgotten pieces of many jigsaw puzzles. All heartfelt and meaningful at the time, left forgotten and not pieced together.

I find this so reflective of my life. So much comes into my mind and words sometimes never meet the page. So, to be part of writing this book, to be part of something which will make such a difference to those who read it, is truly an honour.

When I came to write the words, they didn't appear. They were lost. Blocked by negative thoughts such as 'not good enough', 'too much' and 'too little', I also felt the stirring of what being part of this gathering of women helped me to see. And that was, that those thoughts were other people's perceptions, part of hurt people's perspectives that I'd taken on as my own.

Through this experience, I got to know those pieces and decided to choose which words would nurture me and which I would hold as true. I choose to accept all parts of me and rewrite my story, this time from the perspective of the woman I am now, once so hurt, now healing and for some parts healed. For the parts of me not fully healed, I give tender loving care and acceptance. For me this is progress, a much kinder place than the 'could've', 'should've' and 'would've'.

This sister circle created a safe space, I felt like a piece of that jigsaw, the jigsaw that connected like-minded women who all honoured each other. It is now my honour to have created a safe space for all parts of me, including my younger self, the woman I am yet to become and also for my own family.

To be part of writing within a circle of sisters feels so wonderful, each of us bringing something to the space, each holding our own jigsaw piece for the bigger picture to emerge. As we shared our stories in the gathering of women, I was struck and in awe, that it was the elder of our sisters who was given the opportunity to share their wisdom first. Respect given, for her age, as would have been given when our ancestors sat in their sacred circles. My heart was touched. I have often wished that I could've been present during those times when women gathered together centuries ago, honouring each other and looking to the elders of the group for council and wisdom. And now it felt as though I was.

Age was seen to carry more than wrinkles and grey hair back then, it was a time to embrace those things as proof of a life loved and lived. I am blessed to be part of circles like these now, holding hands, light shining from within, seeing each in the circle carried by their own light.

When I connect with another's story and take a moment to listen to the elders, I respect each woman, whether older or younger; I feel that I am able to honour them, myself and my ancestors.

Alexandra Fraser Duran

28

She was the type of girl now who slipped off by herself
to commune with the tees and the ground and the sky,
to listen to birds, to hear spirits in the breeze,
to connect with her Self and steady the fizz.
She was the type of girl now who slipped off her boots
to soak up the earth, disperse energy, feel flow,
to listen to her breath, to hear more than could be said,
to connect with source and know all was love.

from 'A Woman's Blessing'

Remembering

I remember making a deal with God.

I asked him to give me a sign, a clear sign, clear enough for me to see. I was 17, my parents had split up and I felt lost. In limbo. My world had been turned upside down. Later that day, I was on the bus coming home from work and a man sat next to me. He looked at me and said 'Nothing is lost, all experiences are valid'. He placed in my hands a book. 'The Alchemist' by Pablo Coelho and then he got off the bus and I never saw him again.

I knew in that moment, I was being looked after by angels, the sign was clear and I gave thanks.

Fast forward thirty something years and I find myself lighting a candle, connecting to God again, inviting myself to go deep inside of me, to connect to my younger self. I'm sitting, about to meditate, burning sage and connecting to ceremonial cacao – I feel her in my heart; my internal and spiritual senses suddenly awaken and I feel a rush of excitement in my back, my nervous system and my whole body.

Going back in time, deep within myself, unlocking past memories, so many precious moments. As I listened to a guided meditation, transported back in time to when I was about seven-years-old. I see her so clearly. I can see what she's wearing, feel what she's feeling and I feel heavenly loved in that moment.

I place my hands on her heart, tell her how much I love her and that I am so proud of her. I tell her she's beautiful and more than enough. Tears are streaming down my face as I realise, I've been her protector all these years – her protector from the future, leaving her breadcrumbs of hope and support, sprinkling of magic in her heart and a thread of luminous light for her to follow when she loses sight of the path.

I want her to know that the rainbows and feathers she believes in so much, were me, supporting her in reconnecting to her path. Guidance from her future self. It's only in this moment that I remember the past memories I've kept in a box, safe and locked, with care. They're now free and in the open.

I see my younger self, kneeling in prayer position with a candle in front of her. She's praying to God, I remember it so well. She talks to him and prays for her family, thanks him for her parents, her sister and she asks him questions.

I felt so deeply connected to the light, I am in tears just now while I am recalling those moments of joy and divine love. I feel my younger self has a deep knowing she can't explain but she feels it in her soul, it feels like a whisper, like a soft caress on her cheek directing her to the next destination. Much as she stumbles through life, sometimes feeling there's no path, somehow, she carries a knowing that everything will be ok.

I want her to know that believing in rainbows, feathers, lighting candles, burning frankincense and closing her eyes, is all a magical way to reconnect to her soul and her divinity. I want to tell her that doing all of these things is such a profound way to be with herself and with her heart. That she will remember and unlock treasures of love, scents, innocence, play, dance, joy and deep acceptance of who she is.

In that same meditation, I was also taken back to when I was 27. I'd had my heart broken. I felt so deeply sad. I saw myself crying and once again asking God 'What have I done wrong?'. I felt so insecure. I wasn't in a good place.

I remember that time so well, just after I my made request to God, I received a phone call from a friend asking me to go for a coffee. I declined but she insisted. I found myself screaming out loud to the universe to give me some hope, I really needed it and as I walked towards the bar, I saw this magnificent rainbow in front of me. I cried. I knew in my heart this was my clear sign that good things were coming. Once more, I gave thanks.

The sacredness of ritual, of connecting to God in this way, I now know has always allowed me to go deeper, to sit with the experience of connecting. I remember countless times where I was held, supported, seen and guided in a different direction - as if someone was doing it for me.

Setting intentions with my eyes closed, helps me to reconnect with those parts long forgotten and hidden. The girl I used to be knew about candles and essences but she was afraid of being ridiculed, afraid of her own light, ashamed that people would laugh at her. It's only in these moments, with myself in ritual, in my sister circle, that I realised how much I've grown through these years. I've overcome so much, experienced so much, I've been a survivor, feeling the imprints of every step in my cells, in my organs, my whole being.

So many emotions felt at once, my heart exploding with joy, sadness, loss, grief, heartbreak, excitement, happiness and deep gratitude for every experience felt, lived and loved. I rediscovered a way to honour myself and to honour my seven-year-old, the girl who always knew that lighting a candle would open a door, a portal

226

to the light, to God so she can connect to her higher self, her soul, her divinity.

Infinite blessings in the form of people, books, experiences, rainbows, feathers, friendships, opportunities, connections and sacred ceremonies have showered my life and I feel in deep gratitude.

I now wake up every morning thanking the girl I used to be for her wisdom and her knowing. She has taught me so much about the miracle of life, the joys of dancing and letting herself go, as if nobody is watching, to make life a play where laughter and fun exists in endless ways. She has taught me to love myself unconditionally so when it rains, I can light a candle, close my eyes, drink cacao and remember that there are threads of light connecting me to all there is.

The woman I am now

It's three am in the morning and I find myself sitting by my daughter's bed in the hospital while she's recovering from a chest infection. I caught a glimpse of myself in a small mirror opposite me. The moonlight is creating a shiny light through the window and reflecting it at the mirror where I can see myself.

I observe that woman and I see her courage, her determination, her sadness, her resilience, her pain and her struggles… but above all, I see her fierce love for her family and herself. She has gone through so much and yet she still looks amazingly beautiful. There's a vulnerability around her that's palpable and raw but that's exactly what makes her so intensely dazzling.

The woman I am now is not afraid of looking at herself in the mirror, as she contemplates her scars, her wounds, her body. Once

227

upon a time, this same body was ostracised for being too fat, too curvy, too sensual, she was afraid of her own power.

Now at almost fifty, I have learnt to fall in love with myself again. With my insecurities, my self-doubts, my fears and perfect imperfections. I have deep compassion for the woman I am now. She's experienced loss that tore her insides apart. She had to learn to pull herself out of dark holes when she thought there was no way out.

This woman now is fearless, passionate, driven, determined, intuitive, vibrant, spiritual. She's had to learn to surrender, to let go and to trust fully in herself.

Through intimate sacred rituals, she's now found new ways of exploring herself more deeply, where spirituality meets sensuality. Lighting candles in her bath with soft music, petals, crystals, rose incense, luxury creams and a glass of wine along with her sex toys - her eternal companions. Creating space for intimacy has deepened her connection to her body.

This woman now knows herself better than ever before. Where she once felt unseen, she now shines. Where she once felt rejected, she now accepts herself. Where she once felt abandoned, she now feels supported by all there is. Where she once felt unheard, she now speaks her truth even if her voice trembles.

This woman now has come a long way. She's turned every broken piece of her into gold, like the Japanese do with pottery. She embraces her flaws and imperfections, she turns them into stronger, more beautiful pieces of art.

This woman now has just started to grasp the meaning of life; she's stepping onto the path of the crone, the wise woman, the elder, the medicine woman, the holder of space, the healer, the mother, the wife, the daughter, the sister to many of her soul friends, she embodies all of it.

She has rediscovered a relationship with herself in a way she didn't expect. She's learned to say NO to protect herself and her own. Her space is now sacred and she enjoys sharing herself with only those who are open to appreciate her fully.

She's also learned to distance herself from friends and family, taking the same NO out into the world, distancing without shame. I accept that others are taking a different path but this is mine and every step forward into it is a step that makes me stronger, more creative and a channel for infinite possibilities.

As I step more and more into my power, I feel younger, sexier and somehow in acceptance of this beautiful transition, I'm finding seismic shifts that loosen the hold that old patterns have over me. It's a beautiful place to be, as unknown and uncomfortable as it can feel some days.

The woman I am now has stepped out of her comfort zone once more to become an author for the first time in her life, almost in my fifth decade. Sharing sacred space with thirty-five other women in this process has been an absolute honour.

Ceremonial cacao and the need to be held by other women has been my sacred connection. To be held in such a way, to feel in a safe container of support, where I can let myself go fully, knowing I'm not alone and I'm being heard without judgement, is truly a gift.

I feel the journey unfolding before my eyes...I see this is just the beginning of a new adventure. I hear my crone whispering in my ears, 'You can do it, you are strong, you are intelligent, don't be afraid'.

I'm not always ready to listen and when I'm anxious or upset, it's easy to tune out the whisper. But when I'm calm, in a meditative state, drinking cacao and lighting a candle, I often hear the answers to questions I've asked for a long time. I receive insights to problems but most importantly, I feel unconditional love.

Some people might call this voice their guardian angel, spirit guide or higher self. I truly believe it's my higher self, reaching out to me. When I allow the voice of my higher intelligence to flow through me, I'm in communion with the most sacred aspect of me and I find that truly enlightening.

I'm excited to turn fifty this year. I tell my body how grateful I am to have been able to bear children, to have lost one and feel the pain, to feel the tender touch on my skin when my kids hug me and kiss me, to feel good in my own skin despite the scars of childbirth and child loss.

Contrary to many of societies beliefs, I genuinely feel excited to turn fifty. It's a blessing I feel, to turn this age, when some could not. I feel I have more to give and to share. I want to play, dance and have fun with life, to embrace change with open arms and receive the many blessings I know are yet to come.

I want to wear funky clothes, beautiful colourful summery dresses with equally comfortable open sandals where I can show my beautiful olive skin, my new tattoos and create a new pathway for the woman I am yet to become.

The woman I am yet to become

It's a glorious sunny day somewhere in a beautiful location along the Mediterranean. She's walking along the sea, bare feet connecting her to the water, she's looking so healthy, so light, so shiny and beautiful. Her skin is finally released from years and

230

years of wearing layers and layers of clothing and now it's free, in the open, revealing her natural mocha colour.

She's wearing a gorgeous two-piece white silk dress where I can see her glorious olive skin, her lean figure looking fit and young. I notice she's wearing a necklace with a clear quartz crystal so big I can't stop looking at it. She feels so good as she's walking towards me.

This is the woman I've seen in my meditations while drinking cacao. Seeing her so clearly, so close, so vivid has touched my heart deeply. She whispers messages in my ears as she places her hands on my heart.

I feel like a traveller through time and space taking me to see my future self. Such a privilege to easily connect with her with my eyes closed, in ritual, drinking cacao and in silence. The act of creating a ritual in order to connect with the woman I am yet to become is so powerful and so deeply humbling for me.

As I go deeper into this journey, I see a magnificent house at the top of a mountain. I feel the warm breeze caressing the trees, I see the rocks and colourful plants alongside a path taking me to see my future home. Everything feels so familiar yet still unknown. I'm being taken inside a sacred sanctuary next to her home where we're both sitting in contemplation. This is where all the magic happens, the sister circles, the intuitive readings, the gatherings, the healing, the rituals, the dance, the singing, the sharing, the silence, the sounds, the sage, the deep commitment to create change and of course ceremonial cacao.

This is the place she always imagined. A circular shaped building with individual rooms alongside. I can see the name of this place so gracefully drawn at the front 'Maya Healing Centre'. This name is to honour the daughter she lost prematurely.

231

I feel Maya's spirit soul all over. This vision was shown to me for the first time sitting with mama Ayahuasca. I feel my daughter and my mum helping this vision come reality for me.

I sense this woman, my older self, she's not distracted by the 'this and that' of life, she responds to stimuli in her environment, she's unwavering in the pursuit of her inner standing. Anything can be thrown at her, from every side and still, she stands in her own place, not rooted but gracefully responding with the rhythm of her own inner world.

As I sit there, she tells me there's no need to rush anything. That everything has a time and a place and that everything is unfolding as it should be right now. She tells me that every experience she's had, has shaped her into the woman she is now; resilient, calm, strong and extremely intuitive. She knows how hard it's been at times but she also says that after we're forced to face the uncomfortable, to have our comfort ripped from us in order to reach the sacred, it's a blessing and indeed, in many cases, a prerequisite.

She holds my hands and reassures me that I'm doing just fine. She says she's helping me, by leaving imprints of her in every step I take, in every decision I make so I'm just following a thread. I feel so happy to hear this.

She invites me to go outside and contemplate the view. We stand there together in my visions... the mountains, trees, blue skies all around us and the Mediterranean Sea in the distance. This view nourishes her, makes her feel complete. I'm in awe of so much beauty, my eyes are filled with tears of this powerful vision. Breakfast with her family where I sense she drinks cacao outside on the terrace. This place feels welcoming, I feel it's where she connects with the world and where she does her healing. She's become a humble but powerful and recognised healer.

I asked her how it all happened, how it all come together. She told me that when I stopped chasing my tail, I became more present in my daily actions. I stopped comparing myself to others and started believing in myself, then it all flowed and manifested naturally and easily.

She tells me about cycles and trust and that she planted these seeds before she was born. I remember in that moment, how I say to my family that I will blossom with age and it seems I do. She then takes her gorgeous necklace and gives it to me. I wear it and I feel goosebumps all over my spine. She says her energy is imprinted there and I will know what my next decision to my next destination will be when I connect with it.

I am in so much gratitude for this experience. She hugs me and we become one in that moment. I feel the girl I used to be, the woman I am now and the woman I am yet to become, intertwined and lifted from the earth creating a magic circle of the three aspects, in a vortex of light where time and space does not exist. We are travellers through time, reconnecting and remembering at our essence who we truly are.

I feel so proud of the woman I am yet to become. She has courage, determination and so much love for herself. She's in that place I always dreamt of and it feels very, very good.

As I come out of meditation and back into the now, I feel in a new place of hope, of admiration and a smile comes to my face. Meditating with the woman I am yet to become puts me, I believe, in receiving mode, opening my arms to the universe, so it can shower me with the golden flow of universal abundance.

I finish this ritual with a prayer and a candle - honouring my seven-year-old self, my twenty-seven-year-old self, the woman I am now and the woman I am yet to become.

A'ho

Mahala Gehna

77

'One sunrise at a time' she thought,
'just one sunrise at a time'.

from 'Sacred'

Letting go of grief

When I went into this immersion, 22 days of ritual and sisterhood, I thought of myself as someone who did a little bit of ritual already and so this was right up my street. I had thought this was something I was already doing because I used cacao once a month and I had a personal daily ritual.

However, I soon came to realise that my daily ritual was very much about connecting with the Divine and very much not about connecting with myself. As I took a look at the things I was doing in my life, I realised I facilitated lots of things for other women but I didn't participate in things like that very often for myself or if I did, I didn't allow myself to fully immerse in it. It became clear this was something I'd been avoiding.

And so, I was not prepared for the connections I might feel with myself now, with the girl I used to be and the woman I am yet to become. I was not prepared for the revelations that came. Nor was I prepared for how resistant I would feel, even having committed to going through this process.

I felt resistance to the rituals several times a week. And even at the end, I was keen to be involved in writing this book but as soon as we started, it became clear I was going to be delving even further into myself - the resistance came straight back up again. It was just really interesting to me but also not actually that surprising.

One of the things I wasn't expecting and so not prepared for, was the sheer level of grief I encountered, particularly during the first week's rituals, in particular being guided into meditation seeing myself as a child. It began in such a lovely way, seeing myself playing with my best friends at school and in the street I lived in. I saw us playing Cagney and Lacey on our bikes, which was our favourite thing to play! But then what I saw changed and the grief hit me like a brick. I saw my nine-year-old self and my first experience of being sexualised, of being sexually assaulted really. It was a touch, that I think was supposed to appear innocent but was accompanied by words which made it clear, it definitely was not. During the meditation I discovered just how much grief I'd been holding on to. I'd known it had affected me a lot at the time but I had also assumed I'd left it behind as I got older. I know that at the time I felt violated and I felt scared about where it might go. I remembered the next time we stayed at that family's home overnight (they were family friends), I was so grateful that the room I stayed in had a key and would lock. I locked the door because I was petrified he might come in.

I was so sure I'd left all that behind, I hadn't realised how much it had affected me as I grew up and through my whole life too. Of course, it led to remembering that this wasn't an isolated incident. It was the only time he ever touched me inappropriately. However, it wasn't the only time someone in authority ever made inappropriate comments or assaulted me and it brought up so much grief for me but it also brought up fear for my daughters.

I know that in so many ways, this is just what women go through and I don't want them to have to go through it. I don't think society has changed that much in the last 35 to 40 years, enough for me to feel that my daughters are safe.

Writing to her

Writing a letter to that little girl, my goodness! I thought, 'Well, I never have things to write for activities like this. I can never think of anything'. Mama cacao had different ideas. I sat with my cacao, did my morning mantra practice and then dived into the letter. I

237

wrote four pages without even pausing, without having to think; it just came out. Just flowed. And with it came tears. So many tears. Thank goodness I was the only person in the house when I was doing this!

I did so many of the rituals while my children were asleep in the morning, getting up extra early so I could do them without interruption and knowing that if I went into my day without having done them, I would struggle to find time. But on this morning, I hadn't been able to do it before the school run, so I came home and just put everything else on pause. I'm so pleased that's how it happened.

It wasn't just the tears that came but the grief again, the crying, absolute howling in anguish, noises I have never heard from me before. So much anguish, so much that I let go of. From my early teens, I knew I wasn't made to follow the crowd, whether it be fashion or thoughts or trends or whatever else. I always felt different and yet always felt the pressure - I don't know where from entirely - to conform. It might have been from society, friends, from parents, probably from myself for the main part. Either way, I was scared stiff of standing out, to really explore who I wanted to be. I'd like to say that changed, that I explored more and more...who I was...who I wanted to be...but it stuck with me, even through my forties; this idea that I should conform to expectations, that I have to be a certain way.

Some of what I wrote, was trying to find understanding for the decisions I'd made, some of it was forgiving myself and some of it was suggesting forgiveness for certain people. And I also chose to ask for forgiveness from my younger self, explaining to the woman I am now and my past self, why I chose to change my name completely.

Rather than doing something quite common in the breakup of a marriage and changing my last name, I actually changed my name entirely - to something completely different. I chose a new surname for myself and I chose a new first name. I wanted to tell my younger self that I wasn't casting her aside, that it wasn't a case of leaving her behind, denying her or letting *her* go. It wasn't about her at all!

I don't think, until I wrote this letter, that I fully understood why I changed my name. I just knew I had to do it. As I wrote the explanation, so much made sense. The girl and the woman who belonged to the old name settled too often for second best, for what was available, what was easy, instead of what she wanted. And more than that, she'd made so many poor decisions...so many alarm bells ignored, red flags ignored.

I wrote in the letter 'you know, those flags and bells weren't there for decoration girl'. It's not that I didn't see the dangers, the problems in the choices I was making, the situations I was getting into. It was that I actively chose to ignore my intuition and do it anyway. And it wasn't about feeling the fear and doing it anyway, it was more about 'how bad could it really be?'. The answer often was very fucking bad!

And so, in that letter, I had to forgive myself for those decisions. You can't keep on (although I have tried very hard), you just can't keep on beating yourself up over those decisions! At some point, you've got to let it go and move on.

This was the point I chose to do that.

I forgave my younger self for some of the ridiculous decisions she made and I decided to draw a line under them. And that's what changing my name was about. It wasn't about leaving that woman behind but saying, once and for all, that part of my life is over. We're not making those decisions anymore. I'm not the woman who was sexually assaulted. I'm not the woman who had a stalker and was harassed. I'm not the woman who spent nearly twenty years in an abusive relationship. That's not me anymore. And the only way I could come to terms with some of those things, especially the realisation that I'd put up with an abusive marriage for so long, was to change my name. In writing that letter to my younger self, all of that came up. When I changed my name, I thought I had one set of reasons for doing so but that reason was not, as it turns out, the actual reason. And it only occurred to me, when I was writing that letter, exactly what I had done.

Those early rituals in that first week, gave me the space and the chance to finally properly acknowledge the things that had happened to me, to try and understand them, to try to understand the effect they'd had on me and to grieve for the girl I used to be. I also grieved for the person I could have been, if I'd have been less afraid of standing out. I grieved for the loss of feeling safe. Once I'd grieved, once I'd let it out, I got the chance to leave it behind or at least, to not let it define me anymore. To say 'Okay, it happened. It had huge effect. It was horrible. But it's done. It's not happening anymore and you can let it go'.

The deepest of healing through ritual

I healed a lot during this process, possibly more than I have through the work I'd done in the previous two years. I think I came further, much more quickly in these 22 days. Before this sister circle, I was using different methods for healing and they were working, I was healing. I'd come a very long way but there was further to go, more depth and I wasn't sure how to get there.

Ritual showed me how to get there, this daily ritual especially, the daily association with mama cacao made the difference. So, I did a deep healing and learned so much about myself. I learned that I need to trust myself and my intuition. It's always been spot on but I've ignored it in the past and I'd have saved myself so much pain if I'd have listened.

I also learned that I have the skills, knowledge and wisdom to not always have to refer to someone else. I need to trust myself to do that.

During this process, one of the oracle cards I pulled was Anandamayi Ma with the message 'I am my own guru'. I pulled this card during a ritual which involved a meditation. It showed me that my 'magic', my gift, was ritual, my role was there waiting for me and it was time to step into it. Combined with what I was being told in this immersion process about trusting myself, it all came together.

This meditation came as we were finishing our focus on the women we are now and as we started looking at the women we are yet to become. I was getting the same messages from those rituals also, that I'm a leader. All of these messages came within a few days of each other and I thought 'you'd better start listening to these. It's time to stop hiding behind the fear, the anxiety, the past and just get on with it'.

That's the part I've always struggled with but now, with the daily practice of sitting with cacao, it was making a difference. I already had a daily practice of mantra meditation and chanting, it was great but adding the ceremonial cacao deepened the level that I was getting to and after the 22 days of ritual in sister circle, I knew I didn't want to let it go.

So, I've continued. Every morning I get up, have a shower and get dressed. I make my cacao and I make it mindfully, in its own little ceremony really and then I take the cup up to my meditation space where my altar is, I say a prayer to mama cacao, set my intentions for the day's session and drink.

My mantra session usually consists of three short mantras to Ganesha, Durga and Lakshmi but now I have cacao too, I'm able to add a fourth, longer mantra. I've known I needed to use it for a long time but I've shied away from it because it's deep. It's part of a 60-day process of changing or eliminating an unwanted action or emotion, replacing it with something positive and beneficial. It sounds easy when I write it like that but I don't find it so! And I've never felt ready for it before. Even now, I feel the resistance to it but now I know that I can work through that and get to where I need to be.

It sounds like I've got this daily practice thing down to a fine art but I've started this 60 day process several times since I finished the immersion. If I miss a day, I have to start again. And I've missed days. I'm a single mum, running a business, with chronic illnesses, who is naturally a night owl, not a morning person and so life and sleep do still sometimes get in the way of my morning plans. But it happens a lot less than it used to – a lot less. And each time I falter, I beat myself up about it a little less, reaffirm my commitment to the process and start again. I have faith that at some point, I will complete the 60 days. I'm OK with that.

I think it's obvious by now that my relationship with cacao has changed a lot – from once a month to every day! She has allowed me to connect with myself, get deep, heal, commit and create. This immersion gave me so much more than I was expecting, healing, focus and understanding, as well as forgiveness, confidence, connection and direction.

Lou Moore

122

To dance with music so loud,
that each cell had no choice but to throb to a new vibration,
head shaking, rhythm pumping,
entering to get lost,
all thought slipping away,
making space for emotion to rise,
cocooning her Self in fire.
She burned and burned and burned.
Her cure. Her medicine. Her fix.

from 'HELD'

Bringing back the faeries

I am four years old. I gather the fallen petals and cheekily some of those still clinging tightly to the rose bushes. I'm making rose petal perfume and I have a row of buckets (my cauldrons) all at different stages in my spell making process.

In the darkly creosoted shed I inspect the newts. I wasn't afraid to handle them and I'm caring for them temporarily in makeshift water-side homes in discarded Quality Street tins. As I open the rusty gate, the rest of the world opens up before me – the wilder part of our garden, the most incredible acre and it feels as though it's all mine. My kingdom. I am safe here and most at home. Imagination, exploration and play just roll in to one. I skip past the old pony stable – more recently made home by a passing tortoise, that I named Thomas. There's an orchard of fruit trees and rows of hay-covered strawberry plants. My skip to the bottom of the garden passes mushrooms…which do not harm me, although they may explain my most vivid recollections!

In the mornings, the dew droplets capture reflections of streaming sunlight. In the late afternoon, I hear wood pigeons cooing and see squirrels chasing one another high in the surrounding trees. Behold, the most magical place awaits – the blackberry bushes. The end of the garden drops away to views of a nearby housing estate, roads and busyness but from up here, the brambles create a barrier between my world and theirs. Here reside the faeries – my faery friends. Although only two have revealed themselves to me, I know there are more and they can see me. They are the size of my Sindy dolls and as delicate as the images in my Flower Fairy books. They're as beautiful to me, as I am to them, with my curls starting to loosen and becoming straighter, turning naturally from fair to strawberry blonde to a dark brown as I grow.

This process of continuous colour and style change continues in my adulthood, a little less naturally though.

I am as carefree as my faeries, dancing and noticing natural gifts offered to me as the seasons change. I'm learning to read and my choice of books allows my imagination to drift between the pages, imaginative play and my exploration of every creature, plant and tree. Every whisper of the breeze and ray of light is a wonder. I only share these enchanting moments at the bottom of my grandparent's garden with my little brother. I take him by the hand and point out all my favourite places. We return with grubby knees, fingers and faces stained from the soft fruits and berries.

Fast forward a little over forty years and I was easily able to recapture these moments in guided meditation. My own children are now teenagers and no longer tolerant of my attempts to capture their imaginations with enchantment and adventure.

When I accepted the invitation to revisit the girl I used to be, it was easy to return to this time and age. To sit with her...me. To witness the curiosity and wonder of the elements and mother earth at a time in my life when everything was still new. I took a walk in nature and gathered fallen gifts from trees – just as I once did. I allowed myself to see the world around me through my childhood eyes. To not feel any sense of limitation or restriction in my physical body, to feel totally free of all responsibility or time restraints, meant I noticed the magic once more. As if it had never left, in fact, it hadn't left...I just forgot to look for it.

I inhaled the freshness of the day – the musty dampness in the woods, feeling the sunlight upon my face as I skipped and foraged and returned home with mud beneath my nails and leaves caught in my hair. I had not yet experienced change at this young age. But relocation after relocation, puberty, a deep craving to belong, fit in

247

and find my tribe saw my daydreams equated to odd. I was labelled naughty and not able to conform. These childhood forages were before my constant chatter and before I tried to squeeze myself into the box I was supposed to be in. Fuck, did I resist...yet I wanted 'in' so badly.

I wrote a letter to myself, the younger me, reminding me how loved I truly was and always will be. Words have always come easily to me, although narrative is usually, and constantly in my head. I lit a candle for my younger self, smudged to clear my space, drank cacao and allowed the words to pour from my heart to my page. As they did, I opened to an innate knowing that things had never been as rosy beneath the surface. That I had clung so tightly to that seemingly perfect family bond – remaining in denial for a long while. I hadn't wanted to speak out loud of the obvious power struggles and controlling behaviour. I told my younger self that times will get tough, that illness, sorrow and grief will ravish through my elders and I will find myself being the one to care and look after those who had once cared for me. I told her that I would feel resentful in being the one left behind, that I will feel trapped, I would crave escapism and a change of scenery.

My only opportunity for change has often been yet another hair colour but I will always find solace deep in the woods and freedom in wide open space. I will always find magic amongst the trees – a connection with the rhythms of nature. This opportunity to spend time with my four-year-old self taught me so much and rekindled a sense of playfulness. An urge to dance with myself and my faerie folk, the letter became a reminder to look for the joy and enchantment all around me and to create my own rituals to bring forth the extraordinary into what had begun to feel quite ordinary and mundane.

I now add treasures that I find on my daily walks to my alter and nourish myself and my family with seasonal produce. From my understanding of Ayurveda, I know that I too will experience a greater sense of balance when I can realign and live in harmony with mother earth. This is the most wonderful gift for me – from such a young age. It was not long after, having scoured the many books upon my parents' shelves, that I conjured up my own notion of witchcraft. I formed a firm belief that my bedtime terrors (of being paralysed in the middle of a house fire) were an indication of me being a trialled witch in a previous existence.

I was born intuitive and insightful. I was so wise – wise beyond my years. I've been following a linear route through life and it hadn't occurred to me to revisit the lessons learned at every turn. To quote one of my most favourite films (and evoking another memory from around that same age as I first watched it, with tears rolling down my cheeks as the closing titles appeared), 'you've always had the power my dear, you just had to learn it for yourself' Glinda, The Good Witch of the South, The Wonderful Wizard of Oz.

Joining dots

It should have been easy to spend time with the woman I am now. I am here after all, day in day out, in this body and this mind that I've already spent so much time observing…judging and criticising – but that's normal, right? I decided to do this, I blocked out the time in my diary and I would spend time with myself – and a group of unknown women from three continents and differing times zones.

I didn't expect to have so many revelations and link so many pieces and parts of myself together. I didn't expect to join so many dots but I'm usually game. Up for anything – so here goes!

In recent years I've had surgeries. Big, whopping life changing surgeries which I felt were necessary to preserve my life. These surgeries were not made available to my mum, my paternal grandmother, her sisters and nieces. There was no pre-warning and preventative methods that my dad could have taken, nor my grandfather. I was offered these surgeries due to genetics and risk factors and whilst I'm a mum to boys, who were still very young at that time, I made the decision, signed the forms and subsequently had removed from me what were perhaps my most womanly assets - my breasts, my ovaries and my fallopian tubes.

As these ticking time bombs were taken, I have suddenly begun to feel more 'woman' than I ever have! I have never struggled with my identity or gender yet, despite my frolics with faeries and love for flowing dresses (with big boots!), I've never felt part of any girl tribes or gatherings of women.

We moved about a lot - not long after my visits to the faery garden. We relocated several times and each time, I found it more difficult to fit in. I always seemed to be the odd one, the quirky one, the one who was a little bit different - a different accent, different interests, different musical tastes. I did make friends. Usually short term, before I moved on, or they moved on physically and metaphorically. I found myself comfortable in the company of the boys. They got the same music as me. I suppose I was a tomboy but I was also very comfortable in my own feminine skin. I was happy climbing a tree or playing soldiers whilst wearing my ra-ra skirt and pixie boots!

But I never did feel that I belonged – constantly divided between my own quirkiness and a deep longing to fit in (remember me trying to squish myself into that bloody box?). In fact, as I became a mother, I allowed myself to feel more and more intimidated by other women. Mum and toddler groups became my idea of hell on earth!

But…as the palo santo smoke cleared, I realise, I have reached a point where I'm SO comfortable in the company of other women, I no longer feel judged. My own 'not-enoughness' has finally packed her shitty little bags. Hallelujah, I finally feel able to spend time in the company of women. I relish time in women's circles - to hear other women, to not be afraid to share my story, my path, my deepest hopes and fears and for us to all mutually share the magic that is all around us.

To look for the magic in everyday moments and to know that the path I've always known is shared by so many others, is wonderful. My people are OUT THERE!

I finally feel a connection and feel so blessed to have so many wonderful and beautiful women to now call friends. I have friends who notice when I've not been around, friends who notice when I need to be lifted, as much as I dedicate my soul to lifting them. The time spent honouring the woman I am now became a joy, carving out time for daily ritual, sacred bathing and bodily worship.

It also became a time to go deep within. I truly believe I retreated, deep into my own cave. Spending time in my own shadows during this time, I was able to notice patterns within my life's journey. It was intense – there was times when my body and soul just wanted to sleep and sleep, not to block out the revelations but to heal inner wounds that are so deep within my psyche. As shafts of light were shone upon the cave walls, these realisations revealed themselves to me. I was finally ready to speak of the cracks within the family unit – this hierarchal power that had perhaps repeated itself through the generations or maybe just spawned this one time - out of love.

It would be easy now to look back and realise myself as a pawn in a game, yet I choose not to be a victim. I choose not to be resentful, on behalf of myself or anyone else. I try hard. I feel I am now shaped by sorrow and pity but going so deep in this understanding, has moulded me into this resilient and strong and uniquely independent wild woman.

There is still time to heal some wounds, to reform alliance and bond. Perhaps one day I will write another letter, as I've done so often in my mind, that tells of this knowing. Perhaps this chapter, the one I'm writing now, will be enough to declare my utmost respect and gratitude to my true hero and teacher.

The woman I am now has days of looking in the mirror and not caring for my own reflection. I have days when surgical menopause feels so cruel. My body no longer carries the same energy and stamina it once did. I have days when the effects of my surgeries drain me. I don't always recognise this new body and I feel that I am prematurely ageing.

Yet self-care practises that start off indulgent and luxurious soon become living rituals. I am here learning to be unapologetic - embracing my shadows and no longer afraid to retreat, to create space to learn and to grow. I light a candle for myself every day to remind myself that I shine so brightly. As I meditate and write in my journal, I revisit the girl I once was and visualise myself as the woman I am yet to become. But mostly, I settle comfortably in my own heart space, in the present moment, in this beautiful cavern of light, fully aware of myself as I am, right now.

I see myself with whichever hair style and colour I'm currently carrying. Right now, my hair is blue. I hadn't intended for the blue dye to be absorbed and to last this long but whilst it is, I embrace it. I am a forty-five-year-old mother of teenage boys, a carer for my grandmother, a wife, daughter, sister, aunt. I am a teacher and a holder of space and I am totally rocking my own style. I'm not afraid to stand out and to shine. I have learned to dance, as I once did with the faeries and now without needing to be fuelled by alcohol to mask the fear of being judged, I am, most days, learning to love my new curves. Sculpting my own divine self with sesame oil. When I'm tired and weary, shackled by responsibilities, I remind myself that I still have so much time – so much more magic to cast and adventures to have.

She is right there

There she is, that older, wiser and more radiant version of myself. Her hair now wavy and long, the grey finally showing in its full glory, interweaved with all the other colours worn over the years. This is me...the elder, the crone, the wise woman.

When I visualise how I looked and 'will' look, my hair is usually my most apparent and obvious attribute. Perhaps my hair could tell the story of my life! But in this next phase, no longer do I hide the hereditary curse of grey. My hair is as wild and free as I often long to be once more.

And this is where this vision of the woman I am yet to become quite often becomes a yearning. During those times when I'm floored by my health and energy levels, I see this vibrant and radiant older version of myself and I can't wait to be her!

When I followed the guided meditation, I met her and spent time with her. She came so close, she could hold me tight. She wasn't my mum or my nan or any of my spirited loved ones who've look over me in the past and often return in guided journeys these days. She is ME and she brings a message that I am no longer disconnected and distant from my future self.

The integration is already beginning. When I see my future self, I notice that my eyes sparkle with childlike innocence as I spend time in nature…mountains, meadows, forests, by water. I no longer feel restrained by time and commitments. Instead, I have time to explore with wonder and rediscover how it was for me, way back in a time when the world seemed still very new.

I have felt stuck for quite some time. I have these urges you see…to run away. Not in a 'detrimental to my family' kind of way but moments to get away for a walk, a wild night out with friends, to be amongst a crowd at a gig or festival. To be part of a women's circle to just simply find a space to sit and breathe.

Strangely, during this time of isolation, when there hasn't been the opportunity to travel very far, to be amongst a crowd or a wide-open space, I've finally found a sense of connection with my closest surroundings. I can observe the effects of the change in seasons and the gifts that the elements have, within my own garden, the local woods and the tree lined streets that I walk most days.

I am starting to feel more at home and often draw an oracle card or write in my journal that there are glimmers of contentment and acceptance of where I am right now. Perhaps this is the start of the integration with my older wiser self. No longer rushing to get there.

As I prepared for the final ceremony in our sister circle immersion, I filled a jar with water, I added crystals and flowers; I charged it with reiki and moon magic and blessed it daily upon my altar.

During this final online gathering of women, sisters from all around the world, sisters I'd spent sacred time with, I drew oracle cards that depicted the water element and time for a deep dive.

During that final journey to spend time with the woman I am yet to become, she gave me a gift of liquid. I see now that this message is to 'flow' rather than live my life defined by distinct stages. I have permission to flow with a greater sense of ease, to release those feelings of stagnation and entrapment.

A flow state for me is being as accepting of the little ripples, as the big turbulent waves. Just as the waves upon the oceans of this planet ebb and flow, I have permission to return to the woman I am now, the girl I once was and visit my future self in order to tap into my own source…my wisdom…my knowing.

And I now have my daily rituals as an opportunity to celebrate myself. Every day I light a candle just for myself. I drink cacao. I cleanse myself with smudge. I meditate to connect with mother earth, my angels, guides and spirits and infinite realms above which I do not yet understand. I call myself home to my heart space where I no longer visualise different versions of myself but I see me for who I am right now. I write myself a story using my oracle cards and my now trusty journal. I'm surrounded by crystals – chosen for how they make me feel, not any expertise. I have essential oil blends gifted to me by sisters in women's circles. Every day has magical moments and this is all in preparation for the woman I am yet to become.

The woman whose naturally wavy hair reveals her true colours alongside the blonde, brunette, blues and lilacs and pinks. Her clothing flows from her now healthy and nourished body. She absorbs and reflects the light. She speaks softly and she is oh, so wise from the lessons learned in this lifetime...from a deeper understanding of the knowledge gained from the women and the ancestors who walked this earth before her and from the many times, that *she* has walked this earth before.

There is no ego or arrogance. She shares her wisdom with humility and love. She gathers the fruits and gifts from mother nature and prepares the most divine meals. She explores with her loved ones. Her most favourite vantage points are now high upon a mountain - overlooking the depths of the forests, the bodies of water and the entrances to caves and caverns. From here, she can see for many miles and she can breathe.

She is not afraid to call herself a wise woman, a medicine woman, a witch, a crone. She is I and I can't wait to be her. I am becoming her.

Beverley Ross

30

Sacred cacao…her spirit lit her creativity,
bathed her soul in delight,
soothed her senses with love and
flooded her heard with contentment.
Connected, level and balanced,
she had never known beauty so deep.
To feel at home deep inside,
to trust with such force that she couldn't fall,
she was held.

from 'A Woman's Blessing'

Following my fox

My gaze follows the lucky fox, a majestic animal who wanders through the streets under the watchful eye of tonight's full moon. The fox had always felt like the reincarnation of my grandma who transitioned into my guardian angel, aka my 'lucky fox', since her passing some fifteen years ago.

I was forty when I realised foxes appear to me when I have some internal question or something I'm ruminating on. I recall noticing that with each sighting of a fox, I felt somehow reassured, that she was giving me the nod or a blessing from my family lineage that the path I was creating for myself, was the right one.

It was at this time, I found myself craving anything that filled me up with experience. I was hungry for a place in which I could grow. I had this instinctive feeling that I was now being given permission to play and explore and this was my time to delve deeper into a journey to get to know myself.

I kept following my inner guide and over the next two years, I jumped into just about any experience that filled up my happy cup. I learnt a lot about the benefits of meditation, discovering that I could let go of anything I was carrying that made me feel heavy or drained.

My daily practice became my best friend and assisted me in tuning into my inner voice and intuition. I find myself lovingly 'setting up my stall' to sit in the quiet, allowing my mind to empty and find its own rhythm.

I light my candle every morning, it's my ritual. There's something very significant about lighting candles, the flicker of the peaceful flame, for me, indicates that it's time to stop and slide into my day with simplicity and grace.

This is my time. My space and I greet anything that comes in with open arms. I snuggle into my cosy, comfy corner. A corner of my life which is filled with special objects that feel like me.

This is a space my body recognises and automatically takes a deep sigh. I catch a wave of the scent from the candle or the fresh roses I buy myself to adorn my alter with and I smile. I take a sip from a steaming cup which contains thick, dark magic ceremonial cacao, prepared with love for myself in the stillness of dawn. I close my eyes and sink into this moment.

Sitting in silence, I allow myself to settle as my breath opens up a world in-between awake and asleep. The door opens to a vast place that can't be explained, a space which feels expansive and yet so intimate and homely. This ritual of breathing into the spaces that sit just beneath the surface of life, a serene place where I meet and listen to myself, is a magical place. It's where I'm able to gather and connect with all of the women within me, the place I meet all of my aspects, the girl I used to be, the woman I am now and the woman I am yet to become.

The gathering of women

In the winter season, I find myself drawn once more, into a community that holds space for women to gather and to meet each of these parts of themselves collectively. The winter hibernation feeling in my body is waning and I'm yearning for something that stretches me out and re-energises me. And so, we gather together and sit in circle several times enjoying personal meditation, sharing and daily ritual.

A candle lighting ceremony marks my first devotional meditation time, it's mesmerising light dances around at the front of the space dedicated to myself. I can feel this energetic pulse running through me as I lay back in anticipation of this experience. I'm laid on my bed, eyes closed and I sink into the sounds of the guided meditation which flow softly through my headphones. I set my intention for this journey, I settle, my body knows this space, eyes softly closed, connection to my breath. I'm held in this familiar space of relaxation and a sense of peace and calm flood through me.

Seconds later and to my surprise I arrive at an unexpected point in time. I'd just become a mother for the first time and whilst looking at this tiny human, I feel an abundance of love. I also feel overwhelmed and out of my depth. I'm twenty-two and I've just given birth to my first son. I'd always wanted to be a mother, so I wonder 'Why did I feel like I'd been hit by an out-of-control bus?'.

I sit with my new-born son in his nursery, soothing him as he cries. As I look down at him, tears fall from my eyes onto his pure white baby grow, it's now that I hear it. I hear a whisper, one that comes from within. It's so quiet that I almost miss it. 'Don't worry everything is going to be ok'. The same words simultaneously fall out of my mouth as a whisper and onto my now sleeping child. I feel a wave of relief and peace wash over me.

I've found that my body loves meditation in the early hours, before my day begins and before my mind fills up with thoughts. I find my comfy seat and sit in stillness in the present, I light my candle and I stretch myself out, out of all the places where my body feels stuck in this moment. My body tingles with excitement as the energy flows into the newly stretched creases of myself. I follow the urge to move my whole self and intuitively let my body dance its own magical movement, for as long as it needs. After a huge settling deep breath in and out, I come to my place of stillness in my physical self, which is now calmer and ready for this, my second meditation in this sister circle.

I greet the soles of my feet where the pins and needles of my own body's energy stir, I follow the movement of energy up my body, each nook, each curve. Guided through my whole self, I take my time to awaken and re-energise each part that supports me in this journey. I linger on any part that feels like it needs more, the areas that crave something else and I lean in, to listen closer to what's needed.

I'm transported through every experience that brought me to this space in time, like a potent spell being cast, the memories flow like a river of reminders that I'm both courageous and resilient.

Through this practice I learn to hold space for myself, I am able to access the parts of me that need a voice, that need additional love or support. I listen closely to her musings which illuminate the instinctive guidance for what's needed in the next moment. We walk together, I am her and she is me, I feel the deep connection to her, I smile and greet the woman I am now.

I find myself craving the next meditation and when I find a quieter part of my day, when I know I won't be disturbed, I close my eyes once more and tune in. I'm guided to allow my future self to come to me. I settle and immediately a winding path appears, it's lit by a guiding light. This light lands on a woman who greets me, she has a kind, familiar face, one that has weathered many storms but has come out stronger and wiser each time. I feel her heart beating, she has warm hands that, as I touch them, I sense they hold a universe of experiences, people and love.

She's surrounded by a semi-circle of other women. They're looking at her from a distance, she looks as if she has wings, an angelic sight. Looking closer, I realise that they're not wings, they're a semi-circle of women who I recognise as my female ancestors. Years of lineage, experiences and knowledge is right there, being passed down from generation to generation and now to me. I gaze into her eyes and feel a rush of fast paced excitement. She brings me back in, slows me down and with her hand on my heart, she assures me I hold all I need and that everything is perfectly and uniquely timed.

The Wisdom

The invisible thread weaved through each of these three meditations and through each chapter of my life so far, brings me to this moment, as I write this.

I'm an elder now, a wise woman, this is my time, the knowledge is in my hands and heart, I make a promise to express this through living intuitively and authentically. I recall a beautiful practice experienced in one of our gatherings, a ritual of lighting a candle for each of the children in our lives. Dedicating a candle to each of these children and giving each a blessing, evoked a huge emotional response from me and tears flowed throughout this ritual shared in our circle.

Blessing each child felt like a big responsibility, perhaps too big for just one person to hold. I realised in that moment, that it's not just me blessing the next generation, it's the women I shared my gathering with, it's each of my elders too and just like the amazing women that came before me, I will instinctively pass on the most important elements of myself to be handed over and taken forward.

That, I now realise, is The Wisdom.

Louise Harris

140

When she didn't have much to hold on to,
she held on to what she had.
And for those moments,
it seemed the most grounding thing in the world to do.

from 'HELD'

Reclaiming and remembering

So of course, I'm writing a book! That's exactly what my younger self would do. My favourite memory of school was of writing a book. That memory is so clear. Boy did I look forward to that lesson each week. I was so proud of that little book and yet until I gifted myself the journey to meet my inner child, that memory was lost.

One of the many gifts of gathering with my circle of women, was journeying to meet the girls we used to be. I'm finding that each time I visit my younger self, a layer of the barbed wire I have protecting my heart with is removed. I soften. I whisper the encouraging words that she needed to hear and see the pureness of sprit, the pure love that this young version of me was.

My heart bursts as I see my young self, immersed in her story writing, so proud of what she's creating. I'm right there at her side whispering in her ear, to let her know that she should feel proud and to belief in herself.

If she spells a word incorrectly it doesn't mean she can't be a writer. I let her write and mis-spell, I let her know that she's a creative being, she's pure unadulterated creative energy and not to forget that in the years ahead (even though I know she will).

Like so many of those gold dust moments, my childhood magic got lost as comparison, achievement and people pleasing took hold and I became consumed by doing and striving for perfection. My true essence steadily got lost as my life became externally focused. I was lost to the energy of 'being something' that I felt was more pleasing, acceptable and successful.

So, there I stayed, getting more and more lost and further away from my truth. I wasn't looking beyond the material world I was creating, I was unaware of the deep disconnection with my true essence. I'd made it afterall; the big job, the lovely home and the family. Everything ticked off the success box and that was all working...until it wasn't.

Life threw me a big curve ball. I had cancer. This was life and death. And, actually, it needed to be. I'd been so unconsciously unhappy that I needed this big nudge. I'd become lost in external gratification, grasping and addictive patterns. I'd ignored the earlier prods from my higher self to wake up, so the gentle nudges got lounder and louder until I HAD to pay attention. I did. I went inside.

I found the courage to turn my focus inwards and take a look at why I had no voice, literally no vocal cord to speak (cancer in my vocal cords). The journey began. And it began with a re-set of my nervous system and cultivating a quiet mind. From here I woke up. I began to question the story, the strategy for success and happiness that hadn't worked out for me. Who I was, what my truth was, what stirred me and how I channelled the stuck creative energy that was lodged in my body, desperate to be birthed.

I learnt to light a candle for myself, to drink cacao, to gather with women and now... here I am, writing a book about it.

So, as I sit here now, my sacred space cleansed with sage, cacao infusing my energy body and I choose to pause. I place my hand on my heart, a practice I've learned through sacred gatherings. And from here, I receive the essence of this chapter 'returning to the girl I used to be'. The power of this pause, is the gift I give myself now, creating the space for me, my new superpower.

When I gathered in circle with women, we visited our younger selves. There I was, doing my thing, moving freely, taking up space in my bedroom as I moved my body with ease, making creative shapes with my arms and moving my energy with intuitive knowing of what felt good in my body.

I stood and watched the girl I used to be, in admiration.

She knew about movement medicine, she could channel her creative energy with such ease and grace, she was liberated and free in her body. As she rested, spent and sweaty, her heart racing, I took the opportunity to whisper in her ear. I wanted her to hear the words she needed to hear; 'It's safe to be you', 'It's safe to be free and easy in your body, to embody your body and express yourself creatively is your gift' and 'you can dance for you, just like this keep doing it and keep doing it for you, not to perform or please anyone else, just for you'.

And she heard me, because in that moment a memory was laid down that she hasn't forgotten. This rare expression of pure freedom, lightness of body, creative expression and fullness.

And so, that whisper from her older, self-crossed the times and she danced around her bedroom again and again.

This pure connection with her true essence continued for a while, until it didn't.

My journey, therefore, has been to rediscover my true essence. Lost in people pleasing, I abandoned my true self to feel loved, imprinting the energy that 'I have to be different in order to be accepted'. An imprint so deeply established that I forgot the real me and became lost in my story of who I thought I was and what a life well lived should look like.

In the first sacred circle of gather the women, with cacao and a candle to honour the woman I have become; I wondered if the healing journey I've been on these past nine years has cultivated the self-honouring in me required to meet myself where I'm at.

Would I have the courage to show up for myself and my sisters in this healing gathering and speak my truth?

The powerful energy of the feminine gathering infuses each woman in the circle to reach deep into her soul and share her heart, in what is probably one of the most deeply healing journeys we can give ourselves – sister circle space.

Not only do I meet myself where I am in this space but I witness the vulnerability of other women here too, which softens my heart.

I feel the wall, that has kept me bound, melt as I shared my story.

Tears flowed and years of sadness and shame washed through and out of my body.

I couldn't quite believe the rawness of this out-pouring of emotion, I was shocked at myself, as I felt the shame I'd had trapped inside me for years spill out into the circle.

It felt like the biggest, deepest breath I'd ever taken and it emptied my body of a dense energy that had kept ME separated from me.

Those wise women saw me, with all my wounds.

They held that space for me and when that shame dissolved, all that was left, was to feel love.

I was so safe to be 'me' in that sacred space. I told myself, 'These women are your sisters, your sacred tribe and you can choose to heal right here, right now!'

My ancestral wisdom flooded through into my conscious awareness and from that day onwards, I light candles, drink cacao and journal, to channel my forgotten wisdom.

My devotion to my spiritual practice is cemented now, I'm on a pilgrimage to my own healing. Each day I feel and sense more of my true essence. The wounds that kept me bound, dissolve and my sensitivity superpower returns.

The young girl that mixed magic potions, talked to the birds, danced her heart, and expressed in story writing is returning. Day by day I remember more of the girl I used to be and I reclaim her.

I indulge myself in rituals, gathering stones in the woods, collecting my sacred sticks. I talk to the trees and remove my shoes to feel the damp earth between my toes. I feel alive and fuller than I've felt in years. I begin to honour my body in a way that reconnects me with its beauty, its sacred sensuality, I massage my body, especially the parts I turned away from for so many years.

I am ready to fall in love with myself.

Feelings are medicine

In the space of great self-honouring and self-love, I have the courage to lean into my own shadow. Never before have I dared to look at these aspects of myself. As I turn in and shine light on them, I see my patterns of self-aversion, self-sabotage, blaming others and victim mindset that has kept me trapped and small.

This is no fun, I feel empty. In the dark. Who the hell am I and what life am I living? Whose story have I been trying to live up to? The emptiness inside is sometimes overwhelming and every part of my protective self, screams at me 'go shopping', 'meet a friend', 'pour a glass of wine'.

My new expanded version of me, the nourished part, smiles inside. I become the witness, the observer, the screaming protective version of me and I choose to love her for trying to keep me safe. But I don't fall easily into the old pattern anymore. Instead, I light a candle and sit. And sit more. And allow myself to feel it.

It's hard to describe but it's like a heavy brick of energy in my core. I place my hands right there and fill this energy centre with sunlight yellow, breathing right into it, sending it love. I'm crying inside but there are no tears. I feel hard and cold, my face feels old and set. Why can't I let go? I remind myself I'm learning a new skill, that I have a lifetime of training I'm holding onto. I'm more patient with myself. I hold myself, my new acquainted energy of self-love, I play music, I find my inner child, I hold her face and look into her eyes and we dance together. I break. Like a horse being broken in, I finally give in and the tears come. Pure purging, anger, resentment, unexpressed passion. I am burning with feeling that I have never felt.

Another layer shed.

I feel lighter. I feel more proud of myself in that moment, than I have ever felt! I know that arriving at this place of surrender has been a journey, one that took courage and self-mastery and bundles of self-love.

In this safe and sacred container, I live more abundantly which means that when I choose to visit the girl I used to be again, I can comfort her on such a deeper level.

When I've visited her before, I've been taken back to a time when she's deep in shock, scared and unsafe. Every cell in her body wants to cry but she holds it all back. I place her own hand on her heart and tell her what she needed to hear back then, in that moment; 'It's ok to feel your feelings, your feelings are important'.

I allow her to cry and feel vulnerable and I whisper in her ear 'your feelings are your compass, they are your superpower'. I let her know that 'feeling her feelings' is medicine and that by doing so, she will know her truth and be empowered to make wise choices in the years ahead. I hope she hears me.

269

I let her know that one day, when she's older, she may become unwell when her body needs her to pay more attention. I tell her not to be scared and to trust that her intelligent body is reminding her to listen to her inner voice, to speak her truth.

I tell her that she will have surgery on her vocal cords and everything will be ok and that in the journey to healing, she will rediscover her true essence, that her voice will recover and she will learn to know and to speak her truth.

I let her know that she can call on me anytime. And then I jump timelines.

An empowered woman

I love jumping those timelines, going from my younger self to visiting my 75-year-old self, finding her and hearing her wisdom. I admire her silver hair and the fine lines on her mature, yet healthy glowing skin. She speaks the words of my higher self 'keep removing that stale energy from your body' she tells me. 'Purge your body of all those stuffed-down feelings and liberate yourself my love,' I hear.

In that meditation, when I called her in, this sounded like the most precious and wisest of words.

I call in my future self to keep me on track. She knows what's good for me. She teaches me to grow gracefully, to trust my body's wisdom. She helps me discern what I need to know and what I can let go of.

She's guiding me to mature gracefully and I feel younger every day.

'Inspired' is an understatement for this gathering, my journey in sister circle. Every cell in my body knows that I must be in this space for women to gather, in sacred space, to create a ripple effect with this healing journey.

When I time travel to meet my future self, she's doing exactly that. She is filled up watching other women shed their skin and birth themselves anew. I witness her expansion and I grow and expand with them all.

My future self and I heal and grow together now and it's the most powerful, potent medicine.

I graduated from my sister circle immersion as an empowered woman. I acquired the tools to support myself when I enter the void of not knowing, I hold space for myself to ask the big questions, to question everything about myself and my life 'what still serves me and what no longer does'.

I can hold myself compassionately, I can time travel, I can sit with my candle and ceremonial cacao and I can journal, trusting that from the space of the unknown, I really will emerge as a bigger more expanded version of myself.

Being with sisters continues to be a safe place to be, it's empowering and self-honouring to share my vulnerabilities and I heal through being with other women. This journey is so rich for me. It's a roller coaster, the gift that keeps on giving.

By sitting in sacred circle, I faced my deepest fears, I witnessed my wounds, I was inspired to enter the void and find peace within in it. Life became more graceful.

I am a work in progress, there's more grip to let go of, more protective personality hiding my gifts but I am devoted to becoming the eternal inner child. I can't hit the high notes but I can move my body and dance my magical child. I'm learning to see the fairies again and I have a daily dose of tree counselling. I'm on the path, awakening my magical child with all her gifts. I've already claimed the big one; deeper self-love and I wish this for every human on this planet.

Jagdeep Kaur (Jags)

60

Holding little hands, lighting sage and
singing mantras into the night...that's what delighted her soul.

from 'Sacred'

Becoming the big sister

My twelve-year-old daughter once said to me, 'Your words will change the world' and here I am today, sharing my story with you. At the time it felt like those words were being narrated to me by the twelve-year-old me.

As a child I was never keen on playing with dolls or tea sets. We never really had the luxury of expensive toys or books. With both working parents, my life growing up was very simple.

My favourite play time was writing onto an old piece of wooden board, held up against the wall in our veranda. I would write for an imaginary group/class of people. This was my favourite play time where I was shining my own light. In my mind's eye, I had a vision to share and maybe a lot to say but I would always shy away when in public and most of the time, I was shut down for being a young Indian girl.

Culturally Indian girls do not speak in front of their elders. We are only seen and not heard. Having grown up in a strict middle-class family with values and systems deeply embedded into me, I only understood structures and control. Religion was our saviour and disrespecting it, meant disrespecting God.

As the years went by, I got more entangled in the rights and wrongs of life, wearing the mask of a good girl. I lost my voice to express myself and the passion and joy to create and have fun. All this started to turn into rage, angst and sadness, rebelling and questioning all the beliefs and all structures. Something wanted out.

My dreams carried messages from that deepest part of me. Spirit was calling out for me to listen. The night before our first gathering in sister circle, I had another very clear dream. I was standing by my window, watching the young girls gather. There

274

was a knock at the door and when I answered it, it was one of the girls from the neighbourhood. She handed me eight sticks and then left.

I woke up bemused of course, I had no idea what this dream meant. Little did I know that when we sat on-line in sister circle, I would be gathering with eight women from around the world – each woman had already chosen her sacred stick – so there were eight sticks!

So, there I was, I found myself collecting sticks, lighting my candles and setting my intentions, with eight women, with a sense that I had a greater purpose than to be caught up in a tapestry weaved by others.

Where does one start? I knew something had to change. I had to get out of my 'monkey mind' and learn to trust myself again. I needed to learn to sit with all the chaos and all the confusion. I had to learn to become my own space holder first.

As a child, I would watch my parents and my grandparents wake up in the early hours of the morning and say their prayers before they would begin their day. This was the norm in our household and is even today. The prayers were mainly reciting a verse from the holy book or a form of chanting. My younger self couldn't really comprehend the purpose behind all the chanting or the praying, no-one ever explained it to me. I felt that prayer and ritual was just something the elders practiced and everyone would follow, more as a form of respect and maybe to continue a legacy.

Some of my generation might have understood the meaning behind all these practices, others weren't interested in knowing why at all. And I never really had an elder I could speak to or ask questions, which I remember left the 'little me' in despair.

275

It wasn't until a lot later in my life that I really understood the power of prayer, the power of setting an intention and the magic that unfolds with ritual. And so, I wanted to do this for my younger self. I wanted to show her what happens when I place my hand on my heart and what unfolds when I set an intention from the deepest part of my being.

How sacred this medicine is, to connect to something greater, to vibrate with the universe, to step into my inner world and create magic from that place. That day, I became a big sister to my younger self.

I wrote a letter to her. I sat with my pen and my paper and I sat with my cacao. I had so much to say, so much to share but my mind went blank. I needed to express thoughts, words and feelings to her from the deepest part of me. This was going to be ground breaking for the both of us!

As I closed my eyes, there she was, in that same place, writing on her board. Watching her in that space, words started to flow. I was writing in a language that my heart was speaking. Maybe, just like she would have done.

My Dear Younger Self,

I want to share with you my love, how you are going to have a massive impact on those around you, with those you share space with. You will perform your own rituals, set your own intentions and unravel an ancient wisdom. With your words, you will empower those around you. Your love and your light will touch the hearts of many. With bravery, you will rewrite the legacy of pain and suffering. Standing up in courage, even on the days you question your purpose, you will become the

phoenix, the fire and the ashes. Miracles will find you and the
universe will sing your melody.

Something was changing. Something was shifting, a softness, a heart-cracking open moment. Illusions and confusions dissolving. She was starting to understand the power of connection through intention. She was understanding that ritual was a prayer. It was a vibration to be embodied into her (our) being.

I was becoming the big sister, guiding my younger self to trust and to feel safe through rituals.

Ancient womb wisdom

I didn't quite understand the purpose of ceremonial cacao when it first came into my life. You know when they say everything happens for a reason? Well before plant medicine become a part of my everyday life, I always had a niggling feeling that something needed to change.

In my close relationships, because of my background, I was always trying to prove something, to be a good girl, the best student, the perfect girlfriend/wife and mother. Entangled in this illusion we call 'perfection', somewhere between people pleasing and the good girl theory, I was left heart broken and empty.

I found myself alone, even among the many I thought I knew and with that, my armour got heavier each day. When I lost my dad, grief struck me like lightening. I felt rejected and abandoned, I lacked support and my rock had turned to dust.

I needed comfort but my younger self also needed re-assurance that she was going to be ok. Deep in my core, I knew it was just me and that little girl alone on this journey, so, we walked hand in

277

hand, trusting the void we were stepping into, my mind asking 'How am I going to do this?' and 'How am I going to unshackle myself from all the good and bad without getting caught up in the narrative?'.

The narrative was all I'd known and that story was distracting me. It was creating chaos and confusion, even fear. I needed to learn not to get caught up in the illusion. I didn't want to hide behind a mask anymore.

So, when cacao came into my life and when I drank it every day, within the sister circle, I set my intentions and felt a gentle presence in the room.

Memories came pouring back to me, tears rolled down my cheeks. Cacao asked me to sit with her. I could feel the elements taking care of me, the ground holding me and the air flowing in and out of my lungs as I leaned deeper into cacao.

I was being stripped of all the illusions, the facades, as I let go of what was controlling me and surrendered to the unconditional love that was permeating through every part of my being, I was becoming the fire, the ashes and the phoenix all at once – just like I told my younger self she would.

Drinking my cacao and sitting in stillness each day has brought me clarity I never expected. Cacao has given me a sense of direction, helped me see what I needed to do.

I started to create more memories and express how I felt from my heart. I began to have fun (once I threw the rule book out the window)! I had no idea that this ascension would be my 'descent' into my womb space. It was time to face my shadows and insecurities and they were buried away there. I began facing each one of them. I felt the rawness of my own truth. I began to listen to the songs that my soul was singing and started to dance and move.

I had the feeling I was unravelling ancient wisdom within me that lay deep in my womb. Just like the moon moves through her phases, I was renewing myself and letting go of parts that didn't serve me. I was in sync with the cycles of the moon and she was teaching me the power of blood magic as I sat with cacao on my yoni steam.

I was learning to honour my creative centre, my shakti. This was ritual for me. It was sacred medicine and I was embodying it into my daily life. I was taking back my power and freeing myself with each breath I took. Bit by bit, I let go of all that was controlling me, letting go too of the need to know, detaching myself from the need to be validated by others.

My perspective began to change with each surrender, something started to surface, something bigger and greater. This was when I knew, I was held and guided by a greater power, the power of all the women who had walked before me, my elders, my ancestors and the power of plant medicine.

The more I leaned into plant medicine and my self-care rituals, the more I shared and spoke with confidence. Words now flow from my soul, from my wiser self. 'Inspiration pours from your words' I was told once, 'I wish you could see what I see', said another. The woman I am becoming is changing her relationships and her conversations. Magic happens now when I set my intention to change the narrative of my own story. As I drink my cacao, set my intentions and light my candles, it all makes sense now!

Liberation

In comparison to all the other girls, I was the only curvy girl in my family. I had small breasts and a rather large bottom. Being conscious of my body shape, I would wear oversized tee shirts to hide what I felt were imperfections. I was one among many of my generation who felt disempowered by the way we looked. I saw women hide behind baggy clothing or even cosmetic surgery, just so they could be accepted by society and I too was stuck there. 'Why did one have to fit in?' I questioned, 'Why is it wrong to be different?'

To stand in ritual with myself, naked in front of the mirror, in honour of myself, my vulnerability staring right back at me was empowering!

I had put some soft music on in the background but by the time I was naked, I could barely hear it. The warm light from the candles I'd lit had softened the contours of my body. This body! That I had refused to honour and accept because I'd been so stuck in the dogma that'd been passed from generations!

And yet, when I saw my body now, the shape of my breasts felt alluring, even after nursing my daughter, my hips gently rocking side to side, my pelvic throne holding me together, powerfully claiming all she had been through! From the birthing of my beautiful daughter to all the emotions of rage, anger, grief, it was a witness to it all. I wanted to indulge in my own sensuality! I wanted to become my own lover. My eyes, the windows to my soul, glistening with the flickering candlelight. My lips softly pouting as my yoni submerged herself with the amrit from the sacred rivers of my womb. I could hear my heart beating from between my breasts. My life force, asking to surrender even deeper, accepting the change that was upon me, ending the turmoil, wanting to purify me of all the stigma.

I asked myself 'Am I ready to step into this vortex?' and 'Am I ready to let go?'. My body encouraging me to surrender because it no longer wanted to endure anymore pain from holding onto old narratives. This felt very familiar, I'd been here before. The divine feminine, the wise woman screaming to be liberated.

'How am I going to do this all over again?' I heard myself think. The noise had to stop! I was being asked to listen deeper, to listen to the voice of my soul. Allowing my heart to crack open one more time, it had so much more to say and so much more to share, I only had to let go and surrender.

That morning I prepared myself a yoni steam (a ritual that had become a regular self-care practice) and plant medicine, which always brings me right back to where I need to be…being present, feeling my body move and letting go of the ego.

I felt the power and presence of all the women from my lineage, my great grandmothers, my grandmothers, the shamans holding space for me. Today was the ceremony of my initiation. Sitting in a wide legged child's pose, I could feel the warmth of the steam rising up and kissing the walls of my yoni, my hips moving back and forth calling me to lean into this dark space where all the stigma and the shame lived.

How much was I carrying?

Was this liberating all the women that came before me?

The gentle rocking of my pelvis, my breath barely there, I could feel my legs and hips softening into the ground and the rest of me followed. Feeling the raw depth of my own sensuality and presence, I anchored my root into the core of mother earth. I felt her warmth and the love of a mother, as she took me into her embrace. Her deep presence rippled through my yoni, permeating through my pelvis and every living cell in my body, arousing and filling me with sexual energy.

The immense power of the Goddess, Maa Shakti was bestowing upon me, as I came into a sacred union with myself. Daring to walk only in love, I was becoming the alchemist, transforming and standing in my own power. Honouring my own higher truth, despite all the fears rising.

I knew I had to transmute this sexual energy to a higher purpose, creating and sharing from this space. Growing up I'd no-one to guide me into how to truly embody the feminine essence but here I am today eloquent in empowerment and embodiment practices, recognising the greater power that lies beneath our vulnerability.

And once again, I sat honouring my womb and my heart that holds such primordial wisdom. Rewriting my story and moving past the dogma that has been handed down to me through ' MY ' lineage.

I am liberated.

Eleshia Harris

64

Self nurture was her ritual,
her own wishes worshipped,
her most fantasized dreams imagined.
Boundaries protected,
respecting and protecting those of her sisters in return.
That's how she became an empress.

from 'A Woman's Blessing'

The woman I am now

I'd heard of sister circles before but I had never been drawn to join one. Over the decades I'd been hurt by female friends and family that I considered to be close, so the thought of airing my feelings and thoughts to strangers petrified the hell out of me. It wasn't until a friend of mine invited me to hers, that I actually considered this may just be the right time to dedicate some more time to myself. I'd been on a real self-discovery journey for the previous eighteen months and I was ready to release what I'd been holding onto so tightly.

I had spent the last eight and a half years, scratch that, I had spent my whole life keeping myself small and taking care of everyone else's needs before mine and I knew it was time to start to look after myself wholeheartedly without any excuses. I knew the task ahead was going to be *so* difficult for me. People pleasing is in my DNA but I kept on telling myself that by helping others, I was helping my anxiety.

I was excited to see where the journey would take me, I was also really scared. I'd buried so much over the years, it was my natural coping mechanism, so I really didn't know if it was time to unpack memories, thoughts or emotions but I decided to trust the process. I wanted to set a good example for my young daughter, I didn't want her to witness or to have to deal with any of my past trauma in her future. Yes, I knew this was the beginning of a brand-new experience but I wasn't new to having to deal with trauma and the after effects, so I braced myself.

I had already done some work on myself, I'd started to use my voice publicly on podcasts and I wanted to stay true to my main topic, which is ensuring that I'm investing in me first.

So, there I was, about to light a candle for myself for the first time. I'd lit candles before but this felt so different! I did it with an intention and it warmed me up instantly from the inside out. Taking that moment to light a candle just for myself signified so much more than the lighting of your average candle. It was all about me. I was lighting it for nobody else but me and I loved how that made me feel.

As my tendency was to put others first, I had no real boundaries set at all. Through digging deeper, I recognised it was time to stop being an 'enabler' for some of the most important people in my life. It was time to reclaim my power and lead from my heart.

It was such a scary practice for me but I felt comforted by lighting a candle for myself over the days and weeks that followed. I really started to feel more empowered, to confidently stand up for my beliefs and stay strong when they were tested…and tested they were!

People really didn't like it when they stopped getting their own way and it was really difficult for me not to go back to giving in but knowing how much I needed to make a change, I stayed true to my promise and continued to take a chance on me.

This will continue to be a work in process but I'm extremely happy that I've given myself the space to work on myself. I've benefited the most but equally so have my family, friends, clients and all the new people who meet me.

There's nothing to fear

Surrendering to my inner critic, it would be so easy to agree with all of the limiting beliefs I've had imprinted on my heart but where would that leave me?

My parents were both from different Caribbean islands and growing up I was always told that I'd have to work harder than my friends to be seen and heard in this world. I don't blame them, they too were told the same by their parents, they were just trying to protect me.

But those messages of over-achieving sank in whatever the good intentions. From my late teens I worked on career plans - A, B and C! I wanted to prove to others and myself that I was more than capable and deserving of having the life I desired. I took every course and certification available because I wanted to ensure that nobody could question my abilities. I would hide behind the excuse that I was multi passionate and I wanted to be the best at everything but what I realised, both through this sister circle immersion and my own inner work, is that I was limiting myself from focusing on my true desires, abilities and purpose because I was afraid of judgement and rejection.

Those feelings were compounded when my mum died. I knew before the doctor even came in to tell us that she had left us. I remember sitting there feeling totally numb but also thinking about the long list of people I would have to contact and all the people who were congregating outside the hospital waiting room, that I would have to face. I was also worried how I was going to break the news to my brother on the autism spectrum.

I went into full-on people pleasing mode, I had to make sure everyone else was ok. I didn't think about what *I* was feeling once. I was the strong one. 'Oh Eleshia you're so strong, I don't know how you cope with everything' they said.

This had been my title for so long anyway, I just assumed the position and got on with the role. What I didn't realise, was how it was going to affect me, later on in my life. I'd been programmed

286

from a young age to put others first, it was a learnt behaviour. I'd seen my mum do it all her life and I saw myself doing the same. Overnight I took on the matriarch role, I took care of every last detail of the funeral and all of her affairs.

I had always believed that holding it together and being strong, putting others first, was the best way to achieve my goals. What I realised through this sister circle immersion and through the other deep internal work I had done, was that I'd helped everyone one else achieve their plans and yet I'd failed to please myself.

The weight of being the matriarch at such a young age, took its toll on my body. After eighteen months, I exploded from the inside out, the grief I held onto showed itself firstly by nearly choking me in a restaurant. Out of nowhere, I developed a nut allergy. A few months later and after being referred to an allergy specialist, I had another attack. This time after having a set of eyelash extensions applied for my holiday. I remember being on the plane and wanting to rip every single one of my own lashes out, I was in so much pain.

The pain kept on showing up. I could handle eliminating certain foods and products. What I couldn't handle was being told I wouldn't be able to have children naturally. This news absolutely devastated me and was definitely the pinnacle turning point of my life. I knew I needed to make huge changes if I wanted to become a mum and so the journey began of putting myself and my needs first. Giving up control and asking for what I really wanted became a daily practice.

I never once questioned how I was going to heal myself. I knew the answers would reveal themselves to me.

One of those answers, came in the form of a ritual for the seven-year-old I used to be. I read about this ritual slowly and felt my whole body tremble. I didn't want to cast my mind back to my seven-year-old self. I didn't want to cast my mind back to the good or the bad memories! I wanted to skip this day altogether and just move onto the next ritual but I knew if I did that, I'd be left wondering what would have come up. I asked myself what I was worried about and what I might be protecting myself from.

When I really thought about it, I was overwhelmed by the fact that I didn't know how to activate her. I didn't even know what to do to remember her. It was suggested that we make a playlist of all the songs she used to listen to back then, I loved that idea and as I played one song, I remembered another and then the next and the next and the next.

Before I knew it, I'd made a six-hour long playlist and was dancing around my office remembering all the various memories of hearing particular songs for the first time.

Music has always been such a huge part of my life. Both my parents loved music so much, I continue to eye up my dad's record collection and I always recognise songs from the first few seconds! As I remembered, I realised there was absolutely nothing to be afraid of. Whatever emotions I was holding on to, melted slowly away with every song.

I belted out words I hadn't sung for years, feeling such release and finally, I was ready to light a candle for her, to put pen to paper and write a letter to thank her. I thanked her for having courage, as she helped me shape the woman I have become now.

Acknowledging her, has brought those feelings of judgement and rejection to the surface for me as an adult, to see through an adult's eyes, that I hold my own approval and I can put myself first.

Remembering cacao

One morning during our sister circle, I woke up at 4.30am. My head was spinning, so much information in it, all relevant but I couldn't make sense of any of it.

It was all messed up and I couldn't stop it from moving around, so I got up. Quietly I moved around, careful not to wake the house up. I don't often get time on my own in the morning and I really wanted this time to myself. I even wanted to enjoy listening to my mums annoying clock in the background. Before she went into the hospital for the last time, she was going to get rid of it but now I can't bring myself to give it away.

So that morning, without even considering it or questioning it, I reached for cacao, went downstairs and prepared it. If I'm being really honest, I hardly drink it. I listen to others in the circle talking about drinking cacao every day and I feel disconnected. I didn't know why until that morning.

In my culture it's our tradition to drink cacao tea. We drink it for the plant based medicinal purposes. We'd mostly drink it in the winter and I remember we'd have it without fail every Christmas morning with our Caribbean breakfast. It wasn't always easy to obtain the sticks or balls in the UK, so as I got older, I noticed we'd just drink it on special occasions.

As I mixed up my cacao that morning, it bought up all kinds of strong feelings. The strongest feeling was guilt. I'd been holding back from connecting with the ceremonial aspect of drinking cacao every day. The expense of it was one reason but more to the point, I'd been resisting encouraging the deeper inner connection to myself, my traditions and my mum. I wanted to be over that but I was still scared to go there, deep down I knew things would have to change and I didn't want to hear my inner voice, I was petrified of what it would say.

That day though, I gained the courage without even realising it. I stepped into the woman I want to be, the woman I am yet to become. And as I held my cup to my heart and set my intention, I heard everything I needed to hear.

I heard my mum's voice loud and clear. I heard her guiding words speaking to me softly, she was responding to questions I didn't even realise I needed answering. I could feel her presence in the dark room, whilst I sipped my cacao. My memory took me back to our time together so vividly. The gratitude I felt for this moment was so deep. I hadn't realised how much I'd needed that to move forward with my life.

The scarcity that I'd held onto, of not being able to afford or find more cacao when I ran low, disappeared. I explored why I'd felt this strong resistance to use what I had so sparingly and recognised that it was a childhood memory. But we always had enough, my mum made sure of that. And so, I reminded myself 'there's always enough'.

Growing up, my mum's friends were like her sister circle. They didn't do all the rituals but they were there for each other, every step of the way. They provided the love, the support and anything else they needed. I felt the same when I was part of my own sister circle all these years later...held, seen and part of a community. And now whenever I need a little more support, I remember to go back to drinking my cacao, to go back to my heritage and my family roots.

Maila Salmaso

24

Wild feminine healing force surrendering to the sand,
throwing magic in the air.
Ritual, trusting universal law,
her power to create, rising, powerful, healing force,
intention and inspiration a potent feminine brew.
Bravery forged, an expression of her wildness,
all to show the divine feminine future.
Her very own sparkly, glittery flame.

from 'A Woman's Blessing'

Blessing the wilder version of me

I have noticed all my life, that in order for me to be able to do something important, I have to reach a certain frequency, a certain vibration, that's over and above distractions...others needing my attention for instance.

I found there were always some things I resisted doing, because I didn't have the right environment for instance, the proper place or the most beautiful surrounding to do it in. Somehow, sometimes I find these are necessary. Twenty-five years ago though, finding just the right environment to do something was a must! I wasn't aware of it, looking back, I feel I was living in a bubble of my own, paranoid to some extent and certainly alone.

So, even now, as I'm writing this, I haven't quite got over that. Most of the 'self' work I've done in the past five years, was a call. I've been responding to my soul voice, listening to my body, what it wants to tell me and as a result of that, I have found myself in communication with my guides and spirits.

I remember the first time I read about sister circles and gathering, it was almost like an electric shock to my system. Like my body and my guides were actually saying out loud, 'It's for you! You have to do it! Jump in! It's the right circle to work with and lean into'.

I remember also that I was too busy and rather than declare my interest, I decided to keep the intention in my heart, nurturing it like a bird would nurture a nest, in the warmest spot in my heart, not closed or sealed but there to grow and mature.

A few months later, I joined, I was ready! The excitement was so much that I jumped in, completely blind, knowing I needed to do this, a higher call was beckoning me. I knew there was a reason for me to be there and I wanted to find out what that reason was.

What I did know, was that I wanted to experience a real women's circle and I wanted to understand it fully, navigate it, be open to the women and be feminine in my approach.

At the opening ceremony, it was clear, we were all equal…there were no differences…we were all women, regardless of background, money, shape, ability…we were equal. We were all the same there, there to share something intimate with other women, to find support, understanding, to be vulnerable, to accept and understand ourselves more deeply. What I also understood was that there were no stupid questions or thoughts…because another woman was experiencing the same – the same pain, fears, doubts and voids. Aaahhhhhh…the relief! I wasn't alone anymore.

We were there for sharing and the healing, we were there to release, to disintegrate old monsters and it was so beautiful, so soothing. I felt no comparison, no judgement, no 'why?' or 'how comes?' only support.

I felt like we were a grid of support. The armour and barriers I'd built up over my thirty-six years of earthly experience, finally had a place to melt.

My healing process generally is not fast. Often it takes a long time of integration after deep healing journeys. However, that first week of sister circle, was the deepest and most profound destruction of childhood trauma I had been through and it was ultimately healed.

I wasn't alone in my crying anymore, I wasn't alone in my pain, I didn't need to do everything on my own, I was not obliged to close my mind off to support. Someone was listening to me, not to fix me but to truly listen and support. I found my sisters validated my words, they validated my silence and they were just there…to witness me, nothing else.

293

I'd met a lot of resistance in doing pleasurable things for myself in the past but in this circle, I noticed I released that, I felt able to flow with the WHOLE of who I was in complete trust. My wound wasn't bleeding anymore.

Before the circle I had created time for ritual but I soon realised the rituals I had practised, hadn't been deep enough to make a true difference to me. Within this sister circle space, even though it came at a time when I'd just started a new job, was co-living in a difficult partnership and I was commuting every day, I still brilliantly, somehow found time – even if I was a little behind schedule, I found my space, the perfect vibration, the golden thread if you like and I started to dance with my pen.

I wrote a letter to the girl I used to be.

I wrote and wrote and wrote, such an overflow of emotions, memories and visions from the past!

Everything was extremely vivid, clear and right there for me, on a silver plate, to be observed with fresh new eyes. Like a condor, I was seeing a bigger picture from above. From that different perspective, everything was there, raw, actual, unfiltered. I was no longer seeing myself from a victim's perspective but from my adult perspective, taking total responsibility for the past, looking at it for what it really was. I looked at the facts, completely detached, it was nude. And with that nudity, came a boiling over of tears – a mixture of old pain, shame and exhaustion mixed with liberation, joy and love.

I found myself full of unconditional love for that little soul, the girl I used to be and more than that, for life itself, for the nature of events and their timing. When things have to happen, they happen and they generate great change.

My soul, I realised, was ready. Nothing could have been different, everything had been perfect, not in spite of but *because* of all the pain, the lessons and spilled blood. I felt so worthy of that soul process, it was a crystallizing of my senses and an opening of my awareness for the woman I am now.

The ritual of writing that letter had a profound effect. I embraced the fact that nothing is impossible and everything is possible. EVERYTHING! Even the furthest thing I can imagine runs through my veins way before I can actually do it.

I've realised that change is possible, I am not my mother or my father. I'm not what my uncle or my granny told me, I am ME and I have discovered who I am. I don't even feel as though I'm my parents' child anymore, I don't have their biology, I chose them because my role of earth was bigger. Now that I'm really open to the billions of experiences and possibilities my life brings, I can understand why I chose them.

And ALL of these revelations came to be while commuting on the underground from Clapham Junction to Hampstead Heath! I can hardly believe that. It turns out, that THAT was my perfect place, the lovely and comfy nest I needed in a surprisingly empty train. I adored writing that letter, there on the train, in an empty carriage. It really has been a little gem of a ritual.

I later buried it, in a forest in the mountains of Northern Italy. A place I know so well, with the most beautiful memories of that little fairy girl. I sealed the letter in the ground, with my moon blood and cacao.

It felt like a coming home, like the most plush, velvet, pinky-purple long dress on the most beautiful and comfortable of sofas carved from mahogany wood!

Following that burial ritual, an irrepressible need emerged for me to stop living the identity that had been shaped by others throughout my teenagehood. Somehow my soul, my inner child, had begun to scream 'ENOUGH! Open your eyes and mind, YOU ARE NOT THAT'.

And right there, I broke that loop. I'd kept myself defined by trauma, because I'd kept the feelings and emotions of them running…with absolutely no clue what the opposite could sound or look like.

When I felt totally and completely safe, when I'd created a nest I could open fully in, I found the wilder version of myself. Seeing that waterfall of cacao blessing that letter, I opened my Self, my mind, my essence, my core and my perception.

I've broadened my earthly life possibilities, experiences, skills and future beyond what I knew possible.

Embodiment

Embodying the woman I am now, means seeing the reality of my habits while at the same time, being aware of how my barriers are coming down, of how I'm listening to my higher and truest self, accepting who I am, as a whole. And through that process, I recognise I binge eat. When I've written that before, I've written it in brackets…but this time, no brackets, I acknowledge it, observe it, express it and let it be.

This time there is not hiding or rejection. I'm not ashamed of it and I don't blame myself or anyone else anymore. Instead, I am listening. I am listening to myself, my mouth, my taste buds, my stomach, my legs and my heart.

As I write this, I am eating. A mixture of real breakfast hunger and also the kind of anxious excitement of feeling scared to be great, with a hint of resistance to soak into the woman I am now.

You see…everything changed for me when, in one of the rituals, I told myself:

'I LOVE YOU'

I was far away from my home country. I was alone with my feelings and my cat! I will remember that moment forever. I'd told myself that before but I said the words without anything moving inside me…THIS time, I anchored myself to my eyes in the mirror, the light from the mirror became bright and vibrant. Every cell in my body started to shake. My eyes became luminous, a different energy started to show up, they got bigger and bigger, suddenly a big smile widened. It was like seeing the eyes of someone else, like this person was looking at me and then looking into my own eyes back and the words 'I LOVE YOU' flew out.

My body started to vibrate, palpitations of joy and surprise mixed with magic filled the air around me and I was soaked in love. I could not leave that mirror. I stared at the person looking into my eyes and I was staring into the eyes of this other person.

The warmth and the reverence, the esteem, the honour, the respect coming from my heart centre and expanding into the rest of my body, well, it was unbelievable.

I had a few tears of joy, they were hot teardrops saying, 'The time is right, you are ready, recognise yourself, recognise who you are, release the veil of doubt. You are joy, beauty, potential, power, medicine, you are 'il cammino' ('the path' in Italian).'

And then, I knew that walking my path was a conscious act now. I knew that some invisible part of me was ready to expand

and accept that path. I felt more able to fully walk my talk. My defences were down, I was free.

A large part of this process (that I really connected with and has helped me bridge between the dimensions) is my sacred stick. At the beginning of this immersion, I was asked to find my 'stick'. I had no idea how this would help me walk my path - being present but in the past and being present but in the future, no time and no space, only PRESENT.

My stick has reactivated within me so much creativity, the joy of my inner child in creating, using colours, using the touch of the hands and channelling magic in rituals. My stick has helped me in REALLY feeling the rituals – to the point that I vibrate! I end up feeling my organs move and understanding that they're actually talking to me, directing me in which colour to use, what to write and where to place my sacred dreams.

My stick has somehow increased my awareness, both inside and around me. I'm not judged, there's no need, it's all mine, my creation, my messages, my reflection of the present moment. It's been part of my bleeding, painful, sad moments and a manifestation of my joyful, wishful and creative moments. It has been the anchoring of beliefs and has given me the trust to be in the present moment, with present wishes and present emotions.

Sacred silence

There was a time when the ground used to collapse under my feet, the only sensations I had were those of being lost, incapable, hopeless. Those times were my darkest voice and normality for me, my way of surviving was to fill that void with drugs and alcohol – they were the only things that made me feel capable, fulfilled and gave me the push I needed to carry on and deal with my life. And that lasted until it didn't.

In my thirties, everything broke down around me. The veil of illusion, you could say that synthetic substances gave me, fell away and I could see. I started to get a sense of the earth, mother earth. I felt like she was contacting me through my body. I started to feel the sharpest pains of nature, something I realised, didn't align with my cellular system...and there...was the beginning of my journey with plants...plant medicine.

It took a few more years to be able to recognise and hear the call from the realms of nature and plant medicines. But when I did...oh my girl...I heard every message very clearly and I listened very carefully. I have followed every single call.

I now know I was experiencing a gap in my consciousness, something that no-one from my native culture could teach me. This was something my soul knew and had known for a very long time. My knowing was rooted in my senses, ancient memory. I started to smell familiar smells and see landscapes when I closed my eyes, I could no longer stop the connection to mother earth, it was like something invisible was pushing me beyond and over my boundaries. I had no choice but to start breaking down the limits that had been created for me by my family, the society I lived in, my own mind even.

Slowly, step by step I saw all the limitations and started to break every one of them. The connection between my mind and my body became much more apparent, almost like the link was recreated by my soul. The embodiment of this is a daily ritual began in the form of drinking ceremonial cacao, being in silence, lighting candles and sitting in sister circle.

Silence has become something I crave now, like a neutral place where everything can be integrated…my thoughts, wishes, desires, projects, my emotions, healing…it's where I work things out, give myself love and nourishment.

The silence is where I listen.

I hear so much in the silence. I've learned to navigate it rather than get lost in the void. Silence used to be cold for me, an absence of something but as I began to crave it and sit in it, I became so comfortable with it. Silence is my ally and I will always sit with it now, I feel it's my right and that my wellbeing depends on it.

It's changed things forever for me now.

Sacred silence has been the last 'tessera' (tile, mosaic piece) in the process of healing wounds, lighting three candles for the three aspects of me – the girl I used to be, the woman I am now and the woman I am yet to become. They awaken in me when I light those candles, I live my life fully now, without my energy seeping away. I realise now that I'll never live life fully without obstacles, limitations or being in 'self-sabotage' mode but these rituals have liberated me completely.

Virginia Gonzalez Pinto Medrano

25

Standing in the crashing waves,
holding her drum to the gods of the oceans,
offering herself and her spells,
they took her breath away and replaced it with bliss.
Vital energy rushing through her veins, she hollered so they
could hear.
Every woman, calling them to gather, ancient DNA,
she'd held them a thousand times before
and today, they would remember.

from 'Sacred'

Embodying my feminine

I never thought I would embody myself into a sister circle. For so many years, I neglected the feminine in me, I neglected my feminine body and it started when I was ten years old.

Me, running fast down a broken pathway, wearing a blue and pink flowery dress, every moment back then was a chance to play. We were coming back from church; it was a Sunday. Nothing mattered to me, not even the fact that I'd been to church and I didn't believe in any of it! I was running home, to take off that dress and play, we were going to have a big Sunday fire.

Now THAT was a ritual I knew how to be part of! Fire, in my culture, was for men. So, at night time, there was my chance, to be part of that ritual with fire, to be with the men and I unconsciously choose my masculinity over my femininity.

I was the third of three girls, no-one really cared, I could take the place as the tom boy, so I did! And I had SO much more freedom, feeling it would be so much easier to close my emotions down, to close my feelings down and go against the beauty standards that even at aged ten, I was beginning to become so acutely aware of.

It was around this time we found out my mum had lung cancer. I grew angry, angry at everything. I was angry at life itself and resentment start growing inside me. I knew instantly she didn't have long. And three months after my 16th birthday, she died.

I was broken. There was no real happiness anymore, I tried to hide the pain and the resentment at her for leaving me. I finally left, to take care of my grandmother, my mum's mum. Losing her daughter before her own passing had destroyed her and she developed senile dementia. Pretty soon, I had to let her go too...and the anger kept on rising.

302

I got into fights, physical fights and chose a path of self-destruction. I transformed into a strong aggressive 'I can do it all' superhuman. Depressed and lost, finding joy in extreme moments, usually under the influence of something that would take me away from this 3D life, where the pain was so strong.

I see now, the joy of that little girl transformed in abuse, drug abuse, I burned years in months maybe even days! I have no regrets at all. I learned so much. I connected with so many people, my mind expanded and my creativity too…but I never felt any real joy. I don't think I even recognised it.

In my darker moments, I found a way to connect to myself….by connecting to the moon! I felt so alone and misunderstood that it was grandmother moon I reached out to. She was my companion, jumping out the window to look at her and to speak with her. I shared the magic of nature together with her.

Fast forward many years later, at aged thirty-five, I shared these memories with my sisters in circle. It was so powerful. I heard stories from one woman and then another and those memories triggered emotions and other experiences in me, as though their stories had happened to me also. They served as reminders of other parts of my own story.

I heard about a sister dealing with dementia, her story reminded me of how I held my grandmother with great honour until her departure and all of those powerful emotions helped me when I made my intentions as I wrote the letter to my younger self. They calmed me.

I really didn't know the power of this but writing that letter showed me, I have the power to go back in time. In my letter, I told my younger self what was going to happen. I told her that it would all bring learning in the end and I told her that she could wear

ANYTHING she wanted, that she could be in her feminine, that joy didn't only come from wearing trousers and that freedom lives within. And it really worked.

Magical Kali woman!

There was a moment I realised I didn't like my body. It was after giving birth. I stared and looked at the changes my body had been through and I realised how difficult it was to remember how it used to look, to remember who I even was.

It was such a difficult time for me, all wrapped up in all the rules of society, how perfect a new mother 'should' be, in front of the camera or on social media and how it caused me so much unworthiness.

Babies, for me, meant lower boobs, a scarred belly, hanging skin, dirty clothes (puke and poop). All those new marks were part of the new me, the new me that was created to be a mother.

When I looked at myself in the mirror as part of my shower ritual, it helped me to realise how scared and separated I'd been from my body. I'd forgotten the more natural ways in which I could seek perfection.

I remembered how I had wanted to be a man, because they were cooler. I had started using some masculine ways of coping, spending time with men mostly, nobody knew or needed to know, that I had emotions other than anger, frustration and resentment. These are the emotions that men in Argentina typically display. And I hid like this for quite a while until one stormy night. I'd been walking in the woods and on that walk, I had suddenly realised that in my 'feminine' body, I could bring a boy onto this earth and learn from and 'with' him!

And so…the first baby I conceived on that stormy night, in my 'girl' body was a boy.

So many changes followed that calling to bring a boy to earth. The responsibility of co-creating a new person, the responsibility to find out who I was, who I was with my partner and as the birth got nearer, layers of fears got all mixed up with well-meaning tips and useless phrases from everyone! And it took its toll.

'Your knees will never hold the weight of a baby they told me. 'If you don't take iron, you'll bleed out and die' they said. But, for me, those phrases triggered the magic and the strength inside me. My middle name is Patricia, my mum's cousins name. She had died after an abortion in exactly the way people were describing to me and yet, I was being introduced to the other side of what it is to be a woman, the magic I was seeking. I was creating another human inside me and I would also be able to feed it from my powerful, creative body.

Twenty-five kilos later, my knees were still taking me for walks, my hips had divided to make space for this new treasure growing inside me and when that happened, I knew I would have the birth I wanted, to be free, to do it as naturally as my body desired. I realised I knew myself and my body better than anyone else.

And I did. With a powerful roar, my baby boy gently came out, no cuts, no blood loss, no stitches - just another magical natural Kali woman bringing a new human to this world.

And this beautiful body appreciation ritual brough this all back. How perfect nature is, how my body had created unique nutrition for my child and in that moment, I was in all my power and gentleness, all at the same time.

I have met myself now

I don't have an everyday relationship with my blood family, my mum died many years ago and everyone went their separate ways afterwards, so I realise now, that over the years I have created my own 'chosen' non-blood family. I have SO many adopted parents and crones all around the world, I've been attracting them all my life. My unique family. People I love. They don't know each other but as time passes it's like they connect somehow.

In not having a close-knit blood-family, I've realised too that I have a certain amount of freedom. No-one telling me what to do for instance although I do miss hearing someone else's experience and advice, learning from their path and battles. Those in my unique chosen family bring that to me instead, gatherings bring that movement to me, this sister circle brought that to me and I'm so thankful for that.

Taking myself into this '22 days of ceremony' was a gift. I knew I would go much deeper into myself than I could on my own, without a sisterhood with me. I took that gift and gave it focus to honour that time for myself fully. I spoke with my family and explained that mummy was going to be having time for herself and they really got it. My kids loved it in fact, each morning asking what ritual was next and I involved them where I could. We lit candles together, I involved them in the painting and they filled my bathtub with petals and the bathroom with candles. I got to show them, through living the example, of what honouring myself is. I hadn't really been used to sharing ritual with them, instead, I would do it on my own or with my sisters in circle. I hadn't realised they would take to it so well, I never imagined how profound it would be.

Through this immersion, I had a strong sense that I'd been taking my 'magic' for granted. That time to myself made me see that even to breathe, to speak, to communicate is so special, so divine. It's easy for me to pay more attention to social media, work and running around like a headless chicken, than to remember to live in the moment.

I also realised that I have good, strong people in my life. I am a woman connected to plants, to animals and to the moon and that thought came to me so strongly one day when I made a big decision – to have my contraceptive implant removed from my arm. I decided to go back to my natural moon cycle, I realised the unnatural hormones that had been causing me to bleed for six months non-stop, needed to stop. I decided to cleanse my body.

Gathering with those women helped me to realise I wanted my own female connection back. I'm only just meeting my real self. I know I want peace and happiness, I know I have to place boundaries, choose myself first and be in right partnership. I'm learning.

And in that learning came the woman I am yet to become in meditation. She had silver long hair, she wore white clothes (as clean as a brand-new canvas still waiting to painted), she was standing at the beach watching the sunset. She extended her arm to me and as I took her hand, I could feel her thin skin. She invited me to get closer, the touch of her skin was the same as my grandmother's, we sat on the beach and I lay my head on her lap while she gently stroked my hair. She told me with a giggly smile 'You are going to be ok!'.

I love noticing synchronicities and through this time there were so many. I had the opportunity to have my hair done unexpectedly, just as we were entering 'the women we are yet to become' stage of the immersion. I told my hairdresser that I'd really love Titania's hair from X-Men – I used to play that with my sister as a child. She had a white stripe in her hair. My hair is very dark Argentinian hair, I've had my hair so many colours...turquoise, purple, white, green, it's been short, long, blonde and red for many years, I even had a rainbow done once! This time, it didn't turn out quite as white as we'd hoped, instead it was a beautiful silvery grey AND it looked very natural.

As soon as I saw it, I remembered my father had same stripe, the same colour in the same place in his hair! That week, I found myself embracing my crone with my new grey stripe and later, I tattooed my friend – she asked for an old wooden arrow with a stone-carved tip, with the words 'one life'...another synchronicity. For me, this was really a beautiful honouring of the Self, a present for the moment, a reminder to live in this unique experience and a reminder of how I want to live my life.

And so...after those three weeks with the girls we used to be, the women we are now and the women we are yet to become, I sit together easily with my younger self, wearing the blue flowered dress and I notice my daughter looks so much like I did. My elder Self comes and sits with us too and we hold hands creating a spiral.

So many symbols appeared in that final meditation...triangles...the moon...the smell of roses! I understood that it's all about invocations and inviting light...a beautiful way to close the 22 day container.

My daughter came to sit with me at the very end, I felt to show me the woman I am now and my son called me 'señora' for the first time. I realised, I am THAT age - woah - I noticed I had taken on my mums patterning of considering age a bad thing (in Argentina, the elders are not respected so much). And yet I've had so many important learnings from the elders in my life.

In this sister circle however, I was the youngest. I 'closed my mouth and learned to listen' (as Rising Appalachia sings). Every unique story is there to be honoured and I'm choosing to honour my life and everything that comes with it, as my path.

Ashleigh Guthrie

139

*She learned with every curve, with every steep hill
and with every deep river crossing in which she almost drowned,
that the landscape was being created just for her.*

from 'HELD'

The girl I used to be – The grieving daughter

'Oh the wonder's you shall see'

Back in 2017, I was twenty-nine. I stepped off the plane in Bali, pale, underweight, feeling and looking like a shell of my former self.

My mum had unexpectedly died the previous year and I'd become so far removed from friends and family in those first six months of grieving that I'd unwittingly become entangled in an emotional and narcissistic toxic relationship. I felt helpless and isolated, too scared to leave.

A living nightmare, panic attacks were my wake-up call. I now know this to be the beginning stages of awakening, my 'dark night of the soul'.

I had reached a point where it was too painful to stay in the reality I was in and so, I answered the call to meet a dear friend in Bali.

It was there, that I sat in my first women's circle. I remember feeling nervous, like a little girl back at her first day of nursery. There were eighteen women, each one taking it in turn to share their name, age, star sign and where they were from.

'My name is Ashleigh Guthrie, age twenty-nine, I currently live in Manchester, UK.

I was born in a humble town called Bolton. I'm a Pisces sun sign'

There were women there as young as eighteen up to late forties. I was curious to hear each woman's voice as they shared what had called them to the circle. I took in each of their faces, noticing the difference in hair textures and colours of skin. When it came to my turn to share, I could barely string a sentence together. Tears

312

streamed down my cheeks, my shoulders collapsed around my broken heart, protecting the little lost girl whose voice struggled to find the words to explain the pain she was carrying - 'My mum died. I feel lost, afraid and abandoned. Please help me'.

I was frozen in grief, guilt, trauma and regret. Guilt for not being the 'perfect daughter', regret for not giving my mum enough of my time or being patient enough.

The story 'you weren't enough' unconsciously looping around my nervous system.

For three days I sat in circle, I shed my tears of vulnerability, I looked into each woman's eye's and saw parts of myself within them, a reflection of hope, a sacred mirror showing me a glimmer of potential, I knew I could find my way to shine again.

And here I was, years later, back in sister circle, online this time. During that first week, I realised that in the last five years, women's circles had provided me a safe space to receive mothering energy and now, I was in connection with sisterhood.

This time was for me and my story as a woman. It felt unfamiliar but I was ready.

One of the most important rituals for me was to speak to that twenty-nine-year-old who'd landed in Bali and reflect to her, as her big sister, how far she'd come! I wanted to let her know that she has *so* many gifts to offer this world, that her story matters, that *she* matters and that she *IS* the gift. I wanted her to know that she is something to celebrate!
This is what I wrote;

To the girl I used to be, oh the wonder's you shall see.
Yes, your heart has been broken, your innocence stolen but,
my darling girl, you shall travel far and wide to find those

313

broken pieces and you shall love yourself back whole. You will discover new lands, new relationships and new opportunities that allow you see beyond what society has told you to be.

You will break through the illusion of control; you will flourish and transform into the most magnificent sovereign swan. You will learn to love like you've never known before and it all starts with you.

You will become your greatest love story.

My darling girl, be patient with yourself, your gift's will reveal themselves in time. Take sex out of the equation when it comes to matters of the heart and see what you are left with. Follow the whispers that set your soul on fire, even if at times you think it sounds crazy, for some it might, but the opinions of others matter not.

Know that mum's spirit lives' on in you, she will inspire you to be brave enough to face the fears, to have courage to take the leap of faith, time and time again. She will show you how to let go of the guilt and regret – forgiveness will set you free. Do not waste time on those who are not ready to receive you, it is you who is being asked to look inside and see your own potential,

"The beauty you see in every sunrise, you are that."

So, dive deep my darling girl, you'll be surprised and delighted when you finally see, it was you all along who held the key.

Your heart is pure, your love is rare, trust in this love, let it guide you home.

Be true to you.

Through sister circle and revisiting the girl I used to be, I learned that if I lead with my heart, my mind will follow, that my vulnerability and intuition are two of my greatest gifts. I learned that women's circles are sacred spaces where it's safe to speak my truth. I discovered that self-care is sexy, that my history does not define my destiny and that there are pearls of wisdom, woven everywhere – a sacred mirror to my own sovereignty.

The Woman I am today – The maturing maiden

Grief says, 'Something is missing. I am all alone'
Love says, 'I'm right here. I never left you'

As I sit here in this sacred space, I'm met with the familiar presence of sadness, I surrender to the heart-breaking awareness that my mum is not here to celebrate and witness who I have become. I allow everything to be, just as it is. Surrounded by sisterhood, honouring the journey I've taken to become the woman I am today; I feel welcomed, warm and embraced by the Elder's.

This gathering of women offered me a powerful and a safe space to move through the loss that comes from the changing of seasons and cycles of life, death and rebirth, the cycles of womanhood. Purging many tears that have waited so long to be expressed, cleansing the heart, a mourning to what has been.

Through the ritual of letting go, combined with ancestral healing, I have been able to release attachments, disappointments, fears, shame, resentments and expectations that have been passed down through my bloodlines, imprinted in my womb. I've reset the story of my 'mother and daughter' bonded by our unconscious traumas and conditioning.

315

For me to grow I realised I needed to create space. The art of ritual has shown me how to mature into my own unique vision of sovereignty and grace. I've learnt to work with the magic of the moon, returning to the natural cycles. As I birth myself anew, I walk a new path, enlightened and embodied as I come into right relationship with the great mother. I hear a new voice that's lovingly guiding me towards seeing the beauty that lies within. I'm reminded that I'm most alive during my deepest moments of pain.

This rite of passage has been a homecoming, an uncoiling of the dark mother archetype. An initiation into the remembering of who I am today. I have felt my body slowly thawing out old trauma's, awakening my sacred NO, connecting to the medicine of sacred rage and bringing a lifetime of crossed boundaries and countless acts of self-sacrifice into the light. An unleashing of wild feminine fury challenged me to say goodbye to the good girl, the people pleaser, peacekeeper and perfectionist.

To be seen as the woman who doesn't always have it together, the woman who can give herself permission to 'lose her shit', has been both vulnerable and at times confusing.

This fiery, fierce energy has taught me how to love myself even more when my crown has slipped and to not hide the parts that fear being judged, rejected or outcast.

I now have a soothing loving voice inside me that says 'Please remember your worth. Please remember that you are a divine spark of creative energy that is longing to be expressed. Remember you are a spiritual being having a human experience. You cannot run away from the power you hold. Come home. Come back to Self'.

Sister circle has been somewhere I could go to be truly seen and held in my times of vulnerability and growth. A community of sister's who have acted as a sacred mirror, reflecting my inner beauty, fears, childlike wonder and innate wisdom. It's a safe space to explore myself and experientially heal the wounds that held me back from leaning deeper into trust.

I said yes to this gathering of women because my inner maiden was longing to be seen and celebrated, so I decided to reclaim my power and celebrate myself! I was excited to celebrate in ceremony with other women who were on the path of awakening also. I wanted to acknowledge and reflect the greatness I saw in each of them, knowing I would receive the same.

In saying yes to myself first, my voice of wisdom has been activated, as old conditioning and fears began to rise and fall away. My fearful voice says, 'what will come through me if I let go of control and surrender into the bigness of this power? What happens if I speak my truth and allow the fullest expression of the divine feminine to flow through me? Will I be persecuted and abandoned?'.

The voice of doubt has been my reminder to stop and smell the roses. An invitation to sit in circle and take a moment to be present with that fear and hold it from a place of curiosity and compassion.

From there, something new started to stir within my soul, something grounded, something real and raw. Shame fell away, my heart began to open and new parts of me were restored. I came into connection with the ever unfolding of the sacred rose and her many thorns.

Through respecting this tribe of sisters and trusting myself to share my intuitive truth, I have found peace in my heart, my spirit renewed. I'm remembering long forgotten gifts and continuously practising patience as new parts of self slowly reveal themselves to me.

One of my favourite rituals to honour the woman I am today was when I made a print of my hand with cacao. I imagined how tiny my hand was when I was born and how that hand had grown into the hand of a thirty-three-year-old woman. I imagined all the things I have held, the people I have touched, the lifelines that had run across each palm.

I drew around the outside of my left hand, inside I wrote all the things I saw within myself, I closed my eyes, took a breath and evoked my internal mirror, I began to write out words within the fingers and inner hand and creatively adorned the drawing of my hand with cacao.

Honouring the woman I am today.
My story is one of great strength.
My heart is brave and bold.
I know there is so much beauty within honest vulnerability.
There is power present when I speak my truth.
I cherish the moments of innocence.
I liberate the real and raw aspects of self by giving them full
artistic expression.
It is time for the woman I am today to shine,
she is ready. I am ready.
It is time to celebrate who she is and
all that she has achieved.
I know you. I see you. I am you.

The woman I am yet to become – Maiden to Mother

'How far are you willing to leap for love?'

On this path of mine I've been asked repeatedly to let go of old identities that needed to fall away in order to rebirth anew.

I've been asked to say goodbye and grieve what has been, to truly see myself reflected in the eyes of another woman, to receive and be received. This, I believe, is one of the greatest acts of love and devotion I can commit to.

Writing about the girl I used to be and the woman I am today has been an emotional experience, a releasing of the past, a cleansing of what has been and yet there has been so much joy to the process. There was resistance to this third aspect because I wasn't feeling as connected to this part of myself. I needed time to sit with what was changing within me, to see the bigger picture.

Rituals, to me, feel like unseen gateways that open me through womblike portals of initiation, where I'm asked to take a leap of faith and trust in love. I don't always know what wants to come through, sometimes It feels like a pounding within my heart, a burning sensation within me, longing to be expressed. There was a particular ritual where I remember experiencing this, when during our immersion, we lit a candle for the children in our lives.

It felt like such an innocent, simple act of love. I'd recently become a bonus mum, so I lit one for my partners son, I lit one for my godson and one for twin boys who were conceived after their mother had been through a conscious conception ceremony.

And then...there was a very clear message to light another candle. One for the potentiality of a spirit baby, a daughter, that was waiting for me in the ether should I choose her. This came with a divine message; 'Who are you to deny yourself the experience of motherhood in this lifetime'.

Previously I'd been adamant that I never wanted children, so I was surprised to feel at peace with this. There was a certain level of matter-of-fact acceptance to it, that if a child should come to me in this lifetime, then so be it, and if not, I trust that all is in accordance with divine will.

I reflected this message into so many areas of my life, I could clearly see where I'd denied myself the gifts of abundance and where I was blocking connection due to fear and unworthiness.

Shortly after this ceremony I followed my intuition to have my copper coil removed. This evoked the initiation of the 'Dark Mother' archetype in me.

I dove into the shadow side of how I felt about being a mother, how my own mother might have felt giving birth to me. My fears, anger, fury and confusion erupted like a volcano with each bleed. The mother wound had been ripped wide open for me to tend to, I mourned the relationship of my maternal lineage, I returned to the original wound of separation and began the next journey of rebirth, an initiation of the woman I am yet to become.

A year on from this gathering of women, my relationship to my body and womb is continuing to evolve. A deep healing with the great mother is taking place, bringing forth a remembering of the intuitive wisdom of womanhood, re-connecting to the cyclic nature and grounded rhythms of life and in this, a returning to the universal light of a mother's love.

The girl I used to be was discovering spirituality for the first time and the awakening process was new and exciting, she was a seeker chasing the mystical boon, addicted to the intensity of the cosmic high's, lost and afraid, she was dissociated and at times, she spiritually bypassed the reality of the pain hidden within the discomfort of the mundane.

There has been a sense of nostalgia and grief in the process of accepting that it doesn't feel or look like that anymore. Speaking to those younger parts of myself as they mature, making more sovereign choices, I realise I am now responsible for the choices I make and I ask myself the question 'What do I desire to create with this life-giving power?'

Knowing now that the woman I am yet to become, is an integration of both the girl I used to be and the woman I am today, I recognise that there is great wisdom already existing within. Taking this time for myself, to sit in ceremony, to listen, to hear the pearls of wisdom that flows through my very being.

'Change doesn't happen outside of oneself but within', as within, so without.

I now realise that permission has already been granted, there was never anyone or anything external standing in my way, only the internal voice of doubt and fear. When I built and strengthened my relationship to sisterhood and the feminine, I began to connect to something far greater, I saw and heard the world with a deeper awareness. I created my stability and security from within.

The woman I am yet to become is rooted deep into the belly of mother earth, she draws her wisdom from within and knows that it is free to flow all around her, for she is connected to the great cosmic womb.

This woman is me; this woman is you.

Casey Mauro

93

She felt the energy of that silent moon.
She knew a big shift was coming.
She knew she'd need every shred of trust.
And that flow would gently find her hand.
She sank into those dark mornings.
Eyes closed, barely-there breath.
And trusted and trusted and trusted.

from 'HELD'

'All you imagine is valid and true'

I cuddled up with my cup of cacao popped on my headphones, closed my eyes, shut out the world and off I went into this sister circle meditation to meet the girl I used to be. Each sip of cacao melted my body deeper and deeper. Anandamide unlocking my brain wave flow state, theobromine activating a heart pumping sensation and phenethylamine giving each of my cells a hug of self-love. Becoming more wave than particle, I dissolved into the bed until I was brought back to my childhood.

A bright-eyed dreamer beyond her earthly years. Observing the little girl I used to be. Plump yet precious smooth skinned with freckles for days. A stab in my gut triggered me to remember how I distained my chubby belly every time I looked in a mirror or sat down and counted my tummy rolls. Oh, how I wish she knew those rolls did not define her worth! I was so damn cute - rolls and all. Looking into my wide brown eyes, clear as day I could see how determined and laser focused I was, immersed in my mind doing my jazz dance isolations in my bedroom. Shoulders up and down, rib cage side to side and hips in spirals. Safe in my bedroom so no one could see the real me. This was my way to the magical land of freedom. Body expression.

Entranced watching my ten-year-old self ungulate her body harder and harder, her tenacity pierced through my heart and became visceral again. Cacao circulating through my blood vessels releasing my emotions that have been locked away. I could feel again. I could feel me again. It was like my soul had been injected back into me. Time dissolved. All my worries and self-criticism no longer existed and I was back home. Home in my freedom to believe the way I once did. Re-membered. I believed in magic and I believed in myself.

324

'I can fly! I can fly if I think happy thoughts!'. Visions of my pet pig Sophie and I rubbing noses and chomping carrots together in the grass on a hot summer day put a smile on my face. Shooting stars and sparkles filled my heart and, in a flash, I was in my backyard. I climbed up the monkey bars to the top of the swing set shaking because this was the moment. My clammy hands gripped tightly to the wooden structure as I looked up to the blue skies and puffy white clouds, ready to become weightless at any moment. I belonged up there with the birds, the clouds and the sun. I leaped from the top of the swing set, sprawled my limbs like a star, with an intense moment of euphoria. 'I can fly!', I believed in myself. A smile on my face and dimples impressed on my cheeks, gravity pulled me back down as I crumbled into the earth below. The sandbox came hard and fast. I barely felt my bones get smashed from the adrenaline of truth that ran through my veins. My faith was unamused by $9.8m/s^2$ gravity business. Physics did not apply to me. I got back up knowing this sandy wedgie was a lie. I grabbed my underwear and pulled it out of my butt cheeks. I did it. I can fly. I scanned the yard to make sure no-one was in the yard so I didn't get in trouble. Mom did not approve of me doing anything slightly 'dangerous'.

OK, coast clear. Back to micro- analysing my brief flight. Then it clicked. My wings. Ah, that's what was missing. I need wings to stay in the sky longer. No biggie. I was amazed how resilient and optimistic my ten-year-old self is and unphased by getting knocked down. Damn girl. My older self would have been disappointed and given up or found something else that she was good at.

My body separated from hers and I had an overwhelming degree of realization. She is so sure of her truth and her inner wisdom. My throat welled up and tears dripped down my face. I had somehow lost that faith. How did I let this relentless little girl die? When did I lose sight of her dreams?

Maybe I didn't.

And at this very moment I re-membered.

In a flash, I was back in my childhood bedroom hugging little Casey. Heart to heart. 'What does she need to hear?' I heard, 'keep believing!' I whispered in her ear, 'keep believing, all you imagine is valid and true!'.

My body trembled as the words resonated so deep within my soul. It was like I was re-infused with sparkles of unwavering faith in each of my cells reverberating from my own words. I had invoked the girl I used to be from dormant to alive again. Tears of relief, joy and clarity now streamed down my face as my body shook uncontrollably. I can't remember the last time I actually cried in such a way.

The girl I used to be is still very much a part of me, I put my hands over my heart as it beat through my chest into my palms. Her heartbeat is my heartbeat. We are one. Grateful for cacao, grateful for ritual, and grateful for this awakening journey back home.

Now it's time to play.

Water warrior goddess emerging

As a professional dancer, I've looked at myself in the mirror my entire life - but I've never accepted the body that was in front of me. Avoiding the here. The now. Continual nit-picking, all the disgust I saw and felt. Pure judgments of how to be different and better. Wishing I could purge it all of it out of me. This Woman I am. I flash back to when I thought I was more fit, more beautiful and younger or flash forward to who I will be in the future. Anything to avoid the reflection in front of me in this moment.

Yet here I am facing my biggest fear. Me. Naked. Naked in the mirror. Cringing at the sight of wanting to be more toned, more vibrant and longer luscious hair. Cursing this Mirror Ritual. Is it over yet? Am I done? Maybe I need more cacao. I look around at the geckos climbing up the walls in my Bali house for support. Then I remembered. My sisters. I am not alone. My sisters were doing the same ritual. We are all in the privacy of our own homes yet all together in our hearts. 'I can do this!'.

A deep breath into my chest and I locked my focus to my hazel eyes, taking the attention away from my body and into my eyes to ease the pain. Something looked different. This time I could see my soul in my eyes. A whole world portal opened up within the dark hole of my pupils, dropping my gut-wrenching disgust of who I saw in the mirror, by spiralling inward and deeper into my soul, I began to breathe and embody this sacred place.

And so, I took that sacred place to another. I knew I had to head to the mountains of Bali to finish this ritual! And right there...secluded...with not a soul around me, just the chirping cicadas and other insect dwellers, I looked around me. 'How did I get here?' I said out loud in wonder.

The sun is just peaking up above the horizon.

The cool dewy morning still hangs heavy and I could hear the rushing water of the waterfall.

What if someone sees me? Fuck it.

'I drove my scooter two hours in the rain to the middle of the island and slept in a tent on the side of a mountain last night for this! I can do this'.

I reached around and untied my bathing suit top until my breasts were exposed to the morning air. I looked down and yup, my nipples were telling me it was a bit chilly out. 'Well hello girls!', I said half-jokingly. I self-consciously crouched in the pool of water just in case someone was watching. Okay, this was enough. No. My stubborn go for it all self was not satisfied. Bottoms too. 'You can do it', I told myself.

I held my breath and off they went.

One foot then the other, I slipped off the rest of my comforts. A chill ran up my spine in exhilaration. I swam underneath the powerful cascading waterfall. At first it hurt being pelted by water droplets so heavy it felt like I was getting ambushed by paint-balls (if you know you know!). I, for sure, thought I was going to lose an eye. The pounding over my entire being became melodic and the realness of the situation was being washed over me. I surrendered. My shoulders relaxed as the waterfall now massaged my previously tense upper neck and back. A release and gentle satisfying smile softened my face. The sound of all my self-deprecating thoughts in my head, being drowned out, rushing over the rocks and down the river before I could hold on to them any longer.

Gone.

Blood pumping, contentment in my soulful eyes and elegant collar bones level across my chest. The muddy floor of the waterfall under my feet held me, the sun shining invigorated me and the water was washing me clean. I was being held by mother nature. Mama Bali. Just like being held in circle with my sisters. I am beautiful. I am sexy. I am free. 'Express yourself Casey, intimately!', whispered an inner voice. I swayed with the flow of water stirring up the natural rhythms of my hips. Swirling, tapping and dancing from the tips of my toes to the ends of each strand of hair radiating in ecstasy while being showered and restored by the freshest mineral water on all the island.

Each droplet kissed my lips as I sipped in the liquid elixir shining like diamonds in the morning sun. The wild dance of the feminine. I am sexy. I am flying. I am free! 'AHHHH', 'YEWWWW', my soprano voice sang with the birds above so radiant and alive. In nature and naked is my happy place. The courage I needed to feel comfortable in my skin no matter where I was. Supported by the girl I used to be and my sisters. This was no longer a fantasy. I closed my eyes and rolled my head back living in the moment as the woman I am now. Spreading my wings. I am flying. I am free.

This beautiful gathering of women had led me to that dream-like but actually real adventure with myself. When I got back home and looked again into that mirror, I took in this brand-new Water Warrior Goddess that had become of me! Scanning my body from head to toe, I was seeing me for the first time. Proud to be me. Entranced by this being in front of me, white wings emerged from my back muscles laced with rose gold. 'My wings! They are here', there was a goddess with shimmering wings standing before me. I believed again. The believer of the girl she used to be, is in me. I put my hands over my bare chest to make sure this was real. Yes, I could feel the pulsing life force of my heart. The Woman I am Now.

The woman I am yet to become smells the roses!

Encore! Encore! I gaze out, heart exploding from adrenaline with
gratitude and love. Centre stage under the spotlight as sweat drips
down my back.
A goofy large smile is glued on my face.
The audience is standing and applauding as dozens of roses are being
thrown at me. There are petals sticking to my lashes, curls and body.
I bow in reverence for their support.
I would not be the woman I am today nor the woman I am yet to
become if it wasn't for the support of my sisters.
For Cacao. For Nature.

In our final sister circle ceremony together, each woman was honoured with a rose petal shower (you can legit order bags of rose petals and get them delivered to your villa…only in Bali!). I would never have had a problem sprinkling other women in roses, giving them healing touch and supporting them but to receive it? No thanks. But hey, I'd opened up a lot in those past 22 days and by being in Bali full stop, so this, 'I came to Bali and found myself' ritual? Well…just stab me with the thorns in my jugular now so I bleed a slow and dramatic death! Me…and a flower shower…with rose petals…yes!

As we honoured each woman in turn, I was all 'when is it going to be my turn?' inside.

'Casey, your turn?', oh shit! The internal friction was visceral. I looked down at my bare feet on the earth, with rounded shoulders I avoided making eye contact with the other women as I stepped into the middle of the circle. I escaped by closing my eyes and going to my safe place. 'If I can't see them, they can't see me'. That's how it works, right?

I'm used to other women stealing my ideas or competing with me, so I never felt comfortable opening up out of fear. This ritual was asking a lot. But these women had been nothing but lovely. So, I was confident in my stories, it was fun to share but this was different, I was unsure *who* the woman I was to become, the woman they were honouring, was.

I'm a performer, so I need a rehearsal and perfection before I present her to the world. With no costume to cover up my flaws, I felt ugly, washed up and unclear, could I really trust these women to embrace my 'messy' with their genuine support?

It was like a dream I didn't want to wake up from, an energetic vortex sweeping me up and showering me with love, seducing me with nature and connection, oxytocin tickling my cells from the inside, while my sisters hugged me on the outside.

Cacao circulated through my veins igniting the woman I am yet to become, pushing all the right buttons, it was undeniably a real electrical pulse.

My left brained masculine mind intervened and snapped my nervous system into a high sympathetic state from the uncomfortable sensation of pleasure. 'Make it stop!', 'Stop dopamine, phenethylamine, anandamide stop!'

I couldn't tell if it was pleasure or pain but no...this was fucking amazing! I couldn't wipe the stupid grin off my face. A wave of surrender washed over my entire being. My head flew back, mouth opened and I caught rose petals in my mouth like snowflakes. The girl I used to be giggling and the woman I am now breaking through my masculine mold. I embraced the love and tenderness from my sisters. Life force was radiating from my soul, 'oh my gosh this feels so good and I don't care who sees!'.

Right there, in that moment, I felt supported and encouraged to explore the wholeness of me.

The rose petal ceremony grounded me, the physical weight of my elder sisters' hands on my body reminded me, it's ok to be uncomfortable, it's ok to receive support.

It's like they knew what I was going through. I'm used to hiding my mistakes, wild quirks and raw feminine personality but I was missing out on this beauty of experiencing life. I was too busy covering up the parts of me that I thought were too feminine/masculine to fit in, yet it's the blending of those polarities to be my authentic self, that's my mission.

In sister circle, I'm given the space to practice, to be in my masculine and feminine, to be ok with the feminine; emotional, nurtured, sensitive, trusted, creative, receptive, sexy and soft to the end range of my abilities. It's also ok to be action oriented, analytical, disciplined, logical and structured.

I don't know exactly how this is going to play out and this vulnerability scares me. It isn't perfect and predictable. It's hard to swallow. I want to analyse and understand it all. I'm experiencing the dark side of my current reality, unlearning and unwiring perfectionism.

All the late-night rehearsals, academic accolades, failed attempts of superficial satisfaction, searching for the perfect partner, perfect home, perfect situation in an attempt to find myself and apparently all I needed was a shower in rose petals to figure this out!

This is what ritual and sister circles did for me, they were safe. Outside of that, I may need more confidence before my true self is shown to my closest friends and family.

I'm known for my scientific mind, it's relatable to the masculine world. My femininity has been used as sex appeal for the entertainment industry. I could hide behind makeup, lashes, corsets and heels pretending this is not me but a costume of protection for an excuse to actually be in my feminine self. I don't want to save that for the stage now, I want to swivel my hips and be showered in roses!

This woman I am yet to become is safe in my head, still hesitant to be seen fully. Thank goodness for the rituals from this gathering, as they continue to nourish me almost a year later!

A'ho

Wakanda Rose

108

Asking for connection to her higher self was how she started all
of her conversations,
in the physical realm and the energetic.
She needed to hear everything.

from 'Sacred'

Dissolving fear

Fear. It drives me, controls me, contorts me into a place of reaction. Fear was the main driver of my life for as long as I can remember.

When I was six years old, I was unable to sleep out of fear, then, by twelve, I was struggling to eat out of fear.

By fifteen, I found myself unable to socialise out of fear after a big trauma impacted me and people around me changed how they were with me. Then at eighteen, I found myself living the dream of being signed to a record label, yet feeling overwhelmed by fear and pain inside.

Something in me at twenty-two years old paved the way for me to start changing my relationship with fear.

Looking back as the woman I am now, I recognise that what I felt then was my first experience of self-worth. Oh, how I loved that feeling! I had a deep desire for it to grow. A part of me inside, rose from the ashes of pain and fear, deciding enough was enough, I was ready to claim my life!

It was my first true taste of being in sacred ritual with others and honouring myself. I'd been aware of this world, one of crystals and incense since childhood when my parents first opened their own esoteric shop, yet I'd never implemented these tools for my own nourishment until then.

Ritual.

Dancing this part out, letting the pain part of me take a step back, allowing her to enter into deep rest, for the true me to emerge. Gathering with women who understood and beamed acceptance to me. Ritual. A sacred act of acceptance.

Gathering with the women to light candles for all the parts of me engulfed by fear. Each candle taking a bit more of the fear and pain away. Until one day, it no longer gripped me like it once did.

336

Ritual. Candles. Magic in tangible reality. I was the alchemist of my own life.

The girl I used to be would spiral from any emotion, feeling everything so intensely. She was too much for other people to witness and too much to feel in my own body. My mind screamed at me 'I'm too much', a construct thrust upon me from people of my past.

'I'm fine' became my catch phrase. I'd never let anyone in, keeping the world at arms-length. Repressing. Avoiding. Escaping. A routine I was addicted to, yet yearned to escape from. Bringing this part of me to the gathering of the woman where I talked about previous lovers who'd expressed my 'too much', 'too ugly', 'too fat', 'too uncontrollable' and now I was telling myself that.

Ritual.

Allowing me to own these parts and talk about these parts with other women who had experienced this for themselves.

I found I was accepting my Wild Woman and allowing her to beam in full force, regardless of what others could say. In loving my inner world and finding the juiciness of it all, fear became my greatest ally and has been ever since.

The art of ritual paved the way for me to truly flourish, to be able to accept and allow everything that wants to be alive inside of me without spiralling. I allow tears to flow without my mind trying to repress them. My sacred rage is danced out without spiralling into hurting myself or others. Thoughts are allowed to flow through me without latching onto them and judging myself.

Ritual saves lives, it saved me.

Choosing

Being twenty-four-years-old brought with it some of the most life challenging moments I've faced yet in this lifetime. I was rear ended at 70mph and that led to a traumatic brain injury.

Seizures, stroke episodes, neurological damage and physical injuries, my descent into the darkness was not over. There were more defining moments coming. A cheating fiancé, encounters with a blacksmith, all key moments that tore me open.

A defining choice felt real to me. 'Do I become the pain, the chaos, the heart-breaks, the trauma I'd experienced so far?'. Oh, that path felt easy, almost juicy to embody the energy of vengeance.

'Or do I do anything I can to escape, repress and deny the pain?' – that was definitely a wounded default I could go to.

Neither of these were the path I chose to walk, I decided I would carve my own. Enough was enough, I was going to save myself. Again.

I deepened my connection in sacred gatherings with those who accepted my tears and pain, as well as growing my relationship with my beautiful family. I created daily rituals to honour myself; dancing each emotion out, drumming to the medicine wheel daily, feeling that sacred connection to something greater than me. Rattling and singing to myself, bringing my soul home. Writing out the pain I was authentically feeling with no holding back, then burning it all in the fire to transmute it.

Hugging trees till I could breathe again.

Till one day, the trauma, the heartbreaks, no longer felt they controlled me, yes, they were somewhere inside of me, yet they were no longer screaming in pain and fear dictating every move of mine.

338

They are sacred parts of me now, that came alive during my encounters with life, they show me I have lived. WOW! These sacred parts deserve to be held in sacred ways, gathered in sacred circles. Alchemised in the flames of my life.

I did not ascend this experience, no, the goddess beckoned me from the caves, called me to descend deep into my Self and my life. Losing each part of me to truly

Become.

Coming home

Ritual. A sacred act I gift myself to be, to land, to bring me home. A deep breath into being who I truly am rather than playing a part to please those around me.

For three years I've drank cacao every day. It brings me safely into my body, building a relationship with the plant world and feeling the old ways birth through me knowing it's safe to be in the now. Feeling the pain of ancestors come alive in me, especially during the Burning Times and standing amongst it all, to bring that sacred way of being, back in the now knowing it is safe and it is needed. A new way is birthing in this timeline and it weaves the power of the old ways.

We are the ones our ancestor's prayed for.

This current world tried to shut me down. Constantly. Men telling me to shave my sacred yoni to please them. Men not listening to my sacred no and overpowering me. Women throwing me out of their groups for being different. Women projecting deep sisterhood wounding of gossiping, belittling, jealousy, imitation, manipulation. People lying to me and trying to distort my reality to soothe their own selves at the cost of my mind and heart. Men and women telling me I'm mean for putting boundaries in place. Men and women physically beating me up. And so much more. So much trauma and pain trying to shut me down in this lifetime. I stood in the flames of it all, feeling all my past come alive in me and chose me. No more will the echoes of the past dictate my life.

By no means was I an angel, I found myself caught up in projecting wounded patterns also, yet something stronger than all of that pain emerged through ritual.

A new imprint of safety, love and belonging was gifted to me when I started to gather with likeminded women, when I found myself honouring and being honoured by likeminded men and when I sat in ritual for myself.

Before I adapted ritual as a sacred part of my life, being called 'ugly' or 'stupid' or being belittled in any way, would have spiralled me into a frantic place of despair no longer wishing to be alive. Bringing ritual into my life has allowed me to stay centred during chaos and conscious to it all, to love myself regardless and keep in relationship with myself, no matter what. Yes, I feel the pain, I may sway from the best path for me, wounded parts still exist in me, yet I've found a sense of love for myself during all of this.

I gather in ritual, I gather with women, I gather all of me from the anger, the sadness, the joy, ALL of me, safe inside.

Creating space within.

I was twenty-five and integrating all the journeys I'd been on when we gathered and now a year later, as I write this, I want to show other women they are enough as they are, right now, that they deserve to take up space, that they deserve sacred ritual.

Sometimes I've been blocked as I try to write this, ghosts of the past whispering in my ear, yet a stronger voice within, accepts these voices for what they are - other's opinions from *their* wounded place and social programming.

Ritual showed me how to navigate all the noise inside, giving voice to this wounded part of me in sacred space with sisters who reminded me of my worth. So now this stronger voice within shouts for me to hear;

'I am enough'

'I deserve to write my story'

'I accept all of me'

Each day I drum, I sing, I rattle, I smudge, I drink cacao, I create sacred rituals to keep that voice strong and alive inside of me.

Gathering in sacred space led me to being authentic with what was alive in me, regardless of what was deemed 'undesirable' by another. Someone always accepted me. That imprint of acceptance became my own inner voice.

By no means have I ascended the human experience, I'm deep in it but now able to welcome it all in, with the wisdom, 'I am strong enough, accepting enough to deal with anything. I accept me. I am home'.

Pascale Huart

61

Peace.
Recovery and rest.
Nothing more.

from 'Sacred'

Trust

To be honest with you, I had no idea what a sister circle was really about before I joined one.

Growing up in a very masculine household with three older brothers, I'd never really spent a lot of time around women, other than my mum. As you can imagine, I was a complete tomboy! So much so, that one of my first memories as a child, was receiving a beautiful traditional and I now know, expensive doll from my godmother. Both my mum and godmother really loved it. So beautiful and girly! Every girl should have one. However, I was convinced I was being handed a toy car, like the ones I'd seen my older brothers play with so many times. Seconds after it was handed to me, the doll was pretty much wrecked! Both my mum and godmother were completely shocked and it was a very long time before I was trusted with another doll.

So, joining a sister circle didn't come naturally to me. Despite always wanting an older sister while I was growing up, I didn't really know how to be around women. Things changed when I entered teenage hood. Back in high school, I was part of a group of five girls. I loved it. I felt like we were sisters. The sisters I never had. We'd play in the fields on summer days, sing songs together, have girly sleepovers watching chick flicks. Despite having grown up a tomboy, I felt like I really belonged there. Finally, my beautiful feminine energy was allowed time to blossom!

Lunch break was my favourite part of the school day. Time to enjoy with us five girls. However, this day was very different. I remember seeing my friends in the playground and running up to them with a smile on my face. By the time I'd just reached them, they ran away in the opposite direction laughing. Unsure what was going on and thinking it was a game, I chased after them. It didn't

344

take long for me to realise it wasn't a game and they were running away from me.

The day I'll never forget, I could feel so much confusion and sadness. Drama and toxicity, it seemed, had started to slowly seep into our group without me realising and it corroded a beautiful friendship.

What had I done wrong? As I stood there in the playground all alone, I was teleported back a few months earlier. This time I was in my lounge at home waiting by the windows that faced the driveway. Who was I waiting for? My Father. That weekend it was his weekend to come and visit me. The court had allowed him to and so had my mum. I woke up so early that Saturday morning, unable to sleep all night due to excitement! Having waited what felt like light years to be able to see him again, to be reunited with him. Since the moment I was born, we were always two peas in a pod. Inseparable. Now in separate countries, I needed him more than ever. Hours and hours went by. I stood there waiting by the window. My unwavering enthusiasm never left me. Every car I heard, I jumped with excitement. Just to see them drive by. No, that wasn't him. At no point did it even cross my mind that he wouldn't show up. I knew deep down that he wanted to see me as much as I wanted to see him. I remember my mum trying to get hold of him on his phone but there was no answer. Every month I'd wait there, by the window. He never showed up.

The pain burst through my body. I couldn't bear being seen crying in public in the middle of the playground, so I ran to the nearest girls' toilets. I made sure it was the quiet toilets, less used. Standing there in the cubicle alone I'd let out a whale of a cry. Tears continuously pouring out of me, uncontrollably. Part of me trying so hard to quieten my sobbing in case someone walked in.

345

Just like that I was broken all over again.

The girls had no idea how much I needed them at that time. They had no idea what was going on at home for me. At the beginning, they'd given me some glimmers of a normal happy life. What my life should have been like. My home was so chaotic, wounded and hurt. School in comparison felt like my wonderland, a place where I could get away from all that negativity. I could reinvent myself. I could be happy.

That was the last time I allowed myself to fully trust anyone else.

And so, the day of my first sister circle ceremony came and I felt so torn. I knew I needed to do this for myself. I was being called to do it. Yet surely, I would feel so out of place? I hadn't been in a group of girls like that since my teenage years, instead, I'd avoided them, believing I'd get hurt again if I did.

My initial guard was up to protect myself. It happened automatically and almost unconsciously; I didn't have any control of it. A built-in safety mechanism. At the time, I didn't really understand why I was feeling the resistance of being a part of a sister circle. Sitting with cacao and writing this from the heart, it's all becoming so clear to me now.

Seven women sat with me that day in circle. One of four ceremonies. What a magical space. Such a beautiful feminine sacred space. A place to disconnect from the outside and go within. Despite not really feeling sure if I belonged there, I knew I wanted to stay.

During the self-introduction, I remember feeling more and more nervous about speaking. Especially speaking about my past, my family and the girl I used to be. I'd always, *always* avoided this topic, knowing very well that talking about it would open the wounds of the past that hadn't healed.

Almost as soon as I started speaking, I could hear my voice starting to crack, my mouth getting dry, the eyes welling up more and more. I wanted to give such a better first impression of myself. Rather than barely able to get my words out from all of the tears. I felt so embarrassed. But hearing these women speak from the heart about their stories and experiences, being authentic and fully themselves without judgement or criticism, it gave me courage to open up a little more. The experience and feeling of being 100% fully heard, the experience and feeling of being 100% seen. When was the last time I'd experienced that? It was so incredible. Every one of those seven sisters projecting their loving energy onto me. I hadn't ever experienced that before. They didn't even need to say or do anything at all. I could just instantly feel the love, support and healing energy radiating from all of the sisters. Like I was being held in loving arms. It was such a magical experience, I felt like I was able to trust again.

That feeling increased in intensity as we continued to gather in all four ceremonies. The kind of feeling that's hard to put into words but you understand it as soon as you feel it. The energy was so light, warm and soothing. Women of every age gathered together. I didn't know all of the women but through our journey together they'd become my sisters and I was the youngest.

It reminded me of my family. How I'm the youngest of my three brothers. My very own guardian angels. Always there for me. Protecting me and keeping me safe. With the sister circle, I had my own feminine version. Through my childhood my brothers taught me how to be strong and tough, so much so that I'd forgotten about my feminine side, the sweet softness. It was so beautiful being reminded of that. Having sisters who'd walked the womanhood path before me, able to give me better understanding and insights on topics only women would know.

Being a part of the sister circle made me realise that I should cherish and be proud of my womanhood journey. That it's okay to embrace with open arms. It allowed me to connect to that part of me that I'd thought I'd lost for so long.

'Be kind and gentle to yourself' one sister said, 'you only have one body, take good care of it'. Those were the words I so desperately needed to hear. 'Be kind and gentle to yourself'. Something so simple, I can't forget it. Those words will stick with me.

Marking my journey to womanhood

Before this immersion, I can't remember the last time I'd gone out to find and collected a stick! I remember being so confused and unsure why we needed it. I felt strange going out on my afternoon walk to find one. I felt awkward. It seemed so bizarre.

I had no idea how a piece of wood could become so precious to me. Interestingly, it was another stick on the altar at our first gathering that caught my attention, more so than the one I'd found. I swapped it. I have no idea why I was more drawn to it; I always thought all sticks looked the same. But not all of them *feel* the same. This one felt right. The way it felt in the palms of my hands, so beautifully smooth. The lines on the stick felt so unique. Its very own fingerprint.

Gazing at my stick, it made me think of its origins and past. This stick was once a branch of a tree. Once a part of the whole. A tree that grew from the earth below. A tree that saw many sunrises and sunsets. This stick has experienced many days of sun, rain and wind. Experiencing all of the elements. It holds that energy inside it.

This living material made from mother nature. A symbol of life. A representation of growth and strength. It has developed through the cycles of life. Constantly shifting and changing. Never the same. In the same way, I'd gone through my own cycles and rhythms of life already. The continuous change I'd experience from being a little young girl to where I am now. My journey of womanhood. A sacred journey. Filled with its ups and downs.

Its strong roots keeping it stable, nurtured and connected to mother earth. The symbol of its starting point. The starting point of when it was originally only a little seed. That fragile seedling, that over time, grew bigger and stronger.

A tree isn't ashamed of itself. It's not wanting to change into a ladybird. It lovingly accepts itself. All of its self. It isn't worried about growing older. An old tree is seen as wise, strong and powerful. It doesn't fight or resist change. It embraces it. It doesn't want to return to being just a seedling. It stands tall with its marks, lines, flaws, rough texture. A representation of what it's lived through. The experiences it's had. A visual story of its past.

It stands tall no matter what. Through thunder lightning storms, snow and hail. It continued on. This stick also represented a starting point for me. The point when I realised the sacredness of womanhood and became a part of a sister circle. It marks when I understood the power of setting an intention, when I took time to create my sacred space and alter, when I began the ritual of lighting a candle for myself while sitting with mama cacao.

Each moment of my 22 day journey through ritual had been marked with pens, ribbons and string on my precious stick.

Reminders of the journey I'd taken. How a plain boring stick transformed with each day, becoming more and more meaningful as the journey continued! Finally, my stick was decorated and marked with fourteen symbols: white cotton, black ribbon, hessian, black pen marks, brown string and black tipped by the fire on my final closing ceremony. I whispered my deepest secrets and messages to it, like a dear friend or sister, knowing that she'd keep them safe for me.

The last piece on my precious stick, tied on tight with string, is a loving letter written to list the qualities that I consciously invite in from my future self. The qualities that flowed to me were 'positive vibrant energy, courageous, in flow with the universe, a natural beauty, a world explorer, confident, wild free spirit...'.

This stick of mine, creating a sacred bond between me and my future self. A solid bond between myself and nature. Representing the time I spent as a young girl, having fun exploring and climbing trees in my back garden. A bond that connected me to my whole family, my mother, father, three brothers and our black Labrador. A bond that brings me closer to my ancestors and the wise women that came before me. Following our paths of womanhood together. All connected. All one.

Closing my eyes, holding my stick close to my heart, I can feel those bonds and connections. I can feel them all. I'm never alone.

Blossoming

I would never have thought I'd be doing this, sharing something so personal to me.

At five years old, one of my fondest memories, was being with my whole family at the beach during summer in Belgium. I remember feeling completely free, feeling the wind in my hair, the heat of the sun on my skin and the softness of the sand in between my toes. With my bucket and spade in my hands, I was ready to go exploring the shores for shells, stones and pieces of wood. Skipping and jumping over the waves that rolled onto the shore, the feeling of being completely in my element. Gathering shells for the beautiful sandcastles I'd made with help from my older brothers. The sense of such pure aliveness. I haven't thought about that moment until sitting down in my sacred space with my cup of cacao in my hands and listening to the 'the girl you used to be' meditation.

Right there, I was being teleported back to a time where I was most happy and filled with joy. Allowing the memories and emotions to wash over me, to feel them within my core.

The feeling of love and happiness turned to tears…uh-oh', I thought, I felt my eyes well up. 'Keep it together!' I thought to myself, while looking up and trying to wave my hands to dry out my eyes.

The feeling of sadness is something I was never able to fully express, I had years' worth of tears hidden away and stored up inside of me, tears I'd been too scared and ashamed to let out. I feared it would be as catastrophic as a dam bursting its banks.

I took a moment. I inhaled. Paused. Then exhaled. I could feel a change happening inside me. I recognised that for the first moment in a long, long time…

I. Felt. Safe.

I was being held in a loving embrace, the kind of heart-warming bear-hug that I remember my loving mum giving me as a child while sitting on her lap. A deep feeling of safety and security.

I could hear a voice saying, 'it's safe to be able to let go now. Let go of the sadness, pain and suffering'.

And so, I sat still as I held my chest, finally allowing myself to lower the huge dam walls. I still remember the feeling of the first tear running free. Despite its cold dampness, it was so refreshing. The droplet of water finding its way down my cheek, to the corner of my mouth and tasting the saltiness. The taste of emotion being set free. More and more tears followed.

Being set free. That was it. I felt during that short moment, that I had let out the pain I'd been carrying with me for so long, finally saying good-bye to it.

I was so surprised! I'd never imagined it would feel so good! Such a vulnerable moment, I felt so empowered.

Even as I'm writing this now, I still feel unsure whether to include this information…what will people think? Throughout most of my life, I'd tried so hard to keep it all together. But I'm reminded that flowers can't exist in a dry desert. Flowers need rain to flourish. And that flower has blossomed!

E Birch

32

Burn the candle.
Smoke the sage.
Whisper your blessings.
Breathe out your fears.
This moment is yours.

from 'A Woman's Blessing'

Aligned

I felt time swirl around me, as I sat in meditation in ritual with the girl I used to be. As if I was sitting within a vertical vortex of energy, brushing up around my head, down my left arm, under the dark green rug I sat on and back up around me. It caught me off guard, I'd never experienced anything of that calibre before. Within my mind's eye, I smiled at the girl I used to be, as she picked up a stone and smiled back. I told her I'd be back and that she will be me, allowing myself to let go of the heavy sadness I carried in my heart about the loss of connection to that innocent little girl. I placed my hand on her heart before beginning to leave this realm, opening my eyes, the glint of a lone candle sitting on my alter in front of me, light flickering around the room, greeting me back to the reality I had gotten so comfortable in, that I overlooked on the daily.

I felt more present, more alive, yet more still and peaceful. It was as though something had clicked into place in my heart, a lost part of myself. I'd spent years eroding my connection to myself through drug addiction, abusive relationships and suicide attempts, trying desperately to either fill in or destroy the hole I felt was a broken heart, landing me in a desolate, depressive mind state from the womb.

I couldn't pinpoint my depression to a specific event, 'an amalgamation of events' doctors said, 'just medicate her and get her through school'. I had fun as a child but I remember as early as primary school, feeling like there was something different about me, as though I was too sensitive for the world around me. Despondent and withdrawn, I remember looking around the school yard, not wanting to be there, waiting for it to finish and doing the maths. I had another ten weeks of term left, another three terms of the year left. Rinse and repeat for another eight years...then university, then career, then family, then gardening, 'till death and I didn't want any of it.

School wasn't how I wanted to spend my time. None of the conventional lifestyle appealed to me, it looked so empty and hollow. I felt as though I was in a prison, completely out of control, a path laid out before me by societal expectation, no choice in what my life beheld. Withdrawing into a world of fantasy was my only escape of a ravenously deep and dark internal experience that kept me within a fortress of my own creation, away from the beauty of the garden, of carefree fun and connection with others, of being truly present.

As I grew, I felt I could only escape by causing myself pain and trouble, at least then I would know who the culprit was. Collecting reasons to be in pain, I maintained a shred of control in my life.

Looking back and reflecting at how my life unfolded, understanding my parents' own traumas, I can only wonder if, as a child, I'd been tapping into the untold horrific tragedies of *their* lives – the ones they couldn't visit at the time.

After a decade of living in the self-imposed hell of my mind, burning myself alive, reflecting very prominently in my external reality and relationships, I got sick of the pain. My heart broke seeing eyes reflecting back helplessness and worry on the faces of those I loved, as I lay in a hospital bed after trying to take my own life. I realised exiting the earths stage early might rid me of my suffering but that very same suffering would be the only thing I bequeathed to my family, those I wanted to protect.

At sixteen, still too young to know how to transmute and alchemize that amount of darkness and caught in a 'neither here nor there' attitude about life, I decided to stay alive for others. In my non-committal attitude to myself, I let my body be sucked out to sea, by waves of drug induced obliteration, chasing mystical experiences the only way I knew how. Meanwhile getting caught in riptides of drama as I clung to others in a misguided attempt at a life raft. I was just trying to avoid facing or feeling what was under the water's surface, causing me so much pain and panic.

Little did I know, that that very same pain and panic, would be my fire to want for something better.

Eventually those looks of helplessness would become too much, the moment I truly realised what I was doing, to myself and those around me, my heart melted and light flooded in. Over time, I learnt to let go of hurt. I stopped struggling against the tide and let myself be washed ashore. I wanted something better for myself, my life and in turn, for those around me. I was unsure what I wanted but I was sure of what I *didn't* want and that was direction enough.

I started journeying within, slowly gaining some tools to dive into the waters I felt suffocated and half-drowned me. Even so, having collected those tools, I still found myself in this sister circle, having relapsed just a few weeks prior. With my head in my hands, heavy hearted and strained, a concoction of anxiety, adrenaline and self-doubt pumped around my body, after fourteen months of being sober.

I had been doing my own solitary ritual work for the previous couple years which I had to thank for pulling me out of full-blown addiction but this time complacency had led me astray. Coming to the sister circle I felt alone, haunted by skeletons of the past, my mind had its own reservations it tormented me with, 'you're not as strong as you think you are'. Though in my heart I knew I was a hell of a lot stronger than my mind could ever imagine.

I looked around my room, I felt the dense green rug beneath me, feeling like I was properly experiencing it for the first time, although having only just moved to the new place, after putting so much time into recovery at my family home, it was as though I was looking through new eyes. The flicker of the candle looked richer, the walls more animated, as though they were holding me in this state. 'I'm here' they echoed back to me, as I was there for myself. I went to sleep that night feeling a wholeness in my heart, a glint in my spirit and smile on my face.

The next morning, out of the blue I awoke to a message from an old friend saying she had found all these old photos of us as youngsters. A mixture of gratitude, surprise and tears welled up as I remembered the gripping in my chest, aged seventeen, 'what have I done!', looking down at the flood of water drenching my laptop after having knocked a bottle over it. All the photos of my life until that point had just disappeared into the abyss.

And there, as we were going through that week of the girls we used to be, all those photos came back. I flicked through them, I thought I'd never see them again, memories flooded back to me, remembering the girl I used to be, seeing all the fun that my best friend and I had over those years, no matter how terribly I had remembered them, there was so much light and joy we'd shared, within what I had felt solely were dark caverns of the past.

The past felt like it had balance now. I smiled at the night before, paralleling the mornings travels back through time, within the photo album and being with a part of myself I had long forgotten existed. 'Thank you' I whispered silently out into the void, to the deepest parts of myself, as I typed it on my phone screen to my friend for what she'd just sent me.

Inside felt whole and I had just watched the physical world align to match the inner with the outer, a deep sense of gratitude flooding my day.

Lighting candles

After that first meditation, I was brilliantly excited to see what was to unfold over the following three weeks where I would light a candle and sit with myself every day. The profound experience I'd had, was exactly what I'd been chasing. A surrendering, a being…but this was much different, it didn't come at a cost or detriment to anyone.

I lit a candle for myself everyday with my hand on my heart and came into presence with myself. It was as though for the first time while sober, I was truly encountering myself, my soul. I felt stronger, able to carry the weight of the ocean that had previously held me down.

I felt in these moments (in the night, when the house was quiet and the streets were empty) truly alive, as though every part of me was as vividly alight as the candle flame that danced back at me. Time didn't exist, only my heart, as I felt it beat softly and peacefully in my chest. The past and the future didn't matter, I was just me. Alone, I was content, happy, peaceful. Being around people and sharing myself however was the opposite.

I had lived a very unconventional lifestyle, however, some of those parts were good for me, some were self-destructive and I felt the judgement of the social stigma attached to it…for being different, for wanting a different life to most people. The fear of not being understood weighed me down. 'Like trying to fit a square peg into a round hole,' my mum had always said about me.

But now, I was faced with the confronting and startling reality that there was actually an enormous amount of beauty, wonder and love within a more mundane and traditional world. Love was the glue of it all – conventional or unconventional.

Parts of myself, some I'd known, some new to me, came to me each day, each making me more whole then the last. As I came to be present with myself, the scent of palo santo filling my nose, the 'mundane' reality began to light me up for the first time. I could see it in all its glory, as well as the beauty of myself, just as I was. I began to see the value and find satisfaction in the little things. Slowing down, really appreciating every moment, the beauty of imperfection and awkwardness, how perfect life itself really is. The smell of rain in the air, the texture of thread between my fingers, the smile on another's face, the sharing of ideas.

During this sister circle, I began to see the value of feeling my heart and coming from that place, that true little glint inside of me, of sharing, learning from one another's experiences and the art of storytelling and learning together.

I began to see these things but I noticed my walls were still fortified, a moat surrounding me that I still didn't feel I could swim across. Reconciling my rebellion and the part of myself that now saw the undeniable beauty within tradition, proved difficult. It felt as though I was working at odds with myself.

Working the better part of a decade as a sex worker, not knowing how to connect with that deeper essence of myself, I attempted to give others that very same connection I craved. I saw the glint of divine beauty within everyone, the qualities they possessed, their uniqueness, the stories they had to share, the wisdom they held. I'd cherished every moment, I got a peek into the world of another, through their eyes while hiding the weight of my ocean. I shared my body and mind but never my heart or soul.

Never truly letting anyone in, for fear that I'd be misunderstood and rejected, I found shelter within this more denounced pocket of society. Everything glittered, the mystique of it all, the comradery and laughter within the four walls of the 'girls room'. I connected deeply with these women and was understood on a level beyond words.

They saw things similarly to me, we spoke about the necessity of touch and connection with one another as humans, all having a human experience, in a world filled with tragedy. I smiled when one woman described to me how when she'd hug a client, she would envision her soul projected into his body and hugging his soul. Most wouldn't let go, bodies starved of affection. I grinned, enlivened, 'I do the same thing'.

I brimmed with confidence and elation at work or with close friends or family, the ones I knew I was safe to be myself around. Invaluable relationships were formed. I often felt though that this haven came with the cost of connection with the outside world. Times when I had to socialise with anyone not within my inner circle, were filled with fear of what they'd think.

Well intentioned friends or lovers who believed how I was living was not 'the way,' thought they knew what was best for me and tried to change or save me. Sometimes I let them convince me. Every time I began listening to others, I lost myself, trying to be who someone else thought I should be.

Thinking I was wrong for who I was and how I wanted to live, I constantly second guessed what to say when the dreaded question came of 'What do you do for work?'

I was unable to share my life with extended family on Christmas, robbing my mum of what to say when her friends asked her what I was doing with my life. I felt the burden of shame while attempting to dismantle the walls within my mind, at a crossroads between how I'd been living and how I wanted to be, not knowing how to be open and honest about who I was but not wanting to live in fear anymore, locked inside, walls too high.

Fears lurked in the corners of my mind, echoes of the past...'you're too much' my mind would recite back to me, finding ammunition as to why I'd never be accepted, why my presence wasn't ever wanted, why, if anything, it was worse for the people surrounding me.

I'd spent most of my life struggling with a state of mind that created a tightness in my throat, anxiety and sweating when I was expected to talk or share myself in any way.

The moments each morning where I lit my candle and sat on my own, gave me much needed shelter and solace, allowing me to become truly acquainted with those unattended parts of myself.

I didn't need to run to any person, place or thing to escape anymore, I was content and happy just being, I could be there for myself and know in that moment, everything was okay.

The release

I was terrified by my need to connect. I was led to the sister circle through serendipity, so I understood it was no coincidence my being there. I sat as I watched and listened to the other women speak, sharing their experiences, their feelings, their stories. I realised that even though our paths were all different, the feelings we held inside weren't so different. At my turn to speak, a mixture

361

of excitement and fear welled up within me, once again choking me, as I tried to express my thoughts and feelings. The old stories were activated, fear gripped and restricted me from sharing what I truly wanted to: my experiences and stories, the wisdom and lessons I'd learnt, myself.

Part of me was proud, I knew how far I had come. I had cultivated a unique perspective, a deep compassion for others but was unable to extend that same compassion to myself. A more limited part of me was deeply ashamed, a poison bottle filled with every judgement and criticism society has had on sex workers, people struggling with mental health and drug dependency corked my throat.

Feeling blocked by a disowned part of myself, when I shared how I was feeling within the circle, I spoke about my deep apprehension surrounding voicing my experiences. In the beginning, rather than sharing myself, I shared my walls, for fear everyone else would judge me as harshly as I judged myself. I watched as faces dropped around the circle, as I could see the other women empathising with how I felt, my own heaviness and sadness reflected to me once again in the eyes of those opposite me as it reaffirmed my worst suspicions, I was too much.

In that moment I felt as though I had balls and chains strapped to my ankles, as I plummeted to the bottom of the ocean within, dragging them down with me. This uncomfortable and unpleasant experience showed me that these women were with me! Every word, every emotion, every step of the way. I realised I could've just shared my experiences, as well as the fears I attached to them and more than likely, I'd have been supported.

I realised there was little separating my feelings with others and I wanted to share how I authentically felt, rather than sharing the weight of what I felt. The care I felt within that circle showed me the compassion I needed to have for myself. It was scary to admit that this was exactly what I needed, to be able to share from my heart with others who would receive me in theirs, especially when that was the very thing I'd felt I was incapable of.

I wanted and needed to share myself, not my walls. I couldn't operate within the world as an island anymore, realising the love and empathy I was missing out on. I realised the medicine was in the poison, I learned to stop judging myself and resolved to be truly open about who I was and how I felt, warts and all.

In my thinking I was 'too much' and hiding myself, to defend against my own vulnerability, I had quite literally become 'too much'. The venom and the antidote were two of the same. Slowly, I began the task of draining the moat, tearing down the walls and allowing myself and others inside, allowing myself to feel and be vulnerable, those shackles around my ankles began to unclasp.

As I let my emotions wash over me, all that grief, sadness, anger, shame and pain, they began to dissipate slowly in intensity. I learnt to loosen my grip, let go of resistance, I stopped running and allowed myself to feel everything. I began to feel my emotional landscape broadening. I was able to explore it without the lurking feeling of being stalked as I greeted my emotions and energy.

I walked around, willing to face what I would meet and eventually the sun slowly began to rise, illuminating an oasis, trees…a less threatening reality. I began to feel a widening of emotional experience in the equal and opposite direction, bliss, joy, euphoria, as I melted into a warm pool of tears, a smile on my face as I watched, felt, experienced in awe of every little part of me and the world at large.

I came to know myself more and more each day as I continued to piece together and meet different parts of myself, knowing I was supported and held by the woman I am yet to become, my path profoundly respected and understood by her. I didn't need to drown, escape or carry that ocean anymore because maybe, after all, I am that whole ocean.

AUTHORS REFERENCE PAGE

(with Instagram tags)

Sallie Warman-Watts

Universal Crone Woman, Cacao Carrier, Ceremony & Ritual Holder, Gather the Women facilitator

@visionarysagecrone

Jenni Hallam

Mindset Designer, NLP Master Practitioner, Hypnotherapist and Deep Change Coach. I help people optimise their life experience and achieve their personal and professional goals from a place of consistent wellbeing, designing tailored programmes to fit individuals. Workshop & retreat host, Gather the Women facilitator

@jenni.hallam.coaching

Lesley Readman

Cacao Medicine Carrier, Spiritdance and Chakradance Facilitator

@rosegoddessoftheearth

Mikel Ann Hall
Sister Circles, Cacao Carrier, Breathwork
@mikelannhall

Jennifer Levers
Radiant Real Woman
@radiant.real.women

Angela Pepperell
@angelacpepp

Lynette Marie Allen
Medicine Woman, Wisdom Keeper, Consciousness Coach,
Astrologer, owner of Her Sacred journey. She doesn't have
Instagram but she's contactable through her soul sisters Instagram
@thelynetteallen

Andrea Jackson
Medicine Woman & Sacred Rebel - Owner & Founder of Radiant
Woman Training Temple
@radiantwoman_training_temple

Mairi Taylor
55 & doing her best to come home to herself
@mairitaylor_menopause_rockstar

Julia Anastasiou
Ceremonial Ritualista
@juliaanastasiou108

Ali Hutchinson

Health Coach & Gut Health Specialist. Cacao Ceremonies, Meditation Teacher, Emotional Freedom Technique (EFT)

@alihwellness

Stevie Jane Foster

Teacher of children and young people with Special Educational Needs, Cacao Carrier, Medicine Woman, Homeopath, Yoga and Meditation teacher. Gather the Women facilitator and Ceremony Holder for women to help them to honour the Deep Feminine within.

@sjwangel

Angie Gifford

Crone, Healer, Teacher, Nurturer, Yoga Teacher, Yoga Nidra Guide, Grandmother

@nurturewithangie

Ann Ball

Circle holder

@guruholistics

Emily Madghachian

Love Coach, Creative Arts Facilitator and Youth Mentor

@emily.madghachian

Mykela McAlpine

Medicine Woman, Cacao carrier

@angel_holistics_

Katie (KaT) Thomas
Holistic therapist, Hedgewitch, Intuitive Energy practitioner &
Medicine Woman
@katsholistichedgewitchpantry

Louise Edwards
Gather The Women Facilitator, Dru Yoga Teacher, Cacao Carrier
@in_the_field_of_dreams

Francesca Yogini
Women's spaceholder
@francescayogini

Kirsten 'Kimama' Lapping
Mother, Wife, Medicine Woman, Sacred Mesa Carrier, Cacaoista,
Sacred Circle Holder, Crystal and Energy Worker, Course
Provider with Crystal Moon Holistic Wellbeing C.I.C and work in
our family run shop Crystal Moon Emporium in Sunderland UK
@crystalmoonemporium

Alexandra Fraser Duran
Intuitive healer, Medicine woman, Medical intuitive, Holistic
Practitioner
@maya_holistic_therapies

Mahala Gehna
Sound Therapist, Wild Woman Circle Leader and Certified Cacao
Practitioner
@earthtonessound

Lou Moore
Yoga Teacher, Cacao Medicine Woman, Space Holder, Sorceress of Deep Rest
@gatherwithlou

Beverley Ross
space holder for 1:1 sessions, women's circles and retreats
@beverley76ross

Louise Harris
Holistic wellbeing coach and founder of the mindful being
@mindfulbeing_coachingandyoga

Jagdeep Kaur (Jags)
Medicine Woman, Yoni Steam Facilitator, Cacao Carrier
@_creative_treasures_

Eleshia Harris
Holistic Business Growth & Implementation Coach Helping female business owners get clear on their goals, stay focused and on track to turn desires into revenue
@eleshia_lifestyle

Maila Salmaso
Cacao Guardian, Gather the Women facilitator & Earthkeeper
@pure.cacao.dream

Virginia Gonzalez Pinto Medrano

A channel, tattoo artist, sculptress, mother of two, free spirit, ceremonial practitioner, student of hidden knowledge, lover of life itself

@vir.art.mallorca, @virtattoos

Ashleigh Guthrie

Medicine Woman, Holder of ritual and ceremonial space for women

@ashleighguthrie01

Casey Mauro

Ceremony holder/Cacao carrier

@casey_mauro

Wakanda Rose

Priestess of the Goddess, Medicine Woman, Artist and Musician

@bywakandarose

Pascale Huart

Sacred Cacao Carrier

@pascale_ashley

E Birch

Astrologer

@metacosmios

Lynette Allen

Lynette Allen is a medicine woman, teacher, mentor and an author, who lives in a tiny house in the Balinese mountains. Her journey through medicine work and sacred circles have led her to create 'Gather the Women' sister circles and 'A Woman's Blessing'. She is editor of this book and her previous three books were the Woman's Blessing trilogy medicine books.

A Woman's Blessing
Nourishment for the rise of the feminine

HELD
Guidance for the rise of the feminine

Sacred
Integration for the rise of the feminine

(all available now on Amazon)

Instagram @thelynetteallen

If you would like to join a future Gather the Women 22 day sister circle, you can contact any of the Gather the Women facilitators listed above and you might like to follow @gatherthewomensistercircle on Instagram!

Made in the USA
Las Vegas, NV
21 December 2024